Liverpool
Docks

Liverpool Docks

A Short History

DAVID PAUL

FONTHILL

For my Mum and Dad, who gave me a love of my home town of Liverpool,
and for Jim Brophy, the best teacher at SMA,
who gave me a love of history.

Fonthill Media Language Policy

Fonthill Media publishes in the international English language market. One language edition is published worldwide. As there are minor differences in spelling and presentation, especially with regard to American English and British English, a policy is necessary to define which form of English to use. The Fonthill Policy is to use the form of English native to the author. David Paul was born and educated in Liverpool; therefore British English has been adopted in this publication.

Fonthill Media Limited
Fonthill Media LLC
www.fonthillmedia.com
office@fonthillmedia.com

First published in the United Kingdom and the United States of America 2016

British Library Cataloguing in Publication Data:
A catalogue record for this book is available from the British Library

Copyright © David Paul 2016

ISBN 978-1-78155-518-7

Typeset in 10.5pt on 13pt Sabon
Printed and bound in England

Acknowledgements

During the course of my research for this book and its subsequent writing, I have been helped and guided by many individuals and organisations, without whom I would not have been able to complete the task. Firstly, I must thank my wife Janet for enduring the constant disruption to the domestic routine during the long gestation period of this book. I would also wish to record my thanks to David Stowell, submarine engineer of Barrow-in-Furness, for his help and advice regarding sources of information, especially during the initial research stages. I must also thank Frank Lyons for his helpful comments concerning the Overhead Railway.

I would also wish to record my sincere thanks to the staff of the Maritime Museum at Liverpool, particularly the staff working in the archives—their helpful advice proved invaluable. Similarly, I would like to extend my thanks to the staff at the new central library in Liverpool—a great resource for the city.

The internet proved to be another valuable source of research where there are, understandably, many sites on the history of Liverpool and its docks, far too numerous to mention. With reference to some of the photographs included in the text, I would wish to state that, despite prolonged and exhaustive enquiries, tracking down some copyright holders has not been possible.

Finally, I could not end this section without thanking my son Jon for his constant words of encouragement and helpful suggestions as regards punctuation, style, and grammar.

Contents

Introduction

One constant element runs throughout the whole of Liverpool's long and sometimes illustrious history—the River Mersey. Even as far back as 1207, when King John granted letters patent to Liverpool—often referred to as a Royal Charter—it was the river and its strategic location that, to a very large extent, prompted the action. Indeed, Liverpool's geographical location has often acted as a spur to development; equally, its location has sometimes been viewed as being detrimental to prosperity.

As Liverpool developed from being an insignificant fishing village into a small town, it was the river-borne trade with Ireland and Wales that maybe brought the town's first wave of economic prosperity. The ingenuity and vision of its townsfolk later transformed the area around the 'Pool' into the world's first wet dock—the Old Dock, or Steer's Dock as it was called then.

As trading links were forged and developed, the dock area also underwent a marked transformation, with more docks being built to accommodate the rapid rise in imports and exports passing through the port. It was also during this developmental period that the town's fortunes prospered because of the infamous slave trade, in which the port and its merchants took a leading role. This phenomenal rise to prominence firmly established Liverpool as being a major player in the world's trading centres—a strong position to be in at the beginning of the Industrial Revolution.

With much of Britain's early industrial production being based within 100 miles of the port, and with road and rail networks improving as a direct result of industrial production, it was logical and economically prudent to channel imports of raw materials and exports of finished products through the port.

When the First World War broke out, all of the vast resources of the port were deployed in assisting in the war effort, and not least in this respect was the crucial role played by the Mersey ferries. However, then came the interwar years and depression. World trade was in the throes of deep recession, which was to have a severe effect upon both the port and the city's wellbeing. Unemployment in the country reached a peak during the 1920s and early 1930s, but Liverpool was recording, on average, unemployment figures of almost double the national figure, leading to a general feeling of isolation and civil unrest in the city.

Liverpool and its port were destined to play a crucial role in the Second World War, providing a vital link between the nation and her transatlantic allies, bringing much-needed armaments, food supplies, and other essential provisions that were necessary to sustain the nation. Establishing Liverpool as the strategic operational base for the Atlantic convoys proved to be a vital decision in maintaining the nation's ability to endure the ravages of war and, ultimately, to overcome them. However, the war had brought great losses to the city and its port, with much devastation being inflicted along the whole of the dock estate. Liverpool's shipping companies also suffered great losses, with many of their fleets being severely depleted. The turmoil and industrial unrest along the dock estate continued throughout the '50s, '60s, and '70s, with the port's percentage of trade dropping year by year. The port was, once again, in severe decline. The lack of investment, the growth of the container trade, industrial unrest, entry into the Common Market, and Liverpool's geographical location were all contributory factors in the continuing demise of the port and the city. Nevertheless, through political intervention and a series of business- and city led initiatives, the port began to show some signs of revival. The Royal Seaforth Dock container terminal was opened in 1973, which brought some trade back to the port. With Seaforth acting as a catalyst, plans were brought forward by Peel Ports to develop Liverpool2, an in-river deep water terminal, scheduled to be operational towards the end of 2016. When completed, the terminal will give the port a capacity to handle upwards of 2 million containers per year.

In recent years, the port has also seen the welcome return of cruise ships to the city, and, with the newly completed canal link (opened in 2009), leisure craft now have access to the very centre of the city.

This very brief introduction to the Port of Liverpool aims to focus on some of the more significant events that have moulded the development of the port and, by extension, the city itself. The book does not purport, in any way, to be an academic text, but is aimed at the general reader—charting a path through the development and the highs and lows of the dock estate.

David Paul
Liverpool
24 August 2015

1

Early Days

When the Domesday Book was being written, the hamlet of Liverpool did not even warrant a mention. At that time, Liverpool was a small, insignificant hamlet—referred to as a 'berewick'—in the West Derby Hundred.

It is known that in 1190 there was a small hamlet in the north of England that went by the name of 'Liuerpul', which meant a pool or a creek of muddy water. At that time, the hamlet was little more than a small fishing village. The berewick was centred around an inlet, towards the mouth of the River Mersey, known as the 'Pool'. The dwellings that formed the berewick itself were to the north and west of the Pool. As an inlet, the Pool was not affected by the Mersey's turbulent currents and thus afforded a natural harbour for fishermen's cobles. Indeed, the main and maybe the only commercial trade at the time would have been the sale of fish to neighbouring townships within the West Derby Hundred.

During this time, trade was limited in the extreme, other than in the berewick itself. Apart from the fishing smacks that sailed from the Mersey, the number of other vessels entering the Pool was limited to an occasional smack making its way over from either Ireland or up the coast from Wales. Trading was limited to the sale of cattle and hides and the buying of salt or tar. The berewick was indeed self-sufficient, but whenever other commodities were required (which could not be obtained either in the berewick itself or by normal trading connections) they tended to be brought in from Chester by the lord's bailiff.

On 18 October 1171, Henry II landed an army in Waterford. On the same campaign he also took Dublin, later accepting the fealty of the Irish kings and bishops when they knelt before him and submitted to him as their overlord and High King. When John succeeded his father and became king on 6 April 1199, he immediately went about establishing a series of ports from which he could transport troops to Ireland if and when it became necessary. There were already suitable ports, such as Bristol and Milford Haven in the south-west of the country, but it was important to establish a suitable port in the north-west of the country.

Much of the land in the area were Crown lands, owned by Henry II, but extensive lands that included Litherland, French Lea, and Liverpool, together with a number of other estates were granted to Warin, who was Constable of Lancaster Castle. There is no remaining record of this deed, but there does remain a deed of 1191 when John, son of Henry II, inherited the lands and duly passed the estates granted to Warin to his son Henry. However, the lands were subsequently reclaimed in August 1207 by King John. John's father had invaded Ireland, but there was still a need to keep a military presence. John was aware that, strategically, he could recruit men from his estates in Lancashire and also obtain the necessary supplies and equipment to sustain the assault. What he was lacking, however, was a convenient embarkation port on the north-west coast of England. The ancient port of Chester on the River Dee was the obvious choice, but over the years the river had become shallow and was no longer considered to be suitable for the embarkation and disembarkation of troops. It was also under the control of the independently minded earl and political alliances were too fragile and subject to frequent reversals for the issue to come under serious consideration—the Earl of Chester, who controlled the busy port, had his own political agenda that was not always compatible with the king's.

During 1206, John had occasion to traverse the length of Lancashire on his way to Chester. It is known that on 26 February 1206 he was in Preston and later, on 28 February, he was visiting Chester. There is no record of him passing through Liverpool, but it is highly likely that he did. It was when his attention was drawn to the creek at Liverpool that John recognised the strategic importance of the location and decided on a suitable course of action. His choice of Liverpool at least demonstrated that he had a keen understanding of strategy and could also exercise some vision as a statesman.

The following year, he entered into the exchange of lands with Henry FitzWarine of Lancaster by a Deed of Confirmation; in effect, exchanging parcels of land to suit his purposes. The exchange of lands was effected on 23 August 1207 and, just five days later, on 28 August 1207, John issued letters patent, inviting settlers to come to the new borough where they would gain a number of privileges. The letters patent, which are more commonly referred to as King John's Charter, state:

CARTA REGIS JOHANNIS

Rex omnibus qui burgagia apud villam de Liverpul habere yoluerint, etc. Sciatis quod concessimus omnibus qui burgagia apud Liverpul cepint quod habeant omnes libertates et liberas consuetudines in villa de Liverpul quas aliquis liber burgemotus super mare habet in terra nostra. Et nos vobis mandamus quod secure et in pace nostra illuc veniatis ad burgagia nostra recipienda et hospitanda. Et in hujus rei testimonium has litteras nostras patentes vobis transmittimus. Teste Simon de Pateshill apud Winton xxviii die Aug. anno regni nostri nono.

When translated, the charter reads:

CHARTER OF KING JOHN

> The King to all who may be willing to have burgages at the town of Liverpul, etc. Know ye that we have granted to all who shall take burgages at Liverpul that they shall have all liberties and free customs in the town of Liverpul, which any free borough on the sea hath in our land. And we command you that securely and in our peace you may come there to receive and inhabit our burgages. And in testimony hereof we transmit to you these our letters patent. Witness Simon de Pateshill at Winchester the 28 day of August, in the ninth year of our reign.

John had, by royal fiat, transformed the berewick of Liverpool into a borough overnight. He also granted the new borough extensive privileges. John's actions in creating the Borough of Liverpool were not purely altruistic however, his intention was for the new borough to act as a departure and provisioning port for his proposed conquest of Ireland. People were encouraged, by generous inducements, to settle in the area. The incentives offered in order to entice people to the new charter town of Liverpool included an attractive long and narrow plot of land, known as a burgage, upon which to build a dwelling and 2 acres of land—a Cheshire acre—and all in return for the princely sum of 12 pence per year.

In order to house the people who were moving to the new borough, King John himself designed and laid out the original street plan of Liverpool in the form of a cross. The seven streets were Bonke Street (now Water Street), Castle Street, Chapel Street, Dale Street, Juggler Street (now High Street), Moor Street (now Tithebarn Street), and Whiteacre Street (now Old Hall Street). The burgages were laid out along these streets.

Free borough status also conferred a number of privileges, such as 'all the liberties and free customs which any free borough on the sea or has in our land'. In effect, this gave Liverpool a position equivalent to both Southampton and Bristol. These advantages meant that the tradesmen benefitted from the restrictive trade practices. Later, King Henry III granted additional trading privileges, allowing burgesses exemptions from all tolls throughout the kingdom—a significant concession.

As well as wanting the newly created borough to be an embarkation port for his planned assault on Ireland, John also wished to develop trade through the port so that, when the need arose, he could requisition ships for his own usage. A secondary consideration was to levy tolls on strangers trading in the borough, thus adding much-needed cash into his depleted coffers.

The founder of the borough and Port of Liverpool was undoubtedly King John, and, even from these early times, Liverpool's fate, and that of her population, has been inexorably linked with the River Mersey.

Although Liverpool now had the status of a borough, even by the middle of the sixteenth century the population was still only around 500. Towards the end of the century, there were close on 168 burgages. Many of the inhabitants of the new borough—who were now free men—were already resident in the berewick or came from the neighbouring West Derby.

Although there was some modest growth in trade in the borough over the next few years, it could not be considered to be rapid growth by any stretch of the imagination. However, Liverpool residents did gain some small income from the passing trade that was drawn from the troops passing through the port on their way to Ireland.

Until 1699, Liverpool lay within the parish boundary of Walton-on-the-Hill, but an Act of Parliament changed that status and Liverpool became a parish in its own right. This new status was coincidental with a watershed in the town's development, for it is after that time that the town's population and commercial trading began to grow and thrive.

An extremely significant day in the history of Liverpool was on 23 August 1207. On that date, the hamlet of Liverpool changed hands again. John, now King John, changed the earlier agreement that he had made in 1191 with Henry, Lord of Liverpool and son of Warin. John, wishing now to confer borough status on the hamlet of Liverpool, exchanged the lands that he had granted to Henry in 1191 and, by way of compensation, granted him other estates.

Although King John granted the berewick letters patent in 1207, it must be remembered that these were granted mainly for political reasons and not, in truth, for the wellbeing and furtherance of the subjects who resided in the berewick of Liverpool. At the time, John was intending to invade Ireland, but, as he had somewhat limited access to the busy port of Chester, it suited his purpose to create another port in the north-west as a departure point for his ships. Inducements were given to attract people to the barren wastes of the areas in the immediate vicinity of the town. Later on, again for political reasons, John built a castle at Liverpool and also enclosed Toxteth Park for hunting purposes. Even so, the town was still dwarfed by its inland neighbour, Manchester.

In the early part of the thirteenth century, there was little sea-borne trade leaving the River Mersey. Ireland still continued to be the town's main trading partner, with imports of skins and hides. Liverpool's main exports being coal, cloth, knives, and leather goods, but the port was still predominantly a fishing port. A limited amount of wine was imported from France.

Perhaps the next significant stage in the borough's and ultimately the port's development was the purchase of a charter for £6 13s 4d (about £6.67) from the impoverished King Henry III. The new charter was granted in 1229 and gave the burgesses extensive powers to control the affairs and trade within the borough. The burgesses were now able to elect their own officers, instead of being obligated to the royal bailiff. Property disputes were now settled in the borough's own Portmoot court, rather than having to attend the courts in West Derby. However, the most important right enshrined in the new charter was the right to form a trade association or guild; a guild being an organisation designed to protect members trading interests. Henry decreed that the 'formation of a guild, enacting that no person, unless of that guild, should make merchandise, without the consent of the burgesses'. Burgesses wishing to join the guild had to pay an entrance fee or Hanse. The guild controlled all trade within the boundaries of the borough and no

The ancient wishing gate at Liverpool, painted by F. S. Serres Esq. in 1797. Serres was marine painter to George III.

An engraving of the town of Liverpool, Lancashire. The parish Church of Our Lady and Saint Nicholas can be seen in the centre of the image.

A harbour view showing the parish Church of Our Lady and Saint Nicholas.

one could trade within those boundaries unless they were a member of the guild or were expressly permitted to trade—there was normally a fee charged for this privilege. However, the royal bailiff was still collecting certain dues for the king, and his continued presence in the borough was not welcomed by the burgesses. It soon became common knowledge that the king was only receiving from the bailiff £9 in dues collected; the shrewd burgesses offered to pay the king £10 in return for allowing them to collect all of the dues and, in effect, put an end to the presence of the bailiff.

It is thought that Liverpool castle was built sometime between 1232 and 1235, although no definite evidence survives. What is known, however, is that the castle was built for the king by William de Ferrers, 4th Earl of Derby. The castle was sited at the highest point in the town, overlooking the Pool, and was built to protect King John's new Port of Liverpool. Some further significance must attach to the fact that, although Liverpool was still a very small town, it was represented by two members of parliament in 1295, despite not even being a parish in its own right.

The period between 1300 and 1400 saw very little change in the small fishing village of Liverpool. For instance, when the French were making raids on southern ports in 1338, razing Portsmouth and other coastal towns to the ground, King Edward III needed to mount a counterattack. He requisitioned vessels from many coastal towns; Bristol was required to provide twenty-four boats and Hull sixteen, but Liverpool was only asked to provide one small vessel with a crew of six—an indication of the town's standing at the time. Even by the start of the sixteenth century, it could not be claimed that Liverpool was in any way comparable with the mighty ports of London, Hull, and Bristol. Compared with these ports, Liverpool had what might be considered to be a very slow start. Bristol, one of the pre-eminent ports during the reign of Edward II, had twenty-six ships, whereas Liverpool could only boast one. Even towns on the north-eastern coast of England, such as Hull, had sixteen ships at that time. By the end of the sixteenth century, twelve vessels were regularly using the port; as late as the beginning of the seventeenth century, the figure had only risen to twenty-four vessels. Another measure of the relative importance or otherwise of a port could be gauged from the amount of 'ship's money', which was being paid to the Crown; at the time, Liverpool's payment amounted to £25, whereas Bristol had a liability of £1,000.

The town itself was located a little inland from the River Mersey, on the side of a shallow inlet. The inlet, known as the Pool, had a number of streams feeding into it. At its widest point it was about 1,200 feet wide and then reduced to 150 feet, about 1 mile inland. The Pool could be crossed by a number of bridges and there was also a ferry crossing. Further inland there were sluice-gates that, when opened, served to clean the muddy pool from time to time. The haven thus provided was a shelter for small fishing vessels, but, due to the extremely wide tidal range from the Mersey, the Pool was effectively unsuitable for any other form of trading, as cargoes had to be unloaded on the banks of the river.

The very earliest record of any form of sea defence at Liverpool was recorded in 1551, when the town employed a water bailiff to prevent encroachments and obstructions in the port and to be responsible for the 'care of the harbour and the oversight of the roadstead'. However, in 1561, the old haven, which made a suitable harbour for the small fishing vessels that sailed from the Pool, was destroyed by a hurricane. In 1565, the mayor of the town, Robert Corbett, took remedial action, decreeing that a harbour or breakwater should be built. He also ordered that townsfolk must assist in the work and that every household would be required to provide a labourer, free of charge, until the work was completed. However, even after improvements had been made, the port was still subordinate to the busy port of Chester. There was some residual benefit to the town, resulting from England's conquest of Ireland, as troops were still being transported from the port to quell insurrections. Although the town's prosperity was steadily growing, the population was still somewhat less than 2,000 in 1600.

Various initiatives were taken over the next decades to increase the depth of the 'Pool' in order for the harbour to accommodate larger vessels. To this end a new quay was built in 1635, but the measures taken were ineffective—the roadstead was unsafe and the tides' ferocity often caused much disruption and damage to vessels. As a result, many boats began to anchor on the Cheshire side of the Mersey in the Sloyne, where the ebb and flow of the tide was not as marked.

However, the fortunes of Liverpool and its port were about to change when the first prize ship, the first of many, sailed into the River Mersey in 1563. The vessel was captured by a privateer owned by Sir Thomas Stanley. However, before this enterprise could become firmly established, civil war broke out in England in 1642, as a consequence of tensions between the king and parliament. At the outbreak of war, Liverpool was in the Royalist camp, but in May of the following year, the town was taken by parliamentary soldiers—Roundheads. Elaborate defences were made against the Royalists Cavaliers, who, under Prince Rupert, tried to recapture the town in June 1644. The Roundheads left the town by boat before the Royalists sacked the town. After the Battle of Marston Moor, at which the Royalists suffered a heavy defeat, the whole of the North of England was taken by the parliamentarians.

The Civil War finally ended in 1651. However, before that time, the third and final siege of Liverpool took place, lasting from 20 August to 4 November 1644. Subsequent to that, much of the castle was gradually dismantled and the stone used for other building works.

Towards the end of the seventeenth century, the town of Liverpool began to prosper, as trade with the North American and West Indian colonies began to develop. Clearly, Liverpool was in a strategically advantageous position to profit from this surge in trade.

After the Great Fire of London in 1666, many merchants left the capital and some moved to Liverpool. By the early eighteenth century, the population of the small fishing village had grown; the emerging town now boasted a population of some 7,000 souls. Liverpool's first parish church was St Peter's, which was built in 1704. This newly found status was coincidental with a watershed in the town's development, for it is after that time that the town's population and commercial trading began to grow and thrive.

The beginning of the eighteenth century also saw Liverpool's sea-borne trade expand. In addition to trading with Ireland and Europe in general, vessels from Liverpool now regularly sailed to the West Indies. With the growing importance of the port and the undoubted benefits that it could bring to the salt industry of Cheshire, strenuous efforts were made in the early part of the eighteenth century to make the River Weaver navigable. Once this feat had been achieved, the centre of gravity of the salt trade shifted and ships from various parts of the globe traded in that commodity. Liverpool welcomed vessels from many European countries as well as ships from American ports. The population of Liverpool had grown to 10,446 by this time.

When the revenue of the small town of Liverpool increased due to trade on the River Mersey, the corporation of the town decided that, if trade was to continue to increase, an artificial haven or dock was required to create an anchorage for boats using the river, in order to ensure that they were given better and safer docking facilities; it did not go unnoticed that, by constructing a dock, the town's revenue should increase even further. Many arguments, both for and against, were rehearsed during the time when consideration was being given to the construction of a dock at Liverpool. Not least of the vociferous arguments against its construction came from the cheese-makers of Cheshire. It proved to be the case that their fears were well-founded, in that, virtually as soon as the dock was opened, cheese merchants from London sailed in, capitalising on a new trading opportunity.

In 1708, the corporation of the town decided that a more radical solution was required to alleviate the increasing congestion in the dock. Liverpool's trade with the American colonies was increasing, and consideration was being given to the notion of building a wet dock at Liverpool—this would be the first dock of its kind in the world. At that time, Liverpool was still, in relative terms, a very small town with a population of somewhere in the region of 10,000 souls. The fishing smacks that used the river tended to unload their cargoes in the small shallow inlet from the river known as the Pool. Although tidal, the Pool was ideal for its purpose, but was unable to accommodate larger vessels that occasionally entered the river. These vessels were forced to load and unload in the river itself, which, because of the vagaries of the notorious tides in the Mersey, was not the easiest of tasks. Boats had to load and unload when the tide was out.

Richard Johnson, who was one of the two MPs for Liverpool and a leading figure in the town's commercial community, stated in a letter dated 27 January 1708:

> On Sunday night (25 Jan.), in good time, I saw Mr Sorocold; he would gladly serve us about the Dock; he is a very ingenious man; he is of the opinion it may be very well done, the stones in the Castle will save a great deal of money. He will tell you the charge within three or four hundred (pounds), which is as near as can be computed.

After further discussions, Johnson and his fellow Liverpool MP, Richard Norris, were authorised by the town council to progress the design of the dock with a 'proper person'. At length, following much consideration of the task and expertise required to undertake the project, George Sorocold, a civil engineer of some renown, was commissioned to draw up plans for a wet dock in Liverpool, along similar lines to the dock that was being built at Rotherhithe. He returned to Liverpool in 1709, together with his surveyor:

> One Henry Huss of Derbishire who comes to survey the place where to make a dock with Mr Sorocold and draw a plan and estimate the charges thereof.

Both men were vigilant and thorough in their allotted task, to the extent that they were able to submit their plans later that year. It was clear that the council must have been impressed by their work, as both were granted the Freedom of the Town of Liverpool in recognition of their sterling work and contribution.

Sorocold's plans had rigidly adhered to the brief that he and Huss had been given by the town council, in that they made provision for a dock to be constructed in the vicinity of the Pool. Sorocold was aware that the natural harbour enabled smaller vessels to be loaded and unloaded, but was unable to accommodate larger vessels. His plans envisioned constructing a dock that would facilitate larger vessels being able to load and unload in the new dock, thus negating the effects of the tides. Vessels could enter at high tide and then the huge wooden dock gates would be closed, thus preventing any water from flowing out again. In effect this meant that, as the water level remained constant while the ship was in dock, the time required for loading and unloading could be significantly reduced. A ship could now be unloaded in little more than a day, whereas previously the same operation took almost two weeks because of the ebb and flow of the tides. The economic benefits accruing to the port and the town itself were substantial. The major benefit, as perceived at the time, being the possibility of increasing trade with the American colonies—an objective close to the hearts of both Norris and Johnson. Both men were actively engaged in the tobacco and sugar trade with the American colonies.

A bill was brought before parliament seeking permission to construct a wet dock in the town of Liverpool, amounting to no more than 4 acres, enough to accommodate berths for 100 vessels. In their application to parliament for an artificial haven or dock to be constructed at Liverpool, statements were made:

> The currents of the tides, both ebb and flood, were strong and rapid, especially during high winds and freshes in the river. The harbour was open to the westerly winds and the tempestuous weather, so shipping therefore which lay on the ground between the high and low water-mark or else floated in the current of the tide, to their great damage and destruction.

The act, based on the original survey, plans, and estimates that had been made by Sorocold and Huss, gained assent on 24 March 1710.

When the time came to appoint an engineer to be responsible for the building of the dock, neither Sorocold nor Huss were interested in accepting the position—perhaps being engaged in other projects. As a result of this major set-back, the town council was faced with having to find a competent engineer who would lead and oversee the work, with the knowledge that there were few engineers who were competent enough to take charge of such a mammoth project. However, it was brought to the attention of members of the town council on 17 May 1710 that a certain Thomas Steers was residing in the town and that he was competent enough to be given the responsibility of building the dock.

Although the definitive reason for Steers being given the post of dock engineer is not known, two plausible theories are gaining traction. Firstly, it is often assumed that Steers worked directly under Sorocold on the building of the Howland Wet Dock, which was completed at the beginning of the nineteenth century, and that it was Sorocold himself who recommended to Liverpool town council that Steers should be offered the position, having declined the position himself. An alternative explanation does, however, appear more feasible and suggests that, while on active service with the army, Steers gained valuable civil engineering skills. With increasing trade, the need for improved transport networks assumed a higher priority and so a knowledge of canal and dock design and construction was a skill worth having; Steers was well-placed in this respect. His exemplary work in these areas came to the attention of the Hon. James Stanley—later to become the 10th Earl of Derby—who was commanding the 16th Regiment of Foot in Flanders at the same time that Steers was deployed there. Stanley—who was mayor of Liverpool in 1707 and Lord Lieutenant of Lancashire until 1710—then mentioned Steers's skills and experience to his known associate, Thomas Johnson, and that it was primarily this intervention that was instrumental in Steers being offered the position. However, whichever set of circumstances ultimately led to Steers's appointment, the undeniable fact is that Steers was confirmed in post as Liverpool's first dock engineer on 17 May 1710. However, it is still a mystery as to why he was in Liverpool in the first place.

A glimpse into Steers's background may serve to illustrate his qualifications for the role of dock engineer. It is thought that Thomas Steers was born in 1672, somewhere in the Deptford–Rotherhithe area of Kent, although the exact year and place of his birth is not known. Following his early education, during which time he had gained a solid understanding of mathematics, Steers joined William of Orange's 4th Regiment of Foot (The King's Own) and went on to fight at the Battle of the Boyne in 1690. Later, he fought against the French in the Low Countries until the Peace of Namur was signed in 1697. He probably acquired his understanding of hydraulics during this period. As quartermaster, Steers's role would have given him ample opportunity to assess and evaluate the hydraulic systems employed in the Low Countries. Additionally, he would undoubtedly have been involved with procurement issues as well as conducting a significant amount of surveying and excavation work

On his return to England, Steers married Henrietta Maria Barber. Her father gifted them a dwelling in Queen Street, Rotherhithe. It was at this time that the Wells brothers, John and Richard, were engaged in the construction of a dry dock and shipbuilding yard, Howland Great Dock. There is no evidence to suggest that Steers played any part in its building, and his only professional link with the dock appears to be that he surveyed the whole area—perhaps being employed as a surveyor to the estate

Following his appointment as dock engineer, Steers immediately reconfigured Sorocold's original plans by changing the proposed location of the dock and also the method of construction. The plans were significantly different from those of Sorocold and Huss; Steers's plans envisaged that the wider 'mouth' of the Pool should be closed and the land reclaimed, enabling a dock to be constructed, together with suitable quayside access and gates giving direct access to the river. The concept was both revolutionary and innovative, allowing water to flow in at high tide before the dock gates were closed. The water level in the dock was thus maintained, allowing easier loading and unloading of cargoes without having to consider the changing and turbulent tides in the River Mersey. Sorocold and Huss's earlier plans, although similar in concept, had envisaged the dock being built on virgin land.

Steers's plans were accepted by the council and work commenced. Being an opportunist, Steers, in addition to being responsible for the design of the wet dock, was the major contractor in its construction and also for much of the excavation work, being named as one of the principal undertakers. There were several other sub-contracts for brickwork, masonry, and carpentry work. As dock engineer, Steers was obviously responsible for the oversight of the project, but much of the day-to-day work was left in the capable hands of his assistant, William Braddock.

Due to unforeseen difficulties when the dock was being built, principally due to the amount of soft mud that was encountered during building, it meant that the original budget proved totally inadequate. Also, because costings for the dock construction had been based upon Sorocold's original designs, this factor merely added to what was a significant degree of overspend. The final cost was approaching £12,000, almost double the original estimate. The corporation almost became bankrupt because of the unforeseen expenditure. Therefore, after six years of construction, the trustees were forced to return to parliament for a further act that would allow monies to be raised against the projected income when the dock became fully operational. The additional loan that was secured still did not cover all of the building costs, so land adjacent to the new dock was leased for building in order for the dock project to be finished. The dock, originally known as Steer's Dock and later known as Liverpool Old Dock, was opened to shipping on 31st August 1715. A contemporary record stated:

> 1715 August 31, I went to Liverpool and saw the 'Mulberry', the 'Bachelor' and the 'Robert' all in the dock. They came in this morning, and were the first ships as ever went into it. The 'Mulberry' was the first. Breakfasted at Mr. Owen's. He went with me to a smithy at the lower end of Redcross Street, where I saw an ox roasting.

This later act also included provision for a dry dock and three graving docks to be constructed close by the newly built wet dock. As a result of increasing trade, as had been envisaged, Steers was given the brief in 1718 to draw plans for a dock extension, south of the existing dock. However, not long after the Old Dock had been opened, Steers was the recipient of sustained criticism, as many considered that the dock had been sited on unsuitable ground with inadequate foundations. A major disadvantage to the operational efficiency of the dock was the stream that flowed directly into the dock. The continuous flow of polluted water into the dock caused silting, which in turn meant that, from time to time, the dock had to be completely drained so that the silt could be manually dug out and removed—the only suitable method of overcoming the problem at the time. The regular draining of the dock brought its own particular problems; not only was there a loss in trade during the time that the dock was effectively out of action, but draining the water from the dock lead to a weakening of the walls themselves.

However, in spite of these shortcomings, the Old Dock proved to be a great success, having the advantage of vessels being able to load and unload their cargoes without having to take into account tidal changes in the river itself.

Indeed, significant amounts of trade were taken from London, Bristol, and Chester docks. However, the dock soon became a victim of its own success and could not cope with the increase in the number of ships using the facility.

Shortly afterwards, in 1717, another Act of Parliament was passed, which gave authorisation for a tidal basin and a further three gravings or dry docks to be built close by the newly built wet dock. During the time of their construction, various changes were made to the original dock. This major undertaking was completed by 1721. By now, Steers was well-established as dock master, with a salary of £50 *per annum*, and Braddock was water bailiff. However, in 1724, Steers also assumed this role, but, rather than receive a salary, he was rewarded with a number of additional benefits and fees.

However, after the dock had been operational for a number of years, other shortcomings began to emerge. One of the more significant ones was due to the fact that the entrance to the dock was so narrow and the outer basin of the dock was so small that vessels were unable to run in for shelter. On 11 January 1737, the council made a resolution:

> There is an absolute necessity for an addition to be made to the present dock or basin … and also for a convenient pier to be erected in the open harbour on the north side of the entrance into the present dock, towards Redcross Street, for the safety of all ships when ready to sail from the port, to lie till a fair wind happens, which very often are prevented when in the wet dock by other ships lying before at the entrance.

As a result of this resolution, Steers was then directed, as Liverpool's dock engineer, to conduct a survey and design a second dock—to be known as South Dock. When the initial design phase had been completed, a bill was presented to parliament, seeking permission to build the dock. The Act of Parliament was passed in 1737 and authorised the construction of the dock and basin. The act also gave the council power to borrow £14,000; this figure also included the existing debt of £4,830. The corporation's contribution amounted to £1,000 and the land and foreshore for the dock site. The land amounted to somewhat in excess of 18 acres. A tidal basin was built, having a free surface area of some 4 acres that formed a large outer harbour to the Old Dock, together with three graving docks.

The new wet dock was to be built to the south of the Old Dock. Having been granted permission, tenders were out by 7 June 1738. Steers was once again appointed to oversee the construction work of the new dock and was also named as the principal contractor for the undertaking. As part of the ongoing improvements, the old wooden pier was replaced by a stone-built pier, and, in 1846, a graving dock was built at the north end of the pier. The graving dock was built to enable ships to be built and repaired within the dock system. Unfortunately, because of his untimely death towards the end of 1750, he did not live to see his work finished. On 7 November 1750, immediately following Steers's death, Henry Berry, who had worked alongside Steers as his clerk, was named as the town's dock engineer. The construction work on the dock—later renamed Salthouse Dock—was completed under his direction and opened in 1753.

Before leaving this initial chapter relating to the development of the docks at Liverpool, it may be fitting to add a further footnote about Thomas Steers. Steers was such an important influence on the initial development of the docks at Liverpool, it would not be unreasonable to assume that his activities were restricted to the waterfront alone. However, Steers's sphere of influence and activity was much wider than this. His activities were not solely confined to designing and constructing Liverpool's first wet dock; his knowledge of civil engineering meant that his services were in great demand and, fortunately, his appointment as dock engineer did not preclude him from becoming involved in a number of other civil engineering projects. In looking to some possibilities for the future, Steers surveyed the River Irwell and the River Mersey from Bank Quay in Warrington to Manchester, with the intention of building a canal; the objective here was to analyse the possibility of making a navigable canal from the Mersey into the heart of Manchester, thus enabling textiles and other manufactured products from Manchester and its environs to be more easily transported to Liverpool for export. Similarly, he also examined—with the same objective in mind—the possibility of making the River Douglas navigable. This development would considerably ease the transportation of coal from the mines in and around Wigan to the Port of Liverpool for onward shipment. Steers's first application to parliament to progress these initiatives proved unsuccessful, but a further application in 1720 was successful. In the written parliamentary approval, Steers was named as the undertaker for both projects, together with a number of other undertakers. Work on the Mersey and Irwell Navigation was completed in 1725, extending to over 15 miles in length and including eight locks giving an overall rise of 52 feet; it is believed that Steers himself was the engineer in charge of the project. The construction of the Douglas Navigation was more problematical however, and, as there were several financial obstacles to be overcome, the canal was not opened until 1742.

Different from most 'one-dimensional' occupations today, Steers's professional activities were not confined solely to docks and canals. It could be claimed that he had fingers in several different pies, including having part ownership in a slave ship (the *Dove*) sailing from Liverpool that traded with the West Indies. Continuing in a nautical theme, Steers owned a smithy that manufactured, predominantly, ships anchors. Nevertheless, his sphere of influence was not solely confined to sea-based ventures. Although Steers continued to have a strong affiliation to the docks and associated matters, he was also a man of vision, and in 1720 he collaborated with Sir Cleave Moore and Sir Thomas Johnson to open the Liverpool Waterworks. He also recognised that, if the port was to continue to develop, the transport infrastructure needed to be enhanced. He was appointed as one of the commissioners for the turnpike road from Liverpool to Prescot in 1725. Steers was also the council's representative when he appeared before a parliamentary committee in 1737, which was considering the application for a new Act of Parliament for the Weaver Navigation. It was also Steers's plans that were used when building the church of St George on the site of the Liverpool Castle. In 1739, Steers built a number of dwellings for poor and destitute seafarers. The following year, he opened the Old Ropery Theatre in Liverpool.

Steers was a well-respected figure in the public life of the town, and was active in several different spheres of life, not only in trade and commerce, but also in political and social life. He was fully aware of his position and the responsibilities which they carried. His rise to prominence now encompassed a number of civic responsibilities and honours, including being given the Freedom of Liverpool in 1713 and serving on the town council—he was later to become the Mayor of Liverpool from 1739 until 1740. For a time, Steers was town bailiff in Liverpool and subsequently out-burgess in Wigan. One of Steers's major roles, however, was to be responsible for the construction of Liverpool's fortifications during the time of the second Jacobite revolution of 1745.

In 1746, Steers made a preliminary survey of the River Boyne in Ireland; two years later, he made a complete survey, with the objective of making the river navigable. He was assisted in this project by a young engineer, Henry Berry. Steers was also responsible for completing all of the initial design work for the South Dock, but, due to his untimely death in 1750, was unable to see the completion of the new dock (later to be named the Salthouse Dock). Upon Steers's death, his associate, Henry Berry, was immediately appointed as dock engineer and given the task of completing the building work. The Salthouse Dock was opened in 1753.

In addition to his undoubted pioneering work in creating the world's first wet dock, coupled with his canal work—connecting centres of trade in the surrounding area to Liverpool—Steers's legacy is also reflected in both his political and trading activities in the town. Overall, his time in Liverpool undoubtedly helped, in large measure, lay the foundations of the town's rise to prominence in the eighteenth and nineteenth centuries.

2

Prosperous Times

Between the years of 1534 and 1834, the Spanish government gave written permission for other countries to sell people, as slaves, to Spanish colonies in the New World. The permission, granted as a monopoly, was known as an *Asiento*. However, in an age of colonial expansion, the French, Dutch, and English were all acquiring colonies in the West Indian islands and lands in Guiana. These counties all had ports of supply on the west coast of Africa—bases that were strenuously guarded by their colonial masters. By the beginning of the seventeenth century, it was becoming obvious that the most lucrative trade was the trade in people and, for that reason alone, it soon became a major priority for every sea-faring nation.

During this time, the Spanish War of Succession was being fought in order to determine who would succeed Charles II as King of Spain. When the war ended, a number of European countries, including Spain, Great Britain, France, Portugal, Savoy, and the Dutch Republic, signed a series of peace treaties in March and April of 1713 that were collectively known as the Treaty of Utrecht. Two other major treaties were signed: the Treaty of Rastatt (1714) and the Treaty of Baden (1714). Perhaps the most important outcome of the war, certainly as far as France was concerned, was that Philip of Anjou would become King Philip V of Spain. However, for the British, the benefits that they might derive were economically far more advantageous. Under the terms of the Treaty of Utrecht, Spain gave to Great Britain an *Asiento* that would, initially, be for a period of some thirty years. The clauses in the contract required the British to procure and supply to Spanish colonies 4,800 slaves per year, giving England the monopoly in the burgeoning slave-trade industry to these territories during the eighteenth and early part of the nineteenth century. In effect, this meant that there was now a complete and binding reversal in fortunes, in that the markets of the Americas, which had previously been gifted to the Netherlands and Portugal, were now virtually closed to them, and British traders were the recipients of this highly lucrative trade. It must be remembered that this was in addition to the slave trade that already existed with English colonies. Most of the slaves were, at that time, brought from in and around the region of Sierra Leone.

Cristoforo Colombo (Christopher Columbus) first sighted America on Friday 12 October 1492. His statue, outside of the Palm House in Liverpool's Sefton Park, declares: 'The Discoverer of America was the Maker of Liverpool'.

THE
ASSIENTO;
OR
CONTRACT
FOR

Allowing to the Subjects of *Great Britain* the Liberty of Importing NEGROES into the *Spanish America.*

Sign'd by the CATHOLICK KING at *Madrid*, the Twenty sixth Day of *March*, 1713.

By her Majesties special Command.

LONDON,
Printed by *John Baskett*, Printer to the Queens most Excellent Majesty And by the Assigns of *Thomas Newcomb*, and *Henry Hills*, deceas'd. 1713

At the Peace of Utrecht in 1713, the King of Spain granted to Great Britain the privilege of furnishing African slaves to the Spanish colonies in the Americas.

As a further concession, it was also enshrined into the terms of the Treaty of Utrecht that Britain would be given sovereignty of the formerly Spanish territories of Gibraltar and Minorca.

After the agreement had been signed, the British opened offices in Buenos Aires, Caracas, Cartagena, Havana, Panama, Portobello, and Vera Cruz, with the specific purpose of facilitating arrangements for the smooth operation of the slave trade. The terms of the agreement also provided for one ship, not greater than 500 tons, to be sent to any one of these ports every year (the *navío de permiso*— vessel permit) to trade in general goods. The Spanish did not relinquish all of their rights, ensuring that 25 per cent of the profits went to the King of Spain. A further percentage was given to Queen Anne, in whose name the *Asiento* had been granted in the first place. In the first year of operation following the signing of the treaty, a total of 1,230 African slaves were transported to Jamaica. In 1714, 2,680 slaves were carried, but in 1716–1717 the number had risen to in excess of 13,000; although the terms of the agreement appeared to be very lucrative—£10 being paid for a slave over sixteen years of age and £8 for a slave between the ages of ten and sixteen—the traders were still running at a loss. In part, this might have been due to the fact that it was also stipulated under the agreement that two-thirds of the slaves were to be male, and, of them, 90 per cent were to be adult.

Sometime before the signing of the treaty, the South Sea Company had been established in 1711 as a public-private partnership. The company's primary aim was to reduce the cost of Britain's national debt, and, by way of an investment incentive, the company was also granted a monopoly to trade with South America—a new and developing market. However, the concession was seen as a mixed blessing; trading with the continent of America was controlled by Spain, and, since Britain was still at war with Spain, any trade without a permit from Spain was deemed to be illegal and the only existing permit was the *Asiento* for the slave trade with the French. However, this situation changed in 1713, when the Treaty of Utrecht was signed, transferring the *Asiento* contract from the French to the British. Following some political manoeuvring, the trading rights as outlined in the *Asiento* were then devolved by the British government to the South Sea Company, but, the board of the company was reluctant to take on the slave trade as that was not within its remit. It was therefore agreed that the slaves were to be bought from the London-based Royal African Company, who, since 1672, had had the sole monopoly in the English slave trade along the West African coast. However, in 1698, during the reign of William III, laws were passed that rescinded the company's monopoly and opened the 'African trade' to all English merchants from any British port, with two *provisos*: firstly, they must pay a premium of 10 per cent of the total amount of their trade in order that, ostensibly, the forts and factories on the west coast—in which the company kept their captives—could be adequately maintained; and secondly, they were obliged to pay a £2 premium to the authorities in London, Bristol, or Liverpool. All three of these ports were then required to provide a resident official who would have responsibility for supervising the trade. Given these new incentives, Liverpool merchants entered into the market with aplomb. Therefore, in the same year that Liverpool became a parish, the first recorded slave ship, the aptly named *Liverpool Merchant*, part-owned by Sir Thomas Johnson, sailed from the Mersey on 3 October 1699 bound for West Africa. The ship's captain, having then purchased a 'human cargo' of 220 Africans, set sail for Barbados, where the slaves were sold. As a result of this initiative and a number of other business ventures, Johnson is often hailed as the 'Founder of modern Liverpool'. When the *Liverpool Merchant* returned to her home port on 18 September 1700, following its hugely successful voyage, the town's fathers soon realised the tremendous potential for rich rewards that the trade offered. Indeed, the fortunes that were made became the bedrock from which Liverpool's manufacturers and banking interests were built. Shortly afterwards, another Liverpool vessel, *The Blessing*, owned by Richard Norris, departed for the Gold Coast. In a letter from him to the ship's captain, dated 16 October 1700, Norris instructed him to 'call at Kinsale and then sail to the "windermost part" of the Gold Coast, dispose of the cargo, buy slaves, and make for Barbados; there sell the slaves, freight with sugar, cottons, and ginger, and sail back to Liverpool'. This pattern, once established, became the regular triangular route taken by all slave ships sailing out of Liverpool.

Although slower to enter the slave trade than either Bristol or London, ships sailing from Liverpool were soon beginning to capture much of the market. However, before the start of any slaving voyage, there were numerous preparations to be made by the shareholders in the enterprise. The merchants, who generally formed the largest part of the ship's shareholders, gathered together various items to be exported to Africa; cargoes often included items such as textiles brought in from Manchester and its environs, and iron and steel-ware from Sheffield. On occasions, more exotic textiles formed part of the cargo such as silks that had been imported from India or glass beads and trinkets that generally came from Italy. All in all, the ships carried a wide variety of goods on the first stage of their voyage.

While the merchants were engaged in locating and buying cargo items that could be traded upon arrival on the west coast of Africa, the ship owners were assembling the crew that would undertake the year-long voyage. Ship owners were all too aware that their choice of captain was by far the most important choice they would have to make, for it was largely due to him whether the voyage was successful or not. Having appointed the captain, other officers were then recruited; the first mate, second mate, and often a third and fourth mate. In the later years of the slave trade, Sir William Dolben introduced a bill that would make it mandatory for all slave ships to carry a surgeon, and would also regulate the number of slaves that vessels were allowed to carry on the 'middle passage'. The bill was passed and was given royal assent in July 1788. The surgeon's main role was to ensure that as many slaves as possible survived the trans-Atlantic crossing. This policy was not adopted for any altruistic reasons, but it was more one of expediency; the more slaves that survived the crossing and could then be sold, the higher the profits for the voyage.

Once appointed, the captains of all slave ships were usually issued with clear and precise instructions as to exactly what was expected for them to achieve on the voyage. One such letter, written to Peter Potter on 5 June 1783, declared:

> As you are appointed Commr of our new ship the *Essex* on board such we have shipped a well assorted cargo for the Windward Coast of Africa ... barter your cargo for prime young slaves none less than 4 feet 4 inches high ... [and] ivory.... If you should find the Windward Coast glutted with ships and the prices high, and a probability of lying long there, we recommend you to lay out that part of your cargo adapted for this part of the Coast, and such as will not be suitable for Gaboon, and purchase about 150 negroes, and proceed to Gaboon to dispose of the rest of the cargo for good slaves, ivory and wax ... to stay on Windward Coast if trade brisk and can get away in 4–5 months.... A few presents to the traders now and then will not be lost, and will promote your trade and quick dispatch which is the life of an African voyage, for lying long on the Coast brings distemper into your ship and often proves very fatal in the end....

The instructions were given to ensure that there was no misunderstanding as to exactly what was expected of them, and that was to maximise the profitability on every round trip. Robert Bostock, a ship-owner and slave trader owning four ships—the *Kite*, the *Little Ben* (which could both carry seventy-five slaves), the *Bess* (which could carry 200 slaves), and the *Jemmy* (which could carry 138 slaves)—was very clear when issuing orders following a none-too-successful voyage: 'I hope you will be very careful about your slaves and take none on board but what is Healthy and Young and not make the same excuse you did last Voyage'. Bostock was fully aware that healthy slaves could fetch anything between £36 and £38, instructing the commander of the *Bess* on what to do if sickness broke out: 'if your Cargo is Sickly you must make the best Hand you can of them'.

In 1783, Messrs Fox, Croft and Co. owned the *Bloom*, of which Robert Bostock was master. Following a voyage to Africa, Bostock took a cargo of slaves to America, returning to Liverpool with black ivory, cotton, textiles, gum, hardware molasses, and tobacco. In his letter book, Robert Bostock kept a record of many of the letters that he had written between 1779 and his death in 1793. It is clear from his letters that Robert traded in many commodities, including slaves. From contemporary records, it would appear that Robert owned ten vessels, including the *Bess*, the *Kite*, the *Jemmy*, and the *Little Ben*. A typical voyage of the *Bess* in 1789 recorded the following cargoes for each stage of the voyage: Liverpool to Africa—muskets, pots, and cloth, including 8 yards of best superfine cushtaes, 14 yards of Turkey plods, 8 yards of mixed niccanees, bought in Manchester; Africa to Barbados—220 slaves, ivory, wax, and tortoise-shell; and Barbados to Liverpool—wood, sugar, and cotton.

It is a matter of record that ships departing from Liverpool, on what was to become known as the 'Africa trade'—or the 'triangular trade' as some called it in recognition of the three separate elements involved—carried cargoes of manufactured goods from Liverpool and its environs including pottery, earthenware, clothing, jewellery, linen, and small knives and axes that were brought in and manufactured in nearby towns, mainly in the north of England, such as Manchester and Sheffield. Many of the cargoes being shipped from the Mersey had been sourced within a 40-mile radius of the port; coal from the Wigan coalfields and other mines in the vicinity, and textiles that had been produced in and around Manchester. With the number of inland waterways now being developed, many cargoes were being transported to the port by narrow boat. Liverpool was in a prime location to receive these valuable export cargoes. The ships were bound for West Africa, where the cargo was sold to local traders and another, human cargo, was bought for transportation over to America and the West Indies. The euphemistically called middle passage was the most hazardous part of the whole voyage and lasted, on average, between six and eight weeks. Upon arrival, the human cargoes were sold into slavery. Conditions on board were appalling, with many of enslaved dying or committing suicide. Once the captive Africans were sold into slavery, the holds were filled with tobacco, coffee, sugar cane, wood, cocoa, and rum, to be transported back to Liverpool and sold throughout the country.

In 1730, right at the beginning of the trade, about fifteen ships left the Port of Liverpool, but, at the height of the triangular slave-trading route (between the years of 1760 and 1807) more than 1,100 ships left Liverpool. These were all involved in the 'slavery triangle', transporting at least 80,000 Africans every year, but, a significant proportion, maybe upwards of 10 per cent to 20 per cent, died during the infamous middle passage.

The actual building of the slave ships generated huge amounts of income for the shipyards of the town. It was very important that the boats should be swift-sailing clippers as, by building boats with a good turn of speed, journey times were reduced, which in turn meant that the prospect of high numbers of deaths during the trip would be much reduced. It goes almost without saying that the boats were designed to accommodate the maximum number of slaves in the smallest space. The slave deck, which ran across the ship, was only normally just over 5 feet between decks, thus not even allowing the slaves to stand upright. There was a series of wooden benches, running parallel to each other, which were clamped to the deck itself.

On reaching the west coast of Africa, the manufactured goods that had been brought from Liverpool were sold and the cash from the sale was used to buy as many captured men, women, and children as their ships could accommodate. With its human cargo, the vessel set sail for the new worlds of the West Indies. After selling their 'cargo' to the highest bidder, the ships returned to Liverpool, now carrying sugar, rum, and tobacco back to their home port. The profits from these voyages could be very high and many people participated in the trade. In the short period from 1783 to 1793, Liverpool's slaving ships made a total of 878 round trips and carried 303,737 Africans to be sold as slaves. The human cargo grossed a sum of £15,186,850 when sold in the West Indies. After a number of deductions had been made—the purchase price of the Africans, agents' commission and other fees, and crew costs and maintenance of the ship—the profit for Liverpool traders was still in excess of £12,000,000.

There was a slight turndown in trade at the outbreak of the American War of Independence, which lasted from 1775–1783, but the numbers soon increased again following the end of the war and, by the time that the law against the slave trade was enacted, ships from Liverpool were transporting more than half of all the slaves that were being taken across the Atlantic.

The ship's carpenter normally spent the first part of the voyage, the trip from Liverpool to the African coast, preparing the accommodation for the slaves when they were bought. After reaching the west coast of Africa, the cargo had to be sold before negotiations were held to purchase any captive Africans. The process of negotiating for the human cargo was often a very protracted affair, with only one or two slaves being bought every day. It was not uncommon for captains to take anything up to two months to achieve a full complement of slaves. The notorious middle passage was often quite a rapid run, taking on average six to eight weeks to cross the Atlantic, when there were favourable trade winds, but if conditions were not good the passage could take anything up to ten weeks or even longer. In 1790, Alexander Falcolnbridge, in his book *An Account of the Slave Trade on the Coast of Africa*, wrote:

> From the time of the arrival of the ships to their departure, which is usually near three months, scarce a day passes without some negroes being purchased, and carried on board; sometimes in small, and sometimes in larger numbers. The whole number taken on board depends, in a great measure, on circumstances. In a voyage I once made, our stock of merchandise was exhausted in the purchase of about 380 negroes, which was expected to have procured 500. The number of English and French ships then at Bonny, had so far raised the price of negroes, as to occasion this difference.... I was once upon the coast of Angola, also, when there had not been a slave ship at the river Ambris for five years previous to our arrival, although a place to which many usually resort every year. The failure of the trade for that period, as far as we could learn, had no other effect than to restore peace and confidence among the natives, which, upon the arrival of ships, is immediately destroyed by the inducement then held forth in the purchase of slaves....
>
> Previous to my being in this employ I entertained a belief, as many others have done, that the kings and principal men bred negroes for sale as we do cattle. During the different times I was in the country, I took no little pains to satisfy myself in this particular; but notwithstanding I made many inquiries, I was not able to obtain the least intelligence of this being the case.... All the information I could procure confirms me in the belief that to kidnapping, and to crimes (and many of these fabricated as a pretext) the slave trade owes its chief support....

Upon reaching the west coast of Africa, slave ships would travel to several different ports, buying captured Africans whenever and wherever they could. The major ports on the west coast were rapidly becoming Bonny and Old Calabar. The Africans who had been captured ready for sale were detained in so-called slave forts before being sold and transported across the Atlantic. As trade prospered, local gang-masters organised raids to capture their fellow countrymen for sale to the visiting slave traders. As many slaves died within three years of leaving Africa, the plantations always wanted replacement labour. With more and more captives being needed, desperate tactics were often employed in order to secure a full boat of captives. Teams of man hunters ventured many miles inland, hunting their quarry. It was not unknown for hunters to travel over 200 miles to inland villages, taking as their bounty almost the total population, only leaving behind the old, sick, and infirm. Some more ruthless hunters were reputed to have torched habitations and killed any remaining souls before leaving. After being stripped naked, male captives were chained together before starting out on the long trek to the coast. There was no need to take the precaution of chaining the women and children together, as the effective use of whips was considered adequate to keep them under control. Any captives who died *en route* to the coast were just left—burial was not even considered. Upon reaching the coast, captives were sold to the traders, branded with hot irons, and then taken on board.

As a way of ensuring that only fit and healthy slaves were bought, the ship's commander or its surgeon would thoroughly inspect all slaves to be purchased— men, women and children. When taken on board, slaves were packed together, naked, on wooden shelves nailed to the deck. They were manacled and chained together with little or no room to move. Male slaves, who fetched the highest prices, were also held by leg irons. Due to the extremely limited space, slaves were forced to either kneel or lie down on the deck. There was a separate area where women and children were kept. Although their conditions were marginally better than the men's, they too were ill-treated and often sexually abused by the crew. John Newton wrote:

> When the women and girls are taken on board a ship, naked, trembling, terrified.... They are often exposed to the wanton rudeness of white savages.... Resistance or refusal would be utterly in vain.

When the captain of the slave ship had purchased his full complement of slaves, the ship turned and headed for North America. The voyage across normally took somewhere in the region of two months, but, depending upon the winds, the journey could take anything from seven to ten weeks. It would appear that most slave deaths occurred at the beginning of the voyage to America.

There was undoubtedly intense pressure placed on the captain, not only did he have the responsibility of ensuring that the ship, its crew, and human cargo survived the voyage, but he was also responsible for ensuring that the maximum amount possible was obtained when the slaves were sold and, similarly, he was required to purchase the slaves from the traders in Africa for the lowest possible price—a difficult mission to achieve in all aspects. It was during the period when negotiations were being held and before the ship sailed for the Americas that many of the slave deaths occurred.

The captives' diet during the arduous trans-Atlantic crossing was meagre to say the least, consisting mainly of a daily ration of gruel. Captives refusing to eat were whipped and force-fed. Due to the extremely limited space, disease amongst both crew and slaves spread very rapidly; dysentery, cholera, and other related diseases being the main causes of death—as many as 20 per cent of the slaves did not survive long enough to set out on the crossing. On one voyage of the *Essex*, Captain Peter Potter lost forty-eight Africans out of a total of 330 that he had on board during that particular trip. Similarly, Newton, on only his second triangular voyage, recorded:

> This day buried a fine woman slave, having been ailing some time.... She was taken with a lethal disorder which they seldom recover from.
> ...Scraped the rooms, then smoked the ship with tar, tobacco and brimstone for 2 hours, afterwards washed with vinegar.

Slaves were not even allowed to relieve themselves, having no option other than evacuating where they lay. Those who did survive to face the crossing still had to contend with sea-sickness, terror, inhumane beatings, noxious smells, and inappropriate sexual encounters. It is not an exaggeration to claim that conditions on board for the captives were totally inhumane; for example, there was overcrowding, with captives forced to lie down or crouch down because of lack of space. The ships were often unseaworthy, especially when there was bad weather to contend with mid-Atlantic. There were other forms of ill-treatment and whipping, which often led to slave rebellions, only to be quashed by more whipping with the notorious 'cat o' nine tails'.

During the crossing, the slaves, often numbering hundreds, were brought out onto the weather deck on most days to exercise, but that was only when conditions allowed. This exercise was aimed at keeping them in good health so that profits could be maximised when the slaves came to be sold at the end of the voyage. When the sea-state was not good enough for them to be brought onto the deck, they remained chained below in the fetid conditions and this is when many of the fatalities occurred. It is hardly surprising that only half of the slaves were actually alive or fit to start work when they arrived at their destination. Many of the slaves died on the crossing, with smallpox, diarrhoea, and dysentery being common killers. Also, because of the conditions on board, many slaves arrived crippled or too weak to work. Captives dying *en route* were thrown overboard. The treatment that slaves were subjected to during the middle passage is hardly credible today. Captain Luke Collingwood, master of the *Zong*, fearing that large numbers of his cargo would die because of a shortage of water on board, had 132 slaves thrown overboard. In this way, he could claim on his insurance as the cargo had been lost because of the 'perils of the sea'. He could not have claimed if they had died due to malnutrition—the claim was met.

In his book of 1787, *Thoughts upon the African Slave Trade*, John Newton, erstwhile slave ship captain and slave trader from 1747 to 1754, later ordained minister, hymn writer, and campaigner for abolition, wrote:

> With our ships, the great object is, to be full. When the ship is there, it is thought desirable, she should take as many as possible. The cargo of a vessel of a hundred tons, or little more, is calculated to purchase from two hundred and twenty to two hundred and fifty slaves. Their lodging-rooms below the deck, which are three (for the men, the boys, and the women) besides a place for the sick, are sometimes more than five feet high, and sometimes less; and this height is divided towards the middle, for the slaves lie in two rows, one above the other, on each side of the ship, close to each other, like books upon a shelf. I have known them so close, that the shelf would not, easily, contain one more.

Newton, then writing more than thirty years after leaving the trade, stated:

> The slaves lie in two rows, one above the other, on each side of the ship, close to each other, like books on a shelf. I have known them so close, that the shelf would not easily contain one more ... the poor creatures thus cramped for want of room, are likewise in irons, for the most part both hands and feet, two together, which makes it difficult for them to turn or move, or to attempt to rise or to lie down, without hurting themselves or each other....

It was evident at the time that most ships' captains and certainly the ships' owners did not differentiate between one form of cargo or another. Slaves were viewed as a commodity, rather than being people in their own right. When Newton published his *Thoughts upon the African Slave Trade*, he readily acknowledged that 'I never had a scruple upon this head at the time.... What I did I did igno-rantly; considering it as the line of life which Divine Providence had allotted me'.

Captain Hugh Crow, in one of his later statements, reflected that 'it has always been my decided opinion that the traffic in negroes is permitted by that Providence that rules over all, as a necessary evil'. In his own eyes, Captain Crow treated his slave cargo with kindness and humanity, as can be seen in his autobiography, *Memoirs of the Late Captain Hugh Crow of Liverpool*, wherein he states:

> I always took great pains to promote the health and comfort of all on board, by proper diet, regularity, exercise, and cleanliness, for I considered that on keeping the ship clean and orderly, which was always my hobby, the success of our voyage mainly depended.

Obviously, the concept of 'success' is open to interpretation.

It was a fairly common occurrence for slaves to revolt during the middle passage, but most slave captains were aware of this possibility and had a number of deterrents, which they could bring into force as and when it became necessary. On one voyage, Newton observed:

...that the slaves were forming a plot for an insurrection. Surprised two of them attempting to take off their irons, and upon further search in their rooms, upon the information of three of the boys, found some knives, stones, shot, etc. and a cold chisel. Upon enquiry there appear eight principally concerned to move in projecting the mischief and four boys in supplying them with the above instruments. Put the boys in irons and slightly in the thumbscrews to urge them to a full confession.

Some little while later, he uncovered another revolt being incubated, and 'punished them with the thumb screws and afterwards put them in neck yokes'.

In 1746, a slave-ship captain, Thomas Phillips, in his book *A Journal of a Voyage*, wrote:

I have been informed that some commanders have cut off the legs or arms of the most wilful slaves, to terrify the rest, for they believe that, if they lose a member, they cannot return home again: I was advised by some of my officers to do the same, but I could not be persuaded to entertain the least thought of it, much less to put in practice such barbarity and cruelty to poor creatures who, excepting their want of Christianity and true religion (their misfortune more than fault), are as much the works of God's hands, and no doubt as dear to him as ourselves.

However, slave-ship captains were always conscious of cost, especially when it came to the cost of food for the slaves. A stew or pottage made from mixed beans was usually served twice a day. This meagre diet was supplemented by bread and water. An explicit instruction to Captain Luke Mann from the ship's owners stated:

You must not give your slaves too much provisions; they are accustomed to low diet in their own country.

When John Newton found that he was overspending towards the end of one of his voyages, he issued instructions to 'give the slaves bread now for their breakfast for cannot afford them two hot meals per day'.

It is difficult to describe the extent of the lengths that slavers went to in order to maximise their profits. Newton described how slaves were prepared for sale immediately before reaching their destination:

Wash'd the slaves with fresh water and rubbed them with Bees wax and Florence oil ... their skins dressed over three or four times with a compound of gunpowder, lime juice and oil.

In addition to disease and slave insurrection, slave ships were often ship-wrecked, with over 440 being recorded. More than double this number were seized by privateers and then later, in the nineteenth century, when the slave trade had technically been abolished, more than 1,800 slave ships were impounded by naval anti-slaving patrols.

Both the British and French governments were pressurised into introducing laws designed to regulate conditions on board slave ships. The numbers of captives that could be carried was strictly controlled, rations of food and water were also regulated, and it was also required that a surgeon must be carried on every voyage. In the main, the laws were not designed for the wellbeing of the captives, but rather to ensure the security of the crew and the safe passage of the cargo. However, after it had been decreed that surgeons should sail on every voyage, the number of captives that died during the middle passage was considerably reduced. Surgeons were paid 'head money', an amount that depended upon the number of captives reaching the Americas still alive.

With the ravages and depravations of the middle passage being completed, it was important for the cargo to be disposed of as quickly as possible after docking in America or one of the Caribbean islands. The slaves were sold to work in sugar plantations, coffee plantations, or cotton plantations. More often than not, the ship's owners had agents who would conduct the business on their behalf. The preferred method of purchase was for the prospective new 'owners' to string together all of the slaves that they wished to purchase. If any slaves were not sold, perhaps due to their old age or illness, they were cast adrift and their destinies left to the elements. Of the slaves that did survive the crossing, fewer than 60 per cent survived for longer than one year when sold to work on the plantations. A small number were kept as domestic servants.

On their return across the Atlantic, there were many hazards, which could be encountered, not least of which were hostile approaches from privateers or gale-force winds. It was understandable, therefore, that on sailing into the Mersey many captains were ordered to hoist flags in order to inform their owners of the ship's return. One such instruction issued to William Young from the ship's owner, Thomas Leyland, merely stated:

> On your return to this Port hoist white flags at your fore and main top gallant mast heads, which will be answered at the light house on a pole to the southward of the house....

Upon seeing these flags of identification, the lighthouse at Bidston would send an acknowledgement to the ship. Seeing this acknowledgement, the ship's owner would then also be aware of the imminent arrival of his ship.

The triangular slave-trade route meant that, generally, Africans were not brought to Liverpool to be sold as slaves. There were exceptions, however, with a small number of Africans being brought to Liverpool in the eighteenth century to be sold as house servants. The largest recorded sale in the town was held at the Exchange Coffee House in 1766, when eleven Africans were sold.

During the eighteenth century, the concept and practice of the slave trade was little more than an economic proposition to those involved, and the success of a voyage was measured in terms of the number of slaves who survived the trip, ready to be sold on arrival. Upon arrival at their final destination, the cargoes from the slave ships were sold and added to the wealth of the ship owners and the economic prosperity of the town in general. Many of the slave ship owners, acquiring untold wealth because of the trade, often turned to philanthropy, and many charities were founded by Liverpool's entrepreneurs.

Prosperity was often seen as the justification for perpetuating the practice. Captain Hugh 'Mind-your-Eye' Crow observed that 'the traffic in negroes was permitted by that Providence that rules over all, as a necessary evil'.

He also promulgated the view that English slavers had a genuine regard for human life, unlike some foreign ship owners whose countries carried on with the practice well after England had abolished the slave trade in 1807.

Although difficult to reach an accurate figure, it has been estimated that during the course of the eighteenth century somewhere in the region of 6 million people from Africa were forced into slavery; the major perpetrators of these crimes being countries from the 'Old World'. Also, it cannot be denied that many of the slave ships engaged upon the euphemistically labelled African trade, sailed from the Port of Liverpool, especially towards the latter end of the century. Therefore, it is not difficult to appreciate why slave ship owners wanted to carry as many slaves to the Americas as was physically possible. Economic exigencies being what they are ensured that, even after the slave trade was declared to be illegal, slaves could still be sold for exorbitant figures. Even though there were high mortality rates on most voyages, the trading profits were such as to make the speculative venture still extremely lucrative.

One of the critical advantages that Liverpool merchants gained during the years of the slave trade, which would prove to be beneficial to both the port's and town's future prosperity, was their expert knowledge of the trade and the network of contacts that they established on the African coast. Liverpool traders were savvy as to what types of goods were saleable on the African coast, and, similarly, where there were markets for cargoes on their return to the Mersey.

An Act of Parliament curtailed the monopoly held by the London-based Royal African Company; a monopoly that previously had ensured that the company had sole rights in the enforced transportation of Africans to be sold into slavery in the West Indies. From 1698, when the act came into force, merchants and entrepreneurs from Bristol, Liverpool, and London were free to enter into the slave trade, but in those early days the slave trade was dominated by the ports of London and Bristol. At the start of the eighteenth century, Bristol was gradually increasing its share of the trade and by 1730 had surpassed London in both numbers of slaves traded and the monies accruing from those sales. Although beginning to enter into the market, Liverpool did not play any significant part in the trade at this stage.

Even though the first slave ship to sail from the Mersey was not until 1699, Liverpool's entrepreneurs soon caught up on this lucrative trade, by improving ship design. Ships built in Liverpool were sleek, thus making the trip quicker and reducing the risk of losing too many of the slaves during the middle passage. Also, the hold spaces were built in such a way that, size for size, more slaves could be transported than in other ships.

By the early part of the eighteenth century, Liverpool's 'market share' had increased and Liverpool was the county's leading slave-trading port by the 1740s, overtaking both Bristol and London. By any measure, Liverpool was now the dominant partner in the trade, having more ships engaged in the trade and carrying more slaves across the Atlantic. Liverpool ships continued to dominate the market and the market share had increased to 80 per cent of all UK trade and in excess of 40 per cent of trade throughout Europe by the 1790s.

Number of Slave Ships Sailing from English Ports

Port/Year	1725	1730	1772	1800
London	87	25	39	20
Bristol	63	39	24	5
Liverpool	0	21	92	106

It has been calculated that, at a conservative estimate, a return on capital invested in the slave trade could amount to somewhere in the region of 8 per cent to 10 per cent.

The question as to just why Liverpool had gained an ascendency in this trade has to be asked. There are a number of reasons why the Port of Liverpool achieved pre-eminence in the African trade. The geographical significance of Liverpool's location cannot be underestimated; with the advent of the Industrial Revolution and the construction of a number of inland waterways, Liverpool was in a prime position for exporting goods, such as copperware, pottery, and brassware from Staffordshire and Cheshire, small arms from Birmingham, cutlery from Sheffield, and textiles from Lancashire and Cheshire.

Trading links were also developing between Liverpool and London, which introduced a number of different luxury goods. Liverpool's merchant classes were exercising their business acumen while, at the same time, taking advantage of the benefits accruing from the scale of development occurring in and around the north-west as a result of the Industrial Revolution. The business logic was undeniable; England was producing finished industrial machines and machinery products that were in demand in Africa while, in turn, the so-called New World was in dire need of manual labour. To complete the 'trading loop', there was growing demand for imported Virginian tobacco and West Indian sugar. The geographical location of Liverpool meant that the port was in a strategically favourable position to benefit from the opportunities being presented.

Undoubtedly, it was in large measure due to the expert knowledge and entrepreneurial skills that Liverpool merchants were developing with traders on the African coast. Liverpool's traders were continuing to gain experience of the African markets and were becoming increasingly aware of exactly what commodities would sell and what could not be easily traded. This was another advantage that Liverpool merchants gained over their rivals from London and Bristol.

Another one of the measures that Liverpool's ship owners adopted in order to increase their share of the market was to employ youngsters instead of experienced sailors; in this way, overheads were kept to a minimum. Also, in general terms, Liverpool ships were both bigger and faster than the slave ships sailing out of Bristol, and, when crew costs were added into the equation, it is easy to understand just why Liverpool ship owners became dominant in the slave trade.

However, there was one principal reason why Liverpool ship owners and traders participated in the slave trade for so long, and that was pure economics. The profits that could be accrued through this lucrative trade were immense. Although not everyone subscribed to this view, and some dissenting voices were beginning to be heard in the town. When George Cooke, the actor, was being booed off a Liverpool stage in 1772 for appearing to be the 'worse for wear', he calmly walked to the edge of the stage and stoutly declared:

> I have not come here to be insulted by a pack of men every brick in whose detestable town was cemented by the blood of a Negro.

The audience, to their credit, cheered him; an indication perhaps of the changing attitudes within the town.

When defending the practice, a letter was sent from the town council to one of the Secretaries of State in 1762, declaring 'that the West-Indian and African trade is by far the largest branch of the great and extensive commerce of this town', while also stating:

> That this is the most beneficial commerce, not only to themselves, but to the whole kingdom, as the export is chiefly of the manufactures of the kingdom, British ships and seamen solely employed, and the returns made in the produce of the colonies belonging to Great Britain.

Between the years 1750 and 1807, it has been estimated that upwards of one half of Liverpool's sea-faring trade was with Africa and the West Indies, and that much of Liverpool's wealth was acquired by virtue of this trade.

In the eighteenth century, the town of Liverpool saw its port transformed from being a relatively minor trading centre, handling cargoes from Ireland, some northern European countries, and coastal ports of England and Wales, to a truly international port, with trading partners throughout the commercial world. The slave trade was obviously proving to be a great source of wealth for Liverpool's merchants and traders, but it also provided a respectable living for many of the town's inhabitants, including sailors on slave ships (commanding a higher wage than if sailing on other cargo vessels), dock workers, ship builders, carpenters, gunsmiths, and craftsmen following other allied trades. As with the pattern of current economic activity, a number of auxiliary trades and merchants were well-positioned to profit from the slave-trading activities in Liverpool. Tradesmen who profited from the fitting-out of the boats on the banks of the Mersey included shipwrights, chain makers, sail makers, chandlers, coopers, rope makers, and others. Consequently, the town itself profited from the upsurge of economic activity throughout the eighteenth century. It must not be forgotten that there were huge customs duties, which went directly into government coffers. Profits accruing to the town helped develop the impetus to build more dock facilities along the Mersey. It is understandable why the town's tradesmen had a vested interest in maintaining the trade. Also, industries further afield were also garnering the profits from the trade, most noticeably the mills of Lancashire. Liverpool was fast becoming a significant trading port.

The slave trade had become such a central feature of Liverpool's local economy that between 1787 and 1807 all of the town's mayors had some connection with the slave trade. Many members of the town council were also involved with the trade, as were the town's MPs. Thomas Johnson, a prominent slaver in the town, represented Liverpool at Westminster from 1701 to 1723. His relatives, Richard Gildart and James Gildart, both held the office of mayor in the town. Another leading merchant in the town who made a considerable fortune from his involvement in the slave trade was Foster Cunliffe, mayor of the town on three occasions and also President of the Liverpool Infirmary. Thomas Leyland, who was mayor in 1798, 1814, and 1820, was one of the town's richest men. He made his fortune between 1782 and 1807 by carrying almost 3,500 Africans to Jamaica. Like some others who had made their fortunes through the slave trade, he invested his money in banking; forming the bank Leyland & Bullins. The bank merged with the North & South Wales Bank, which, in 1908, became part of Midland Bank.

During the remainder of the eighteenth century, Liverpool's slave trading activities—and subsequent dominance—continued to grow, seemingly unabated. In 1730, one in every eleven ships sailing from British ports had sailed from Liverpool, but by 1771 this figure had risen to one in every three ships. Towards the turn of the century, five in every eight ships engaged in slave trading were sailing from Liverpool. Seemingly, the slave trade and the profits that followed in its wake were beginning to be seen as being economically, culturally, and socially acceptable. Even the established Church of England was not immune to this profitable trade, with the Archbishop of Canterbury himself not being averse to speaking in favour of the practice—remembering that the church owned slave plantations at Codrington on Barbados.

There were now many hundreds of merchants in the town of Liverpool who invested heavily in the lucrative slave trade, but there were ten merchants whose investments far outstripped all of the smaller investors in the business. The most important and influential of these included William James, William Boats, Miles Barber, William Gregson, and William Davenport among their number. From contemporary records still extant, it is known that William Davenport was achieving an average return of almost 11 per cent on his ventures from 1757 and 1785, but other voyages were far more successful. In 1779 and 1780 the *Hawke*, under the command of Captain John Smale, returned profits of 73 per cent and 149 per cent respectively.

Venture Profits on 110 of Davenport's Slaving Ventures by Period of Investment, 1757–1785

Year	Ventures	Outlay (£)	Return (£)	Profit (£)	Profit (%)
1757–1767	31	16,986	18,392	1,407	8.3
1768–1771	30	20,261	24,165	3,904	19.3
1772–1774	22	21,202	22,906	1,704	8.0
1775–1777	12	18,346	18,487	141	0.8
1778–1785	15	19,583	22,946	3,363	17.2
Totals	110	96,377	106,895	10,519	10.9

With the profits accruing from the slave trade, many merchants and slave ship owners, including brothers Arthur and Benjamin Heywood, chose to diversify and channel their profits into other ventures. A number of small banks were established in Liverpool. The Heywoods, who had made a great deal of money from the slave trade, launched a bank called Arthur Heywood, Sons & Co. The bank was later absorbed into the Bank of Liverpool, which later became Martin's Bank and subsequently Barclay's Bank. However, Liverpool's wealth was not solely being generated from the direct profits accruing from the slave trade. By 1780, almost half of the specially designed slave ships were being built and repaired on the banks of the River Mersey, thus bringing more profits to the town. Other successful merchants chose to invest their profits in sugar, tobacco, and other commodities. In fact, the town's future trading focus was based, in part, on these industries, so it could be claimed in a general sense that the slave trade had had a lasting and beneficial effect upon the town—an effect that was to last well into the middle of the nineteenth century. Another hidden benefit for the town was the ability to avoid having to pay import duty by storing goods on the Isle of Man.

Fortunately for Liverpool, when the slave trade was brought to an end through government legislation, the town continued to thrive, turning to other sources of trade and income. There was a number of influential families in the town, such as the Holts, the Rathbones, and the Bibbys, who were successful in looking for and finding new export markets and new cargoes to export.

During the second half of the eighteenth century, it is fair to say that much of the trade passing through the increasingly busy Port of Liverpool was due to the trade with Africa and the Caribbean. More than half of the town's sea-borne trade could be attributed to this extremely profitable enterprise, with many of the town's leading merchants and politicians investing in and profiting from the trade. Given the prosperity that Liverpool was basking in as a result of the huge profits from the slave trade, it is hardly surprising that when the campaign for abolition was gaining momentum in the 1780s, few of the town's merchants were in favour of abolition. In fact, when viewed from a purely economic perspective, it is perhaps understandable why there was so much opposition to the movement in the town. Not only would the investors in the trade lose, overnight, their lucrative profits, but many local tradesmen and sea-farers would also be forced to seek alternative sources of income. Furthermore, many local and national politicians feared that, if a law was passed abolishing slave trading, then the economic prospects for the town would suffer a significant downturn. When a committee of the House of Commons considered the issues surrounding abolition of the trade, a number of prominent townsfolk spoke in favour of the continuation of the trade. These spokesmen were treated as local heroes and were often showered with gifts and honours—many receiving the freedom of the town.

There were, however, a number of local abolitionists, among whom was William Roscoe. Although not engaging in public debate at the outset, Roscoe was nonetheless active in a less high-profile capacity. William Rathbone and his son were adherents to the cause of abolition.

The arguments, both for and against abolition, were waged for many years, as the economic benefits resulting from the slave trade were just too much for some Liverpool traders to relinquish; trade, in one form or another, continued for many more years until slavery was finally abolished in the British Empire in July 1833.

George Fox, the first leader of the Religious Society of Friends (Quakers), began to question the morality of slavery. Opposition to the practice was also gaining advocates in America, where Quakers there were able to witness plantation slavery first-hand. Anthony Benezet was an ardent campaigner in the abolitionist movement. It was as a result of Benezet's writing that John Wesley, the English evangelist and hymn writer, was able to influence other likeminded Methodists to espouse the principle and practice of abolition. However, from the very earliest days of the slave trade, and indeed throughout the whole period that traders from Liverpool were involved in the notorious trade, there had always dissenting voices. Many churchmen, not just Quakers, objected to the practice on religious grounds alone, whereas others found the brutality and ill-treatment of the slaves as inhumane. Initially, little credence was given to these dissenting voices, as the continuing prosperity of the plantations depended upon African slave labour.

In 1765, the radical activist Granville Sharp was almost a lone voice in campaigning about the injustices of slavery. Following the massacre on board the slave ship *Zong*, Sharp became engaged in a number of court cases, which highlighted the broader issues relating to the slave trade; at that time, he was primarily concerned to stop African people being returned, against their will, to the slave colonies. Then, in 1785, a Cambridge undergraduate, Thomas Clarkson, won a competition with an essay entitled, 'Is it lawful to enslave the un-consenting?'

Clarkson was later introduced to a number of Quakers in London, who also wished to see an end to the slave trade. As a direct result of that meeting, they had the essay published and, once published, it became a rallying cry and catalyst against the continuation of the slave trade; a long-held belief of Quakers being that slavery was immoral and inhumane, as no person has the right to own another. Subsequently, on 22 May 1787, a small group of people founded the Society for Effecting the Abolition of the Slave Trade and worked to change the public perception of the slave trade and its abuses. Its main express purpose, however, as its name suggested, was the total abolition of the slave trade. The twelve-man committee, of whom nine were Quakers, was established and elected as their chairman and secretary two Anglicans, Granville Sharp and Thomas Clarkson, respectively. Clarkson was asked to spearhead the campaign for abolition on a countrywide basis, even though he was not a Quaker himself. Driven by a deeply held belief, Clarkson then approached the task of collecting evidence and materials that would convince a wider public and also MPs that there was a desperate need to put an end to the slave trade. His tireless campaigning ensured that there was a greater general awareness in the country of the need for abolition. It is reckoned that in a relatively short span of time, between the years 1787 and 1794, when Clarkson was engaged upon his nationwide campaign, he travelled somewhat in excess of 35,000 miles—a phenomenal feat by any standards. Clarkson addressed audiences up and down the country, in meeting halls, chapels, and churches, in order to further the abolitionist's campaign. He spent much time talking to sailors so that he could gather information, both about the trade and the conditions on board the slave ships, as it related to the sailors themselves and also to the slaves. He managed to collect many of the objects of torture and restraint that were frequently used on the ships: branding irons, thumb screws, handcuffs, leg-shackles, and a tool that enabled slaves' jaws to be forced open when food was being refused. The importance of ensuring that as many slaves completed the crossing cannot be overemphasised, and, because of this, slaves often tried to commit suicide by refusing to take any food.

As Clarkson continued to collect his material to aid the campaign supporting the abolition of the slave trade, he came to the view that, if other forms of trade could be developed with Africa and the Americas, trade would continue to flourish, contrary to much influential opinion that abolition would spell economic disaster for the towns leading the trade, such as Liverpool and Bristol. Others later came to appreciate the logic of his arguments.

The society was very efficient and structured in its approach to achieving its aims, employing a number of different tactics in order to gain more public and parliamentary support. Their objectives were clear and they had access to both printing and distribution of materials. The society was also gaining a number of influential persons to their ranks, including Josiah Wedgewood and William Wilberforce MP. Wilberforce had become a supporter of the abolitionist cause after having read the evidence that had been presented to him by Thomas Clarkson in 1787, the long-standing campaigner. Following that first meeting, the two formed a relationship that was both profitable and complimentary; profitable in the sense that by working together they were able to change the county's view on slavery, and complimentary in the sense that, although they had different skills, when combined, their case was difficult to refute, presenting a powerful force for abolition. Further assistance was later given by James Stephen, Wilberforce's brother-in-law, when his skills of legal draftsman-ship were put to good use in helping to guide the subsequent bill through its parliamentary stages.

Towards the end of the eighteenth century, social attitudes towards the practice of slave trading were changing, mainly due to the well-orchestrated publicity campaign that had been initiated by the Society for Effecting the Abolition of the Slave Trade; the movement to abolish the slave trade was now beginning to gain more momentum, especially after receiving considerable support from a number of influential persons who were sympathetic to their cause, most notably John Wesley the preacher; Olaudah Equiano, a former slave and ardent abolitionist; William Paley the philosopher; Adam Smith the economist; and Edward Rushton, a blind poet, writer, and bookseller who lived in Liverpool. Rushton became blind when sailing to Dominica with a human cargo in 1773. There was an outbreak of ophthalmia among many of the slaves and he too contracted the illness. Since that event, his abiding passion had been campaigning for the abolition of the slave trade, having witnessed for himself the human degradation on the slave ships.

However, it was undoubtedly the early influence and campaigning of the Quakers that was critical in gaining the initial momentum for the abolitionist movement. Although the group was London-based, the movement had an extremely efficient, countrywide communications system; together with a number of very active local groups and because the society had wide access to printing facilities, the plethora of tracts and other freely available materials that were now being produced and widely distributed were beginning to turn public opinion, generally, towards the cause of the abolitionists. Eyewitness statements were also being used to good advantage at public meetings. Petitions were organised and sent to parliament and more influential people were recruited to the abolitionist ranks; one of the most notable people to join the cause was Josiah Wedgewood, head of the world-famous porcelain manufacturers. His company even produced a piece portraying a kneeling slave, under whom was the statement: 'Am I not a man and a brother?'

As the movement developed, Sharp worked closely with Wilberforce and Clarkson. He also personally lobbied Prime Minister William Pitt and the leader of the opposition, Charles Fox. Meanwhile, Wilberforce and Clarkson led a two-pronged campaign, with Wilberforce leading the parliamentary campaign and Clarkson leading the hugely influential public campaign. Clarkson, by this time an ordained minister in the Church of England, forsook his clerical career and chose instead to channel his undoubted talents and energies into overcoming the public's indifference and apathy towards the slave trade. During the course of his nationwide speaking engagements, he collected further information, which added weight to the already impressive body of evidence building against the continuation of the trade. Clarkson, often in much physical danger himself, spoke to sailors from the slave ships and collected trading information and data from official sources.

However, the abolitionists did not hold a monopoly on powerful allies. The anti-abolitionists took strength from a letter dated 10 June 1805, written by Lord Nelson to Mr Simon Taylor—a plantation owner in Jamaica—in which Nelson declared:

> ...I have ever been and shall die a firm friend to our colonial system. I was bred as you know in the good old school, and taught to appreciate the value of our West India possessions, and neither in the field nor in the senate, shall their interest be infringed while I have an arm to fight in their defence or a tongue to launch my voice against the damnable and cursed doctrine of Wilberforce and his hypocritical allies, and I hope my berth in heaven will be as exalted as his, who would certainly cause the murder of all our friends and fellow subjects in the colonies.

The effect of the sentiments expressed in this letter made it more difficult to oppose slavery without appearing to be unpatriotic. Liverpool merchants had other vested interests, however, and often argued that by abolishing the slave trade the development of Liverpool as a port would be impaired, if not destroyed. They also alleged that it would destroy trading in the British Empire, citing that Spanish and Portuguese merchants were already in the slave trade. It was perhaps predictable that the general reaction in Liverpool to the abolitionists would be negative in the extreme, with so much wealth being created as a direct result of the profits accruing from the slave trade. One of the town's leading politicians, Banastre Tarleton, was also a member of one of the town's leading anti-abolitionist families. Tarleton's grandfather, father, and three brothers were all active in the slave trade.

Even in the latter part of the eighteenth century when the campaign to abolish the trade had been gaining supporters, there was still much opposition in Liverpool, and when the parliamentary inquiries were held many prominent people from the town spoke in favour of the trade. Indeed, many were given gifts from the town's council, while others were given the freedom of the borough. On 14 February 1788, the Town Corporation of Liverpool officially voiced its opposition to the abolition of the slave trade, by considering and adopting a petition that had been drawn up by Mr Statham. The petition, which was then presented to parliament, read as follows:

> To the honourable the House of Commons, &c. The humble petition of the Mayor, &c., sheweth: That your petitioners, as trustees of the corporate fund of the ancient and loyal town of Liverpool, have always been ready, not only to give every encouragement in their power to the commercial interests of that part of the community more immediately under their care, but as much as possible to strengthen the reins of government, and to promote the public welfare. That the trade of Liverpool, having met with the countenance of this honourable house in many Acts of Parliament, which have been granted at different times during the present century, for the constructing of proper and convenient wet docks for shipping, and more especially for the African ships, which, from their form, require to be constantly afloat, your petitioners have been emboldened to lay out considerable sums of money, and to pledge their corporate seal for other sums to a very large amount for effectuating these good and laudable purposes. That your petitioners have also been happy to see the great increase and different resources of trade which has flowed in upon their town by the numerous canals and other communications from the interior parts of this kingdom, in which many individuals, as well as public bodies of proprietors, are materially interested. And that from these causes, particularly the convenience of the docks, and some other local advantages, added to the enterprising spirit of the people, which has enabled them to carry on the African slave trade with vigour, the town of Liverpool has arrived at a pitch of mercantile consequence which cannot but affect and improve the wealth and prosperity of the kingdom at large.
>
> Your petitioners therefore contemplate with real concern the attempts now making by the petitions lately preferred to your honourable house to obtain a total abolition of the African slave trade, which has hitherto received the sanction of Parliament, and for a long series of years has constituted and still continues to form a very extensive branch of the commerce of Liverpool, and in effect gives strength and energy to the whole; but confiding in the wisdom and justice of the British senate, your petitioners humbly pray to be heard by their Counsel against the abolition of this source of wealth before the honourable house shall proceed to determine upon a point which so essentially concerns the welfare of the town and Port of Liverpool in particular, and the landed interest of the kingdom in general, and which, in their judgment, must also tend to the prejudice of the British manufacturers, must ruin the property of the English merchants in the West Indies, diminish the public revenue, and impair the maritime strength of Great Britain. And your petitioners will ever pray, &c.

The merchant classes in the town, which included many of Liverpool's leading politicians, had too much to lose. At one point, the council even paid £100 for the publication of a pamphlet entitled *Scriptural Researches on the Licitness of the Slave Trade*.

By now, other churches, most notably the non-conformist Methodist and Baptist chapels, aligned themselves with the abolitionist cause, and awareness of the iniquities of the trade tended to be promulgated through organised religion rather than through party political channels. Through these religious groupings, many more working people were able to gain an awareness and understanding of the situation than would otherwise have been the case.

Some other factors began to change opinions as regards enslavement. The abolitionist movement was continuing with its campaign and continued to gain adherents to the cause, but there were other influential factors. A series of slave revolts on plantations in Barbados, Demerara, and Jamaica not only shocked the government, but plantation owners were beginning to wonder if the economic benefits were being outweighed by the costs of insurrection. The balance of political and economic opinion was steadily moving in favour of abolition.

With the mounting success of the abolitionist movement, the London Abolition Committee was now ready to take their arguments for abolition to parliament. However, before that time, a key question had to be addressed and resolved, and that was whether to press for a total end to slavery or the more easily achieved abolition of the slave trade. Abolition was the ultimate objective, but on a pragmatic level it was recognised that abolition of the trade in slaves would be somewhat easier to effect as it was the British government that could impose a ban on slave shipping leaving the country, and Britain was now the dominant partner in the slave trade. The committee opted to press, initially, for the abolition of the slave trade, even though some members wanted to lobby for an outright ban on slavery.

After much discussion, the prime minister charged the Privy Council's Committee for Trade and Foreign Plantations to investigate the slave trade and its effects and consequences for British commerce. The committee was convened in February 1788 and a number of prominent traders from Liverpool attended the hearings in the house and spoke in favour of the anti-abolitionists petition—the traders were keen to continue with the lucrative trade as it was one of the major cornerstones upon which vast fortunes were being made in the town. As a leading merchant and slave trader, and being held in such high esteem by his fellow traders, it was not surprising to find that James Penny had been asked to represent their views before the parliamentary committee—Penny was renowned for his forthright opinions. As a slave ship captain of many years standing, he suggested that life on board slave ships was an enjoyable experience; he stated:

If the Weather is sultry, and there appears the least Perspiration upon their Skins, when they come upon Deck, there are Two Men attending with Cloths to rub them perfectly dry, and another to give them a little Cordial.... They are then supplied with Pipes and Tobacco.... They are amused with Instruments of Music peculiar to their own country ... and when tired of Music and Dancing, they then go to Games of Chance.

Penny asserted that the trade was humane, stating that he 'found himself impelled, both by humanity and interest, to pay every possible attention both to the preservation of the crew and the slaves. Great improvements have been made at Liverpool within these twenty years in the construction of the ships'. He went on to add that 'the slaves here will sleep better than the gentlemen do on shore'. In his continuing testimony, he stated:

> The Slave Ships at Liverpool are built on purpose for this trade, and are accommodated with air ports and gratings for the purpose of keeping the slaves cool. Great improvements have been made at Liverpool within these twenty years in the construction of the ships. The space between the decks is sufficiently large to contain the number of negroes above-mentioned and is plained, very smooth and painted.

When asked the direct question in committee as to 'whether he conceived this trade to be a profitable one in general to the Merchant?', Penny replied:

> ...he would have to beg leave to observe, that should this trade be abolished, it would not only greatly affect the commercial interest, but also the landed property of the County of Lancaster and more particularly, the Town of Liverpool; whose fall, in that case, would be as rapid as its rise has been astonishing.

During the council's investigation, a number of other prominent traders from Liverpool gave evidence, speaking in favour of the practice continuing. Robert Norris, formerly a slave ship commander, gave powerful testimony, claiming:

> ... [Slaves] had sufficient room, sufficient air, and sufficient provisions. When upon deck, they made merry and amused themselves with dancing. As to mortality ... it was trifling. In short, the voyage from Africa to the West Indies was one of the happiest periods of a Negro's life.

However, this evidence was strongly refuted by a former slave, Olaudah Equiano, whose account discredited Norris's statements. Equiano's view stated:

> ... the air soon became unfit for respiration, from a variety of loathsome smells, and brought on a sickness among the slaves, of which many died, thus falling victim to the improvident avarice, as I may call it, of their purchasers.

He went on to say that, when looking around the ship, he saw 'a multitude of black people of every description chained together, every one of their countenance expressing dejection and sorrow'.

For their heroic efforts in front of the committee, James Penny, John Tarleton, Robert Norris, John Matthews, and Archibald Dalzell were given the freedom of the borough on 4 June 1788: 'For the very essential advantage derived to the trade of Liverpool from their evidence in support of the African slave trade and for the public spirit they have manifested on this occasion…' In 1792, sometime after delivering some compelling reasons as to why the slave trade should not be abolished, James Penny was presented with a silver epergne by his fellow anti-abolitionists. Penny continued to be an advocate of the benefits of the slave trade, even when the greater body of opinion was moving against it.

As Clarkson had built up a list of experienced men who had spent time on the slave ships, he was able to marshal persuasive witnesses to add their voices to the abolitionist cause when parliament began its official scrutiny of the trade. What those men said—about the ships and their sailors, about the nature of enslavement on the African coast, about African rebellion and the ensuing violent repression, and about the miseries of the Atlantic crossing—all added up to a picture of systematic brutalisation that shocked even those already opposed to the trade. The evidence being presented to the committee of the council, which had been charged to consider the arguments both for and against the abolition of slavery, was proving extremely damaging to the cause of the anti-abolitionists. A former slave ship surgeon, Alexander Falcolnbridge, testified:

> The men, on being brought aboard the ship, are immediately fastened together, two and two, by handcuffs on their wrists and by irons riveted on their legs. They are then sent down between the decks and placed in an apartment partitioned off for that purpose.… They are frequently stowed so close, as to admit of no other position than lying on their sides. Nor will the height between decks, unless directly under the grating, permit the indulgence of an erect posture; especially where there are platforms, which is generally the case. These platforms are a kind of shelf, about eight or nine feet in breadth, extending from the side of the ship toward the centre. They are placed nearly midway between the decks, at the distance of two or three feet from each deck. Upon these, the Negroes are stowed in the same manner as they are on the deck underneath.

Similarly, when giving his testimony in favour of abolition, Dr Thomas Trotter, who was a physician working on the slave ship *Brookes*, was asked the direct question: 'If slaves had room to turn themselves?' Trotter was unequivocal in his answer:

> No. The slaves that are out of irons are locked spoonways and locked to one another. It is the duty of the first mate to see them stowed in this manner every morning; those which do not get quickly into their places are compelled by the cat and, such was the situation when stowed in this manner, and when the ship had much motion at sea, they were often miserably bruised against the deck or against each other. I have seen their breasts heaving and observed them draw their breath, with all those laborious and anxious efforts for life which we observe in expiring animals subjected by experiment to bad air of various kinds.

During the days of the inquiry, more and more people were being persuaded that here was a form of trade that was hard to justify—even though it yielded such material bounty to Britain.

Following the conclusion of the inquiry, the Privy Council Committee on Trade and Plantations produced an 850-page report on the slave trade, but, when William Wilberforce introduced his bill in 1789, the anti-abolitionists insisted that the Commons should conduct its own investigation into the practice. The West Indies Committee, as the group lobbying against abolition became known, ensured that Wilberforce's bill was not reintroduced to the house until 1791. During this intervening period, the anti-abolitionists organised themselves into a powerful and formidable force. Due to the huge amounts of money involved, and the possible loss in income and livelihood if the bill became law, many town councils (as well as individuals) subscribed to the anti-abolitionist cause. Over £10,000 was sent from Liverpool alone in support of the anti-abolitionists campaign.

Like a number of other abolitionists, William Wilberforce had been converted to evangelical Christianity. It was only after his conversion in 1785 that Wilberforce championed the abolitionist cause. He considered leaving politics, but was persuaded against that course of action by his friend and mentor, John Newton. It was clear from the outset that, if a bill was to stand any chance of success in overcoming the obstacles that would undoubtedly be placed in its way, then a parliamentary champion was what was required. William Wilberforce, the MP for Hull, was the obvious choice. As a MP, Wilberforce had observed the developments relating to the abolition of the slave trade, so Clarkson implored him to lead the abolitionist's campaign in the House of Commons. He was given further encouragement by William Pitt, but it was a letter that he had received from Sir Charles Middleton that finally persuaded him. In today's parlance, Wilberforce certainly had a 'mountain to climb'. There was entrenched opposition facing him in both the House of Commons and also in the House of Lords. A significant number of influential merchants, who included ship owners, entrepreneurs, plantation owners, and other persons in places of influence, had invested huge amounts of capital in the knowledge that the slave trade yielded high returns. Even a cursory glance at some of the statistics relating to the trade demonstrate just how much wealth was being created in the town and just how closely it was aligned to civic and political life and why, therefore, there were so many people in Liverpool who were against abolition. A typical example would be Thomas Leyland, a wealthy merchant and mayor of the town on a number of occasions. He was heavily involved in the slave trade—having had an interest in almost seventy slaving ventures from Liverpool, carrying, in total, more than 22,000 slaves. On one voyage of his jointly owned ship the *Enterprise* in 1794, 356 slaves were sold when they arrived in the New World. Following fees, disbursements, the initial cost of the slaves, and other overheads, the overall profit amounted to just short of £10,000 or almost 100 per cent. From his overall business profits, Leyland later invested in the banking industry.

The abolitionists were not deterred, but progress was slow and sporadic, as there were powerful forces ranged against abolition, including one of the town's leading MPs, General Banastre Tarleton, and, as he came from a slave-owning family, it is perhaps not surprising that he led for the anti-abolitionists when

Wilberforce introduced his first abolition bill in 1789. The debate was lost by 163 to 88 votes. Clearly, it would take a huge effort to overturn all of the vested interests. After much more lobbying throughout the country, another bill was introduced on 2 April 1792. However, Home Secretary Henry Dundas effectively scuppered the bill by introducing an amendment that would ensure that the abolition of the slave trade would be introduced on a 'gradual' basis, which, as far as the anti-abolitionists were concerned, meant never. The amendment was accepted and the bill carried by 230 votes for and 85 votes against, with 1796 being set as the proposed date for the slave trade to cease. However, the bill was not accepted when it came to the House of Lords and it never passed into law.

The fortunes of the abolitionists did improve following the Act of Union in 1800, when 100 Irish MPs entered the house—most of whom favoured abolition.

Another tireless advocate and campaigner against slavery was a young lawyer from Liverpool, William Roscoe. As early as 1771, Roscoe was arguing against the continuation of the slave trade. Although not a natural parliamentarian, Roscoe made a conscious choice to stand for parliament. He returned as a MP for the town in 1806.

A bill to abolish the slave trade was taken to parliament in January 1807 and went to the House of Commons on 10 February 1807. This was more than twenty years after the start of the abolitionist's campaign. The debate in the house, which was introduced by Foreign Secretary Charles James Fox, lasted for more than ten hours.

One of the more significant speeches delivered in the House of Commons during an abolition debate was made by Thomas Fowell Buxton, who declared:

The voyage, the horrors of which are beyond description. For example, the mode of packing. The hold of a slave vessel is from two to four feet high. It is filled with as many human beings as it will contain. They are made to sit down with their heads between their knees: first, a line is placed close to the side of the vessel; then another line, and then the packer, armed with a heavy club, strikes at the feet of this last line in order to make them press as closely as possible against those behind. And so the packing goes on; until, to use the expression of an eyewitness, 'they are wedged together in one mass of living corruption'. Thus it is suffocating for want of air, starving for want of food, parched with thirst for want of water, these poor creatures are compelled to perform a voyage of fourteen hundred miles.

During the passage of the act, which would abolish the slave trade, Roscoe spoke in favour of the act and also voted for it.

The House of Commons voted 283 in favour and 16 votes against; the scenes in the house were unprecedented, in that members rose and cheered wildly. Voting in the House of Lords was 100 votes in favour and 34 votes against. On 25 March 1807, an Act of Parliament entitled 'An Act for the Abolition of the Slave Trade' was given royal assent and finally abolished the notorious slave trade in Britain. There was still, however, a widely held belief in Liverpool that abolition would be the ruin of the town and its port. The ramifications meant that the slave trade was abolished in the British Empire, but it did not abolish slavery itself. It was a common misconception that by abolishing the slave trade, then slavery itself would soon be abolished. This was not the case, and it was not until twenty-six years later that slavery was finally abolished in the British Empire.

Having declared his allegiance to the abolitionist campaign, Roscoe was not welcome in his home town. After the act had been passed, Roscoe returned to an inimical environment in Liverpool, being met by a group of men wielding staves and clubs. The riot that ensued had been organised by some of the town's slave traders and anti-abolitionists. After that reception—just one year after entering the house—Roscoe never returned to Westminster. Throughout the rest of his life, he remained justifiably proud that he had been privileged to cast his vote for the abolition of the slave trade, which, although it had brought countless riches to the town, trailed in its wake untold misery and deprivation. A similar fate had awaited Thomas Clarkson when he had visited the town sometime earlier. When meeting people along the dockside, he was accosted by an angry crowd who tried to push him into one of the docks; this action could have resulted in his untimely death.

The act did not abolish slavery, but brought an end to slave trading—a significantly different reality. Therefore, having achieved its primary objective, the society changed its name from the 'Society for Effecting the Abolition of the Slave Trade' to the 'Anti-Slavery Society'.

Ill-health forced Wilberforce to resign his parliamentary seat, passing leadership of the parliamentary campaign to Thomas Fowell Buxton, but, before resigning, he wrote a last petition. There was a long drawn-out debate, lasting for over three months, during which time the bill made its way through the various committee stages. Then, on 26 July 1833, the Abolition of Slavery Bill finally passed its third reading. Wilberforce himself was not present in the house, but a messenger was sent to inform him of the momentous news. On 29 July 1833, just three days after the bill was passed, William Wilberforce died.

When the act abolishing slavery came into force, planters were compensated to the tune of some £20,000,000. The thousands of former slaves did not receive any compensation.

The last slave ship to sail legally from Liverpool was *Kitty's Amelia*, which left the Mersey on 27 July 1807 under the command of Captain Hugh 'Mind-your-Eye' Crow, a one-eyed Manxman. This date was almost three months after the slave trade had been abolished in Britain; however, Crow had been given clearance before 1 May 1807, when the laws relating to abolition came into force. The *Kitty's Amelia* carried eighteen guns, serving as a concession to England's war with France, but also in acknowledgement of the hostile conditions that he might encounter on his voyage to the Guinea coast of Africa.

3

Docks Development

The eighteenth century heralded a period of unprecedented expansion in trade initiatives and the discovery of new markets, when vessels from Liverpool explored hitherto unknown ports in every part of the world. The expansion in trade also brought with it a significant rise in the town's population. It was estimated that the population in 1760 was somewhere in the region of 25,000, whereas by 1815 that figure stood at 100,000. The volume of shipping through the port also saw a four-fold increase during that period. New dwellings were built to accommodate the influx in the town's population, and it was evident that several new docks would have to be built in order to cope with the increasing trade. The Old Dock had been opened in 1715, but it was not until 1753 that Liverpool's second dock was opened, the Salthouse Dock. George's Dock, built on what was the foreshore in front of the Liverpool Tower and Saint Nicholas' Church, opened in 1771, followed by Duke's Dock and then Manchester Dock. To the south was the King's Dock, opened in 1788, the Queen's Dock, opened in 1796, and the Union Dock, opened in 1816. These docks, together with tidal basins and graving docks, now filled the whole of the Liverpool foreshore as far south as the limits of the town itself, marked by Parliament Street. During this period, the water area of the docks saw a five-fold increase in size, and even then the docks were full to overflowing as soon as they were opened.

The increasing availability of shipping in the Mersey, coupled with dock development and warehouse storage facilities during the eighteenth century, played a part in ensuring that the port achieved pre-eminence during the latter part of the century. Additionally, advantages offered by geographical location of the town must not be underestimated. Lying on the north-west coast of England, the town and Port of Liverpool were ideally placed to profit from a number of regional factors at the beginning of the Industrial Revolution. Liverpool exported coal from the Lancashire coalfields, textiles and fabrics from the nearby town of Manchester, salt from Cheshire, and cutlery and other steel products from Sheffield. Liverpool's merchants and ship owners had become adept at finding new export markets. The trading connections that had been forged during the years of the slave trade were continued following abolition, and new cargoes were exported to and imported from Africa and the Americas. Liverpool as a port and a town was still developing.

Throughout the whole of the period when Liverpool was rising to prominence as a port and an influential town, the dock estate was having to develop in order to keep pace with the ever-increasing demands being made and the number of ships that were using the port.

After Steer's Dock, now called the Old Dock, had come into full usage, plans had been drawn and parliamentary approval sought for a number of new docks to be built. An Act of Parliament of 1737 gave permission for a wet dock of 4 acres surface area to be built to the south side of the Old Dock. The dock, which was opened in 1753, was originally called the South Dock, but the dock was renamed in 1784 and called by the more popular name of Salthouse Dock; this was recognising the close proximity of the salt works, which was owned by the Blackburne brothers of the nearby village of Hale.

The foreshore to the western side of the dock became boat-building yards. The yards continued in business for many years until the land was used to construct another dock, the Albert Dock.

It could not be claimed that the building of the original group of docks at Liverpool lead to a phenomenal increase in trade, but the groundwork and basis for development was clearly being secured. During the construction of the Old Dock, from *circa* 1709 to 1715, the average total tonnage passing through the port was somewhere in the region of 18,371 tons *per annum*. Later, when the third dock act was passed in 1737, the corresponding tonnage had only risen to 19,921 tons *per annum*. However, less than thirty years later, in 1765, the figure had risen to 62,390 tons *per annum*.

It was obvious that, if docks development (and therefore town development) was to be managed effectively, then a controlling group was needed so that development could be structured and regulated. The first Dock Act was passed in 1708 and named the mayor, aldermen, bailiffs, and common council as the trustees of the proposed dock. They were given powers to build the dock and also to levy dues. The trustees were not incorporated, but used the corporation seal. The first dock, the Old Dock, and subsequent docks built during their tenure were managed through the normal committee structure of the council.

A further act was passed in 1811, which gave a degree of autonomy to the committee. The trustees were given their own seal and the finances of the docks were administered separately from those of the corporation. A statutory group consisting of twenty-one members was appointed by the trustees, but the actions of the committee could still be overridden by the town council, who also retained the right to vote sums of money from dock funds. This situation was unacceptable as it effectively meant that the control of the docks was vested in a group who were not representative of ratepayers or indeed of those who used the docks for their daily business. The act of 1825 went some way to redress this imbalance;

the trust remained unaltered, but the committee structure now included eight members who had been directly elected by dock ratepayers, but the council still retained the remaining thirteen seats and the chairman was selected by the council. Although not being totally acceptable, the committee structure remained in this form until another act was presented to parliament in 1851.

During the tenure of the first group of trustees of the docks, a period lasting from 1709 to 1825, a number of docks were built and developed along the banks of the River Mersey, including the Old Dock, Salthouse Dock, George's Dock, Kings Dock, Queen's Dock, Union Dock, and Prince's Dock. At the end of that development period, the total free surface area of the dock estate amounted to in excess of 46 acres, with dock dues payable of £130,911. The dock quayage exceeded 2 miles.

At the time of his death, Steers had been working on the construction of the South Dock. It took another three years after his death for Henry Berry—who had then been appointed as the town's dock engineer—to complete the work. It was later acknowledged that, because for most of his later life Steers had been in poor health, much of the work on the dock could be attributed to Berry. The Liverpool Mercury commented that Salthouse Dock 'was formed under his direction'. When the dock was completed in 1753, Berry was approached concerning making the Sankey Brook navigable; he considered that the proposals were not viable and turned his attention to building a dead water canal. The Sankey Canal Act was passed by parliament in 1762, whereby permission was obtained to extend the canal from Sankey bridges to Fiddlers Ferry. This work, although much removed from Liverpool as such, would on completion work to the benefit of the town.

In recognising that in the very near future more docking area would be required, the corporation once again applied for and were given additional constructive powers. The submission to parliament included the following statement:

> The trade and shipping of the town and port of late years is greatly increased, and the ships and vessels are more numerous and of larger dimensions, and require a greater draught of water than heretofore. That the two wet docks and dry pier already constructed are not sufficient for the reception of the ships resorting thereto; that vessels, especially his Majesty's ships of war stationed at the port, are obliged to lie in the open harbour, exposed to the rage of tempestuous weather and of rapid tides and currents, in imminent danger of shipwreck.

The trustees were given permission to construct a dock on land lying between James Street and Chapel Street—land that was owned by the corporation. The dimensions of the dock were such that it was designed to accommodate larger vessels. Work on building the third dock at Liverpool commenced in 1762, directly after receiving approval from parliament. The new dock was being built to the north of the two existing docks (the Old Dock and the South Dock). During construction, the dock was referred to as the North Dock. However, when it was opened, it was called George's Dock, in honour of the reigning monarch, King

George III. The dock was of modest proportions, having a free surface area of only 3 acres. At the time of construction, it was envisaged that the dock would serve the American and Caribbean markets, but this trade was later lost to another of the new docks, the Princes Dock. Further debts were incurred when more money had to be borrowed to finance the building of the new dock. The dock, designed by Henry Berry, was built at an expense of some £20,000. Construction was completed by 1771, when the dock was opened. By this time, the benefits of having a wet dock were well-known—the major advantage being the efficiency of loading and unloading cargo. Berry had designed the dock such that cargoes could be loaded and unloaded directly from the quayside—another aid to ensure quick turnarounds. With the ever-increasing volume of traffic passing through the port, the dock later underwent extensive modifications. From 1822 to 1825, the dock was extended to almost twice that of its original design size, under the supervision of John Foster Snr. The extension became necessary solely because of increasing trade passing through the port. At the southern end of the dock there was now access to the Dry Dock; the gates of which were 25 feet deep and 36 feet wide. The gates at the northern end were 29 feet deep and 42 feet wide. The basin to the north had dimensions of 163 yards at its southern end, 154 yards at the north, and the east and west sides being some 112 yards in length. When the extensions were completed, the dock was almost twice that of its original design size. The dock was used mainly for the importation of soft fruits and other perishable goods.

To the south of St Nicholas Church, the line of docks began with the wall of the dry basin, from which access was gained to George's Dock. Vessels waiting in the basin came right up to the walls of St Nicholas's Churchyard. From here, the dock wall extended for almost 1½ miles as far a Parliament Street, which, until 1835, marked the southern boundary of the borough.

There was a small bridewell to the north side of George's Dock that was described as being 'damp and offensive' and 'totally dark and unventilated'. The bridewell was replaced by a new one in 1804, which was built in Chapel Street.

In addition to giving the corporation further constructive powers, the act of 1762 also gave permission for the corporation to build lighthouses to assist navigation in and out of the port. Bidston Lighthouse was built in 1771. The lighthouse had an ingenious system, whereby owners were alerted by certain flags flying when one of their vessels was seen approaching the port.

Trade was increasing at a very fast rate. In 1765, tonnage passing through the port amounted to 62,390 tons, but, by the year 1786, the figure had jumped to 151,347 tons. Due to this phenomenal increase in shipping through the port, coupled with the increase in size of the vessels, it was clear that the dock facilities were proving to be unfit for purpose and additional docking area was required. A parliamentary act was passed in 1785 that gave permission for two further docks to be constructed to be built at Liverpool to the south of Salthouse Dock. The docks were to be called King's Dock and Queen's Dock, and both were designed by Henry Berry. Having gained approval, work began immediately, but difficulties were encountered when acquiring the land necessary and making adequate preparation before the dock itself could be constructed. The Duke of Bridgewater had property that directly obstructed the proposed area of dock construction. In 1773, he had constructed a dock and outer channel at the southern end of Salthouse Dock, on land that he had purchased a number of years earlier. He also had built a range of warehouses in the vicinity. The plans for the two new docks were compromised, as, resulting from Bridgewater's intervention, the new docks had to be sited further south, precluding the possibility of inter-connection with Salthouse Dock. Much later, in 1858, the construction of Wapping Basin overcame this problem.

Although the Duke of Bridgewater's dock undoubtedly compromised the construction of King's Dock and Queen's Dock, the town was still the beneficiary of this injection of economic activity, when the canal built for the duke connected the towns of Liverpool and Manchester, enabling cargoes of coal from his mines at Worsley to be easily transported to Liverpool for onward shipment. The coal was delivered to a narrow basin known as Duke's Dock.

James Brindley designed and supervised the building of the Bridgewater Canal, and it is thought that he was also responsible for the design of Duke's Dock. The design of the dock, being formed in the shape of a cross, allowed maximum use of quay space for loading and unloading. The warehouse, which was built integral to the dock, allowed for cargoes to be unloaded directly into storage—the first dockside warehouse to be built in Liverpool.

The dock, still privately owned, was extended in 1841–1845, a direct reflection of the increasing volumes of trade coming via Manchester and its environs to Liverpool. The flourishing cotton industry accounted in large part for this huge increase in business. As a private enterprise, Duke's Dock did not come under the jurisdiction of the Docks Committee and remained the property of the duke's estate for many years. The dock was not incorporated into the Liverpool Dock Estate until 1899, at which time it was being used, mainly, for its commodious warehousing facilities.

The dock was relatively narrow when compared to other docks, but this was a deliberate design feature and reflected the nature of the craft that would be using it—mainly flat-bottomed boats coming from Manchester and environs along the Bridgewater Canal. The warehouses along the dockside were of a particular design, which enabled flats to be loaded and unloaded without being subjected to the vagaries of the weather.

Work on King's Dock commenced in 1785, shortly after permission had been granted by parliament. The building costs were in excess of £25,000. The location of the dock was such that it was somewhat isolated from many of the other docks in the system, due to the positioning of the privately owned Duke's Dock. To enable building of the dock, a number of the small shipbuilding yards in the area were purchased. The dock itself had a free surface area of over 7 acres and the adjacent bonded tobacco warehouse, completed in 1795, also had an equally large footprint. However, the trade was increasing at such a pace that the building of an even larger bonded warehouse soon became a necessity. The tobacco industry itself was now becoming significant in the town's economy and provided employment for many of the town's workforce.

Being contiguous to the King's Tobacco Warehouse, the dock received all the vessels from Virginia and other ports carrying similar cargoes. The dock and surrounding area had facilities for discharging, weighing, and storing the tobacco. Due to the broad quays around the dock and the plethora of facilities, other vessels from Greenland, the Baltic, and America used the dock, bringing timber, lumber, pitch, tar, and other similar goods.

The importance of the dock was reflected in the salary of the dock-master, being 100 guineas *per annum*.

The common entrance basin to King's and Queen's Docks was constructed as an open tidal basin, but, during the reconstruction in 1852, it was converted into a floating dock, with double gates. This gave the added advantage of enabling smaller vessels to enter the dock at half-tide. It had become necessary for King's Dock to be reconstructed in order that Wapping Dock could be built.

The dock covered an area of more than 14 acres, but the dock itself had a total free water surface of 7 acres. The dock was opened on 3 October 1788. There is some dispute as to the first vessel to enter the dock; Troughton's History names the vessel as the *Port-a-Ferry*, whereas other researchers name the 36-ton brigantine *Three Sisters*, the *Amphrite*, or the *Hannah* as being the first vessel to enter the dock.

In 1795, the corporation built a bonded depot on the east side of King's Dock for the safe storage of tobacco. One of the major cargoes being imported through the port was tobacco, most of which was coming from Virginia. By the end of the seventeenth century, Liverpool was the premier port in the country for the importation of tobacco. Although the bonded warehouse was very large, because of the ever-increasing trade, another warehouse—even larger than the first—had to be built. The new warehouse was built in 1811 on the west side of King's dock at a total cost, including purchase of the building plot, of £140,000. Once the new warehouse had been completed, the old one was used for general storage, but it was ultimately demolished so that the new Wapping Dock could be constructed.

The spiritual needs of seafarers were not forgotten. The Seamen's Friend Society or Bethel Union was established for the purpose of improving the religious and moral condition of the seamen of the port. The society found a suitable place of worship and established Day and Sunday Schools. The society also circulated the scriptures and other religious tracts, provided respectable lodging-houses for seamen, and encouraged among them habits of economy and frugality. The society had several meeting rooms and libraries in the neighbourhood of the docks. There was what was known as a Floating Chapel moored at the north-west corner of the dock and used, on a regular basis, for divine services that were held on every Sunday for the benefit of visiting seafarers. Ministers of various denominations performed the services in the chapel. The Bethel Union was chiefly supported by Dissenters.

Berry completed his work on the King's Dock, but after almost forty years of service to the town of Liverpool, he resigned his post before work on the Queen's

Dock had been completed. The person appointed to replace him was Thomas Morris of Lancaster. He was appointed on the same salary as Berry, 100 guineas *per annum*. Queen's Dock opened in 1796, while Morris was still dock engineer. In 1797, he applied for 'a very great increase in salary', but instead was promptly given the sack. When he left Liverpool he took up an appointment at the West India Docks in London.

The Queen's Dock was opened on 17 April 1796 at a cost of £35,000 and named in honour of Queen Charlotte Sofia, wife of the reigning monarch, George III. The first vessel to enter the dock was the American brig *Baltimore*. The dock gates were 42 feet wide and 28 feet deep, and over the entrance was a cast-iron swivel bridge. Much timber was imported through this dock, but vessels from the Baltic and Holland also used this dock. The length of the east side is 460 yards and that on the west side is 435 yards; the north end measures 110 yards, and the south end 90 yards. The dock has cavernous sheds along the east and west sides, whereas the quays towards the south end of the dock were sloped inwards at a considerable angle in order to ease unloading of vessels carrying timber to the port. There were two graving docks on the west side of the dock that opened from King's Dock Basin and extended parallel with the dock itself for about half of its length. The graving docks facilitated maintenance and repair of vessels as and when required. Timber stores occupied the remainder of the space between the southern end of the dock and the river itself.

Initially, the dock was designed to have a water surface area of slightly more than 6 acres, but in 1816—again, due to increased trade through the port—the size of the wet surface area of the dock was increased by a further 4 acres. The work was conducted under the direct supervision of John Foster Sr, who succeeded Thomas Morris as dock engineer. During the reconfiguration of the dock, the opportunity was taken to construct a small dock to the south called the Union Dock. The dock had a free surface area of just over 2 acres, but it did have a large outer basin. In later years, the dock, together with its larger outer basin, underwent many transformations, resulting in the formation of Coburg Dock. Coburg Dock gave direct access to the river.

There was then a considerable gap between the building of Queen's Dock and Prince's Dock, primarily caused by uncertainties in trade due to both the French Revolution and the Napoleonic Wars, when additional dock construction was not high on the list of priorities.

By 1799, the trustees had to return to parliament again in order to seek permission to increase, yet again, the number of docks along the Mersey. The number of ships now entering or leaving the river had increased to 4,518, grossing over 400,000 tons. Permission was granted to construct a further two docks and to borrow £120,000 for their construction; this loan would be offset against the security of rates to be collected.

Although the two new docks had not, as yet, been built, the tonnage through the port continued to increase. The year 1808 saw 5,225 ships passing through the port, with a gross tonnage of some 516,836 tons. The town council, which, at the time, managed both the corporation and the Dock Estate, came under pressure to take some positive action. A report was duly commissioned, which yielded some startling facts. John Rennie had been asked to make some recommendations. In his report, it was noted that at any one time there were 400 sail and 300 sloops or flats either in dock or in the river. On these figures, it was estimated that the size of the docks would have to be at least doubled—and that calculation did not take into account any increase in the number of ships using the docks. It was stated that, if a dock of about 7 acres was built to the north of George's Dock, it would be able to accommodate some seventy vessels having an average size of 200 tons; however, an alternative solution was possible, which would cost significantly less than the proposed new dock to the north of George's Dock and could be built in half the time that would be needed to build the new dock. This solution entailed enlarging King's Dock, Queen's Dock, and George's Dock. However, in order to create the additional 24 acres of water space, which the extension of these three docks would yield, the plan necessitated filling in the Old Dock.

An act, passed by parliament in 1811, was set to made radical and revolutionary changes to the docks' system. Pickton records them as follows:

1. That the south dock authorised by the previous Act, and which had been so strongly recommended by Mr. Rennie, should be abandoned, and that the new north dock should be proceeded with, for the reason, in direct opposition to the report of 1809, 'that it could be made and completed in a much less space of time'.

2. The mayor, aldermen, and burgesses are continued as trustees of the docks, with (for the first time) a common seal; but the management was to be delegated to a committee of twenty-one, selected from the common council, whose proceedings were to be subject to the veto of the council.

3. Dock rates, which had heretofore been limited to the ships, were henceforward to be levied on goods in addition.

4. Power was given to increase the debt to £600,000.

5. Hitherto, whatever lands had been required from the Corporation by the docks had been given without any payment; hereafter any Corporation lands taken for dock purposes were to be valued and paid for by the Dock Trust. The graving docks which had been constructed by the Corporation were transferred by this Act at a price to be settled by a jury.

6. The preamble recites that great additional accommodation would be afforded to the port if the Old Dock were filled up, and a Custom House and other commercial buildings, offices, and conveniences, dock and police offices, and an additional market thereon erected, and a street of communication made from Pool Lane to

Mersey Street. The Act authorises the trustees to erect the Custom House and other offices out of the moneys raised on the rates.

The corporation agreed to pay for the land that had been gained by the filling-in of the Old Dock. The corporation also agreed to meet the costs of enlarging the Queen's Dock.

In 1793, a number of warehouses were built on the east side of the new dock. The warehouses were part of the original plans, but were not constructed until much later. Recalling some of the vast profits which were made from the African trade, the new warehouses were called the Gorée Warehouses—Gorée Island, being an island off Dakar, Senegal. Many slaves were transported from this area of the west coast of Africa. The warehouses were overwhelmed by a catastrophic fire in 1802, which caused irreparable damage.

The Manchester Dock was built to accommodate river craft between the George's Dock and Canning Graving Dock. In 1818, the dock was enlarged and converted into a floating dock for coastal vessels. The water space of the dock is slightly more than 1 acre. Previously, in 1795, an inlet was made at the west end of George's Parade in order to take trade coming from the Chester and Ellesmere Canal.

The corporation agreed to pay for the land that had been gained by the filling-in of the Old Dock. The corporation also agreed to meet the costs of enlarging the Queen's Dock.

There was much heated discussion with regards to the proposals for the remodelling of the docks and much adverse criticism was levelled at the committee for adopting such an ill-conceived plan. The filling-in of the Old Dock was considered by many to be a wilful and useless sacrifice of dock water space, especially as it was located in the very centre of the town.

The Corporation duly paid £15,165 to have Queen's Dock enlarged. The dock trustees were to have met the expense of building the other offices made provision for in the act of 1811, but, in the event, central government forwarded £150,000 for the buildings to be erected and the other £80,000, out of the total cost of £230,000, was paid by the corporation.

September 1826 saw the Old Dock finally cleared of shipping so that the work of remodelling Queen's Dock could begin. Due to a number of technical difficulties that had to be overcome, the foundations of the enlarged dock had to be sunk much deeper than anticipated and this work alone added a further two years to the time of construction. The first stone for the new dock was laid on King George's birthday, 12 August 1828, and work was completed and the dock opened in 1839.

As the original design for Prince's Dock required a large area of land, including the land upon which stood the old fort, strenuous efforts were made to acquire the necessary land. The common council did not, however, own the land upon which the fort stood. This became a contentious issue, as many considered that the fort, which had stood at the bottom of Dutton Street since 1777, could still serve a useful purpose. It was suggested that the plans for the dock should be modified in order that the fort could remain intact. The fort, which stood towards the north end of the proposed site, if it remained *in situ*, would considerably reduce the size of both the proposed dock and the revenue that it would bring. Eventually, £3,975 was paid for vacant possession of the old fort. This meant that work on the original design of the dock could now proceed unimpeded. The fort's barracks were used to house senior employees who were required to live on site during the construction work.

The fort jutted out into the river, but it must be recorded that, when it was demolished so that the dock could be built, no shot had ever been fired from the fort in anger. Indeed, if any significant force had ever entered the river, then the town's protector would not have been the fort, but the turbulent tides, the strong currents, and the shifting channels at the mouth of the river itself. It was for this reason that navigation into the dock system was guided by skilled pilots.

Prince's Dock took eleven years to build—from 1810 until 1821. The several different delays in the dock's construction could be accounted for by a number of different factors, not least of which was the paucity of available labour during the Napoleonic Wars and the difficulty in raising cash at that time. It must also be admitted that there was a degree of mismanagement during the course of construction and maybe an element of accounting fraud, but this would be difficult to substantiate. John Foster Sr was the dock surveyor who had overall responsibility during the construction of the dock, but he was assisted in this role by William Jessop and John Rennie. When the construction of the dock eventually started, it was alleged that Foster ordered too much stone for the building work. It was then further alleged that the surplus stone somehow found its way to the yards of the building company owned by the Foster family. Foster resigned his post when this alleged fraud was discovered.

The dock, having taken so long to construct, was also the biggest dock to be built at Liverpool, having a free surface area of more than 11 acres. The estimated cost was £650,000, although £121,619 was used to purchase the land upon which the dock was built. The dock was totally enclosed with fence-walls; the first dock to be built with these features. The dock's length was 500 yards and the width 106 yards. To the north of the dock there was a basin and to the south there was access to George's Dock Basin. Transit sheds were built on the west quay, enabling ships to discharge their cargoes immediately upon arrival and under the direct scrutiny of the customs officers, there being a customs house nearby. Access to the southern area of the dock system was via George's Basin, George's Dock, and, later, Canning Dock. The dock was specifically designed for the prestigious North American trade.

The dock was eventually opened on 19 July 1821, which coincided with the coronation day of King George IV. Many important guests were invited and assembled on the adjoining quays. There was music and other festivities, and when the first ship entered the dock—the Liverpool-built West Indiaman, the *May*—there was a nineteen-gun salute. This was followed by a procession around the town with much jollity and festivities.

Trade through the port continued to flourish and in 1824 the number of vessels using the port was recorded as 10,001, having a gross tonnage of 1,180,914. The rapid increase in the number of steam-driven vessels using the port contributed to faster and hence shorter voyage times. Further expansion to the docks system was becoming a necessity.

As with many prosperous undertakings, a degree of fraud and malpractice was beginning to become evident to a number of traders. Following sustained pressure, the Dock Complaints Committee was formed, but the members were all self-elected and members of the common council. Frauds were suspected and when uncovered, merchants and ship-owners of the town—who, after all, paid the dock dues—felt that they should have direct representation on the board. A degree of mediation went on amongst the various factions and persons with a legitimate interest, and the constitution of the Dock Committee was eventually changed. It was agreed that eight of the twenty-one members of the committee would be directly elected by the dock ratepayers and that the remainder of the members would be elected, as was previously the case, from the common council. The chairman of the new Dock Committee was to be elected by the common council, who would also retain a veto on proceedings.

The new constitution of the Dock Committee was embodied in the act of 1825. The act also gave permission for the docks to be extended both northwards and southwards. The committee was also empowered to increase its borrowing requirement to £1,000,000.

Foster was secretary and surveyor to the corporation in 1809. Together with his son, he designed and built Prince's Dock.

However, it was considered that, at this juncture in the development of the dock system, a competent engineer was required to have oversight of the construction and design work. Jesse Hartley, a bluff Yorkshireman, but having an impeccable engineering track record, was appointed to the post in 1824.

4

More Developments

As has been alluded to previously, there is a number of factors that need consideration before an efficient port can be established; not least of these was a safe haven for vessels using the port. There must also be ease of access and an infrastructure network that enables cargoes to be brought from and delivered to inland destinations. These elements translate to efficient systems for the handling and berthing of ships, coupled with adequate docking facilities, together with the requisite number of warehouses and quayside facilities. The ancillary services also need to include merchants who are prepared to invest venture capital for the continuation of the trade—banks that will ensure that cash-flow doesn't present any difficulties. Looking to the vessels themselves, there must be established within the port's infrastructure, suitable provision for building, repairing, and victualing ships.

Now that Liverpool was beginning to be associated in a very real and developing way with the import and export trade, it was obvious that two factors were critical if progress was to be continued. The first factor was accessibility to the port and the second was the berthing availability of vessels using the port. The export trade was now becoming increasingly important, with products such as whitened salt, refined sugar, and linen, some metal products from Sheffield, leather goods, hops, coal, glass, textiles, earthenware, and coarse salt from Cheshire to be used for agricultural purposes. Many of the products being exported were manufactured in Liverpool and its environs. The Cheshire salt fields figured highly in the export industry, as did the south west Lancashire coalfields. At the same time, the time of the early Industrial Revolution, there was an emerging pottery industry in Staffordshire, centred on Stoke-on-Trent and the five towns, but, also, nearer to home, there was an embryonic glass industry in Liverpool's near neighbour, St Helens. Close links continued with the long-established trade with Ireland, and there were markets being developed with the West Indies. Much of the imports from Ireland were tobacco, hides, tallow, Muscovado sugar, and linen cloth. There were some iron products being imported from Sweden and, to a lesser extent, wine and other similar products from Spain and Portugal. Considering the accessibility of the port, better communications were being established by the improvement of river navigation systems such as those along the Weaver in Cheshire, the Irwell and Mersey in Lancashire, and also the River Douglas (also in Lancashire). Similarly at this time, the road infrastructure was being developed, linking Liverpool with Manchester, Lancaster, and as far as York. Considering the development of the navigation of the Mersey, a number of sighting beacons were placed in strategic points at the mouth of the river's estuary, and some of the Mersey's notoriously dangerous sandbanks were marked and the known channels to the port were also improved.

It must be recorded that, even though the Old Dock was the first commercial wet dock in the country, sanctioned by the common council of Liverpool and ratified by an Act of Parliament in 1709, the dock was, in essence, a private business enterprise. The dock, together with the dry dock and the retaining wall, which was funded at a later date by Richard Norris, was not an integral part of the docks estate until it was incorporated by the Dock Trustees in 1740. The total cost of the construction programme amounted to almost £30,000 for the dock itself and another £20,000 for the adjacent warehouses and other administration buildings. The central location of the new dock did however act as a focal point for future docks development.

The land that was immediately adjacent to the dock was quickly filled by a glass works, a salt works—which was owned by the Blackburne brothers—and a sugar refinery. Later on, an iron foundry was built and there was also a copper works nearby. There were at least two shipbuilding yards, one of which was owned by John Fisher. There were also ship repair facilities being developed. A timber yard was also soon established and, not too far away, a rope works.

It was becoming clear that Liverpool's rising economic significance was primarily due to the power of its merchants and the capital that they were investing into the town and its industry. Much, but not by any means all, of its increasing wealth was being created by the African trade. It has been argued that, although Liverpool's rapid rise to recognition and economic dominance was due, in part, to the wealth being created by the African trade, there were other markets that were being developed at one and the same time as the African trade market was being exploited. During the earlier part of the eighteenth century, sugar and tobacco imports were already accounting for much of the imported goods that were now coming into Liverpool. For instance, between the years of 1785 and 1810, imports of sugar rose from 16,600 tons to 46,000 tons; similarly, tobacco imports rose from 2,500 tons to 8,400 tons. It is interesting to note that both sugar and tobacco were high in their respective moisture content and, as such, it was often relatively difficult to gauge true weights for customs purposes. Also, it must be said, the whole system was open to abuse through fraudulent returns or direct bribery. However, the system changed in 1700, when customs dues became payable at the newly opened Customs House in Liverpool. Previously, all customs dues on cargoes arriving in Liverpool had been paid at the

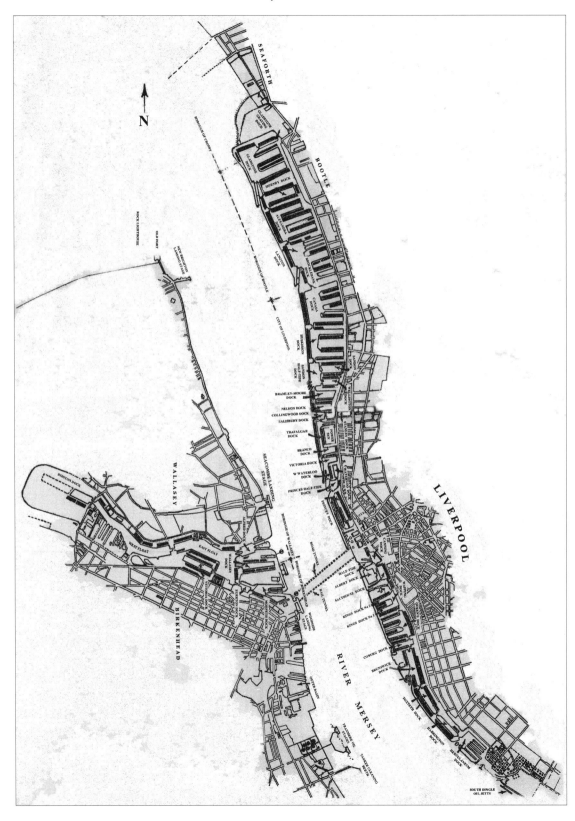

Chester Customs House. The Customs House at Liverpool boasted a far more robust regime.

While there was undoubtedly a significant import trade being developed, there was, at the same time, a burgeoning export trade in salt and coal. The salt, which was being transported from the Cheshire salt mines, and the coal, which was coming from the West Lancashire coal mines, gave rise to much improved communications between the Port of Liverpool and the surrounding environs. Indeed, as early as the start of the seventeenth century, John Holt had declared that, 'it is generally acknowledged to have been the Nursing Mother and to have contributed more to the first rise, gradual increase, and present flourishing state of the Town of Liverpool than any other article of commerce.'

As a direct result of this developing trade, more of the town's men became engaged in the shipping industry, either working directly on the vessels or engaged in the ancillary trades. Salt was an essential commodity for the Newfoundland cod fisheries. The salted fish was taken to the West Indies or to Mediterranean ports where it was exchanged for coffee, wine, and sugar. The coastal trade was also witnessing a resurgence at this time, with clay being brought from Cornwall to feed the demand from the Staffordshire potteries. Also, the town of Liverpool itself needed supplies of salt in order to satisfy the needs of the soap and chemical industries, which were now beginning to develop.

When the act of 1702 was passed, which effectively closed the salt industry to any newcomers, shipments of refined salt from Cheshire were taken down the Weaver and the Mersey to be exported, and similarly the salt that the Blackburne brothers, notably John Blackburne, were refining in Liverpool increased rapidly. Salt from Cheshire increased from 7,954 tons in 1732 to some 14,359 tons by 1752, and this figure did not include the rock salt that was being taken down the Weaver to Liverpool. Huge amounts of coal were required for the emerging industries in and around Liverpool, and much of this was supplied from the Prescot Hall Mine. In 1753, the prices rose, which, in turn, prompted the common council of Liverpool to explore alternative means of supply and improvements in communication between the town and south Lancashire. A turnpike road was built between Liverpool and Prescot, which was later extended to St Helens. The road was further extended to Ashton in 1753. However, the net effect of this was to increase still further the cost of coal reaching the town. Once again, the common council had to rethink their options. A scheme was developed, which would improve the Sankey Navigation. A bill was introduced into parliament on 20 March 1755, which became law 'for making navigable the river or brook called Sankey and the three several branches thereof.'

As both the number and size of vessels using the port increased, it became imperative to develop more and larger docking and dock facilities. The entrepreneurs and engineers of the time were faced with numerous obstacles, including the 30-foot tidal range, the turbulent currents of the Mersey, the acquisition of land upon which to build the docks and the ever-present issue of raising the necessary capital to construct the docks.

The difficulties that had been encountered and overcome with the building of Liverpool's first dock, under the direction of Thomas Steers, were still present. However, a second dock, designed by Thomas Steers, but built in the main by Henry Berry, was opened in 1753. The South Dock, or Salthouse Dock, as it later became known, tended to handle boats arriving from Ireland carrying cargoes of agricultural produce. The dock also handled ships arriving from France and some Mediterranean ports with brandy, wine and fresh fruit. The tidal dock, which had been reconstructed, was known as a 'dry' dock because of the fact that it had no flood gates, and thus became empty at low water. However, when the Old Dock was later filled-in, the dock was converted to a wet dock in 1829 and renamed as Canning Dock.

In 1824, when Jesse Hartley was appointed to the position of dock engineer at Liverpool, the docks of the town had remained in much the same configuration since their inception more than one hundred years ago. The total water surface area of the docks was only 50 acres. However, during Hartley's time, the docks, with the exception of the Prince's Dock, were completely reconstructed. Prince's Dock was opened at the time of King George IV's coronation in 1821. Between 1824 and 1843, the water area of the docks almost doubled in acreage, from 50 acres to 96 acres, and then from 1843 to 1859 there was a phenomenal increase from 96 acres to 213 acres. Therefore, from 1824, and for the next thirty-six years, the docks system and its expansion was under the direct control and guidance of the bluff Yorkshireman, Jesse Hartley. Hartley's single-minded and ambitious plans for extension of the dock system at Liverpool often meant that his dock plans overran estimated budgets. The trustees had been given wide-ranging powers in the act of 1825 to raise capital, but, because of excess expenditure and under estimates, a number of enabling acts had to be granted by parliament in 1828, 1830, 1841, 1844, and 1846.

At a professional level, Hartley's ideas and designs were unsurpassed and were executed with skill, ingenuity, and confidence. He specified that the dock walls that he was responsible for building would be of granite, cemented together with hydraulic lime, which had a consistency almost as hard as the granite itself. On a personal level, Hartley could be despotic, rough, and rude, often resorting to baser expletives.

One of the first projects that Hartley was involved with was the design and construction of the Brunswick Dock; built under the powers of the 1825 act. The dock, built to the south, was opened on 14 April 1832 and was the third largest dock in the docks system at the time of construction, having a total wet surface area of some 12 acres. There was also a half-tide basin of 1½ acres attached to it and two large graving docks, which opened out from its southern end. The dock was built specifically for the importation of timber, having an inclined plane on the east side, designed especially for the unloading of timber. The unique design meant that timber could be discharged straight to the dockside, thus avoiding the need to discharge the cargo onto the shore, as had previously been the case. This was an important advantage, as, because of the increasing volume of timber passing through the port, vessels were having to queue before being unloaded. The new system avoided much of this waiting time outside of the port. Imported timber was used throughout the north and north-west to satisfy the needs of the building programmes, which were being developed across the region. Also, the thriving ship-building industry along the Mersey was always in need of good quality timber. In order for the dock to be constructed, the land which was formerly the site of the old tide-mill reservoir—known as Jackson's Dam—was absorbed into this dock. The lands that were to form part of these docks were owned by the corporation and purchased, by verdict of a jury, for the sum of £95,005.

As much of the timber imported into Liverpool at that time came from New Brunswick in Canada, it was deemed particularly appropriate to name the new dock Brunswick Dock. There is, however, a contrary view as to the derivation of the dock's name, which suggests that the name is derived from George IVs estranged wife, Queen Caroline Amelia Elizabeth of Brunswick-Wolfenbüttel. Later on, when the depth and size of the dock became too small to accommodate the larger ocean-going vessels that were, by that time, using the port, alternative docking facilities were built and Brunswick Dock was predominantly used for ships arriving from South America and West Africa.

Work also continued apace on the north side, with the first stone laid for the Clarence Dock being laid on 5 December 1826. Due to the new dock being built specifically to accommodate the increasing number of steam-driven ships entering the port, the dock was located some distance to the north, in order to minimise the risk of fire from berthing ships. Land had been acquired soon after the 1825 act had been passed. The corporation owned most of the land acquired. A considerable amount of land was purchased, enough to meet the construction requirements of the Clarence Dock, Waterloo Dock, Trafalgar Dock, and Victoria Dock, together with their accompanying basins and quays. The total amount of land purchased was somewhat in excess of 56 acres. Clarence Dock, named in honour of the Duke of Clarence, later King William IV, was opened on 21 May 1830, having a free surface area of 6 acres and the half-tide dock having a surface area of 4 acres.

Due to an underestimation of costs, a further application had to be made to parliament in 1828 to increase the borrowing requirement by a further £200,000. The number of ships using the port in that year was 10,703, having a total tonnage of some 1,311,111 tons. The size of the ships coming into the port was also increasing steadily. In 1811, the average burthen—the cargo carrying capacity of the vessel—was 109 tons. By 1825, this figure had risen to 118 tons, and by 1828 the figure had reached 122 tons. Strenuous efforts were constantly being made so that the dock building programme was at least keeping pace with the increasing volume of trade that was now passing through the port. However, by the time that the Clarence Dock was opened, the funding was once again overstretched and a further loan of another £200,000 had to be secured. The total debt incurred was now in excess of £1,400,000. Perhaps the main reason for this was because Jesse Hartley only worked to the very highest of standards.

The Waterloo Dock, named in honour of the famous battle, was opened on 16 August 1834. The dock was revolutionary in design in that, previously, all docks had been rectangular, with the longer side of the rectangle being parallel to the river's edge. The Waterloo Dock had its shorter length parallel to the river's edge. The advantage of, effectively, turning the dock through 90°, was to make more space along the river front as, with the ever-increasing volume of trade, there was no knowing where the docks system would end. The dock had a water surface area of 5 acres. Since the original dock was built, there have been significant structural changes made.

Other docks that were built during the same expansive period were the Trafalgar Dock and Victoria Dock, both of which were opened in 1836. The docks were built on land that was owned by the corporation. With their adjacent quays and basins they covered some 56 acres. The Brunswick Dock had cost £438,000 to build, and the Clarence Dock, Trafalgar Dock, Waterloo Dock, and the Victoria Dock group cost in excess of £795,000. In the preamble to the earlier 1828 act, it was stated that 'the purchase under the authority of the preceding Act had exceeded the estimates but, as the trade of the port was increasing so rapidly, the utmost expedition was required to accommodate it'. Throughout Hartley's tenure, this statement became somewhat of a recurrent theme. Indeed, by 1847, the overall debt stood at almost £5,000,000.

Hartley's primary concept in docks design was to ensure the maximum number of docking areas covering the least river frontage—a simple but effective planning process. He also introduced other revolutionary concepts in his dock designs. Quay space was extended and covered sheds were built so that goods were protected during loading and unloading. He also had sheds built around some of the older docks.

Victoria Dock and Trafalgar Dock had a combined free surface area of more than 11 acres. Steam vessels using the docks were now increasing in number and for both practical and safety reasons, it became necessary to use different docks for steam vessels and sailing ships. Both Trafalgar Dock and Victoria Dock were appropriated for steam ships.

The composition and constitution of the Dock Board was giving rise to some concern as to the effectiveness of its operation, but the Municipal Reform Act of 1835 did not change the constitution of the board. An effort was made to take the administration and running of the docks completely out of the control of the council, but this move was rejected by parliament.

One of the major issues that was concerning many traders at the time was the fact that there was relatively little storage accommodation near to the docks themselves. Goods were carted and stored in warehouses built in nearby streets. Another of Hartley's concepts, which was not unique to Liverpool, was to build docks that were completely enclosed and surrounded by their own warehouses. In 1810, plans were drawn up and sanctioned by the council (who were the trustees of the docks), which allowed for enclosed docks and warehouses to be built. However, the plans for the docks themselves were accepted when placed before parliament, but the scheme in total, which included the building of warehouses directly adjacent and bordering the docks themselves, was rejected. This was primarily due to the powerful vested interests of the warehouse owners. During the 1820s and 1830s, much capital was expended on building a number of warehouses directly behind the dock area.

However, progress and increased trade were becoming the 'buzz' words along the waterfront and, although parliament had rejected the plans to build integrated docks and warehouse facilities, a new commission was established 'to inquire into the regulations of the Customs and Excise, with a view of facilitating the despatch of business, affording accommodation to trade, and securing and improving the revenue'. The commissioners accepted the wisdom in building integrated docks and recommended that 'a contiguous chain of warehouses adjoining to the docks, surrounded by walls, or otherwise insulated from places of public access'. This latter recommendation, to build walls around the docks and warehouses, was introduced because it was considered by the commissioners that the facilities at Liverpool for bonded warehouses were sadly lacking.

The report was made public on 1 May 1821. Several meetings were held locally, including one that was attended by warehouse proprietors at a local hostelry, the Golden Lion. Although all of the implications of the report were considered in some depth at the meeting, it was felt that the issues were so important to the town as a whole that a public meeting should be convened. This meeting was held at the town hall on Thursday 7 June and presided over by the mayor himself. Just about every prominent merchant in the town was present at the meeting. Following much discussion and debate, the government scheme was roundly criticised and the following motion adopted:

> That the recommendation, if unhappily carried into effect, would involve a complete and ruinous revolution of the warehouse property of the town, estimated to amount in aggregate value to £2,000,000 or thereabouts, which forms a most important part of the property of its inhabitants, and is, in its present extent, much more than adequate to the trade of the port, notwithstanding the unprecedented accumulation of foreign grain, cotton, spirits, and other merchandise which now exists.

The warehouse controversy dragged on for many years and, after the election of the reformed municipal council, the issue gained fresh impetus. Mr Eyre Evans, who was a member of both the council and the Dock Board, fervently believed that all docks built in the future should, automatically, have warehouses around their immediate quayside. Although there was violent opposition from the private warehouse owners, Evans's arguments ultimately carried the day.

A turning point was reached when, in February 1839, Hartley developed and brought forward an ambitious scheme for a completely new dock to be built on the western side of Salthouse Dock. His scheme envisaged a large dock with warehousing facilities completely enclosing it, the dock itself would also be equipped with hydraulic mechanisms to control the opening and closing of the dock gates. Although there was still much opposition to the proposal, the plan was carried in 1841 and the necessary parliamentary approval granted through another act for the dock's construction. At the time of the former act, which had been granted in 1825, 10,001 vessels were passing through the port, whereas latterly the number of ships using the port was now 15,998 and tonnage had increased during that period from 1,180,914 to 2,445,708—more than double in just fifteen years. As a result of the significantly increased usage, the act allowed the port's allowable debt to be increased to £2,284,000.

An Act of Parliament actually fixed the price for the land west of Salthouse Dock that the corporation would be required to pay. The figure set was £221,853 and 16s—a very precise amount. The parcel of land did, however, include a number of graving docks and some other properties. When the cost of the actual construction was taken into account, together with the costs of the associated warehouses, the grand total amounted to £721,736 11s 9d. Although the dock was large, it was not the largest on the docks estate, but did cover about 7½ acres.

The Albert Dock was opened on 30 July 1845 by Prince Albert. After opening the dock, although the prince showed great interest in the hydraulic gates to the dock, he made no comment whatsoever as to the surrounding warehouses, but Picton did have much to say, suggesting that 'the works for strength and durability were unsurpassable', then later added, 'but it is regrettable that no attention has been paid to beauty as well as to strength. The enormous pile of warehouses which looms so large upon the river and in its vastness surpasses the pyramid of Cheops, is simply a hideous pile of naked brickwork'. There was further local discussion concerning the design and style of the new warehouses, with much scorn beginning showered upon Hartley's approach, suggesting that he was too utilitarian and functional in his design concepts. Some merchants suggested that for 'the mere fraction of expense which would have converted the present incarnation of ugliness into something which would have dignified the commercial by allying it with the beautiful'. Be that as it may, the quayside warehouses were an immediate success, so much so that they were soon added to and enlarged.

Earlier, in 1840, a set of gates had been incorporated at Brunswick Tidal Basin, which gave access to both the Union Half Tide Basin and Queens Dock. Following the fitting of the new 70-foot wide gates, the Brunswick Basin was renamed Coburg Dock. The new wet dock could now accommodate ocean-going paddle steamers. Both Coburg Dock and Brunswick Dock became the berthing docks for the American liners and mail packet vessels; however, later on, as improvements were made to the northern docks, ocean-going liners began to berth there. From 1842, Hartley based the South Dockyard headquarters of his construction and repair facility there. In addition to having repair facilities, the dock was also important for grain discharge and storage, having a dockside silo capacity of 62,000 tons.

The concept of a dock-warehouse system was now becoming established, as it was obviously commercially viable. Hartley developed further plans to extend the dock area both to the north of the existing docks and also to the south, so yet more land required for building more docks and warehousing facilities. In 1843, the Earl of Derby, who owned much of the foreshore at the northern end of the docks, was paid £17,500 by the trustees for 1,000 lineal yards, thus enabling the docks to be extended beyond the boundary of the borough to the adjacent township of Kirkdale. The acquisition of this land also incorporated an agreement with the Duchy of Lancaster; £800 was paid when the Duchy agreed to forego any claims to the foreshore. The trustees were now in a position to extend the dock estate northwards.

Similarly, foreshore land was purchased at the southern end of the system between the newly opened Brunswick Dock and the Herculaneum Pottery Works further along the river. Much of this area had been intended for the development of a privately owned dock system, the land being owned by the Harrington Dock Company. More than £50,000 had been spent by the company on preparing and clearing the ground for the construction of two, relatively small, docks, but it was becoming apparent that, because of the number, size, and volume of vessels using the port, it would be difficult to build economically viable docks that were privately funded. The Harrington Dock Company finally acknowledged the economic logic of the situation and a proposal was made to the Dock Committee on 7 October 1843, whereby the property would be purchased by the trustees. Many questions were raised, as the scheme had initially been suggested by the chairman of the company. The purchase did, however, go ahead and the land was bought for £253,000.

The 1844 act ratified these proposals in light of the still-increasing number of vessels that were using the port, now a staggering 18,411 with a gross combined tonnage of 2,632,712 tons. In order to facilitate this new building programme, the borrowing requirement was increased to £1,500,000.

Within the act, there was provision for a number of new docks at the northern extremity of the dock system; these latter developments incorporated a scheme whereby, utilising a series of locks and a canal extension, direct communication could be made with the Leeds–Liverpool Canal, which, again, would add to the commercial wellbeing of both the Port of Liverpool and the towns from which goods were being transported for export through the port. Hartley was now in a position to design and build dock-warehouse systems that would give Liverpool an almost undisputed lead in docks and docking facilities.

The act also gave authorisation for docks to be constructed on the Harrington site, which lay in the southern dock complex. A small dock and two graving docks were built and opened in 1864. The dock became known as the Herculaneum Dock and had a free surface area of some 3½ acres, with lock gates opening directly to the river. Hartley did not live long enough to see the opening of this dock.

With the Port of Liverpool's capacity for handling ships and their cargoes rapidly reaching saturation, even given the proposed new building programme, other avenues for development were being actively considered. One possibility, which was beginning to emerge, related to the creek on the opposite banks of the River Mersey. It had long been known that, similar to the creek, which had originally served Liverpool as a harbour, there was a larger tract of low-lying land (originally a marsh), which extended across the Wirral peninsula to the sea and the high ground that separated the marsh from the sea was known as Walla's-ey or Wallasey Pool. It is at this time that a number of speculative land deals were made on the far side of the Mersey by a number of Wirral's most prominent people, including Mr John Askew, harbour-master of the Port of Liverpool; Mr William Laird, shipbuilder; and Sir John Tobin, a prominent member of Liverpool Corporation, a descendant of a slave-trading family, and Liverpool's mayor in 1819. At one point there had been talk of constructing a canal to cross the peninsula, thus avoiding the currents and other hazards at the mouth of the Mersey, but this proposal was not considered feasible. It was, however, decided to form a company with the idea of re-examining the concept of developing a docks system on that side of the Mersey. The topography of the land was ideal, in that it would be relatively easy to establish rail links between Birkenhead and the Midlands, and similarly between Birkenhead and the coalfields of North Wales. Once established, the rail links would give easier access to the industrial Midlands, Shropshire, and the Black Country. There was little doubt that, if the project was successful, it would be able to rival Liverpool because of its easy access to these locations. Additionally, Laird was developing Birkenhead itself as a prosperous, vibrant community, with ample accommodation for the company's workforce in newly built houses, gas lighting in all of the public building, of which there were many, and open spaces specifically designed for leisure activities—again, another new concept. Birkenhead was developing the potential to rival Liverpool as a hub of business and economic activity.

Mr J. M. Rendel was appointed as the company's chief engineer and surveyor, his main role being to examine the feasibility of constructing docks on that side of the river and, if viable, to prepare extensive plans for the construction of the docks. The next secretive move of the company was to make a bid to purchase extensive lands along the water's edge, which were owned by the corporation. However, rather than make the application through their company, the application to the corporation was made on behalf of a number of private individuals. A number of members of the company attended the council meeting on 30 October 1843. However, they did not declare that they were representatives of the company, but attended as private individuals.

The chairman of the Finance Committee, Mr G. H. Lawrence, appears to have carried quite an influential voice; however, in a naïve statement, he declared:

> The Corporation had expended, including interest, £360,000 on land in Cheshire; that it was a matter of importance to reduce the annual charges to the burgesses; that the sales which had been, and which were proposed to be made, would benefit the funds to the extent of £7,200 per annum, and that there would be still left 725,400 square yards of land.

During the ensuing discussions, little emphasis seems to have been placed upon the original reason for purchasing the land, or indeed why prospective purchasers would be wishing to purchase such a vast tract of land at this time. However, there were few dissenting voices when the proposal was made to sell the land. Mr Isaac Holmes did speak against the proposal, stating that the dock might have been constructed for somewhere in the region of £60,000, which would have relieved some of the congestion problems which were now beginning to occur at the docks in Liverpool. Mr Eyre Evans also spoke against the proposition, suggesting that the area could be used for subsidiary docking for Liverpool. He also said that no inquiry had been undertaken or survey commissioned. He felt that the matter was being approached with too much haste, especially when considering what a valuable asset the land represented. However, when it came to the vote, the land sale was agreed by thirty-one votes to twenty-five. The company bought 206 acres of land for £180,264. It was then proposed to seek permission to build a number of docks on the site. However, Liverpool Corporation and the Dock Committee were totally oblivious of what was about to happen next. Just one week later, on 7 November 1843, there was a meeting of the Birkenhead Commissioners, at which plans were brought forward for a docks scheme on the Birkenhead side of the Mersey. The meeting was informed that plans had been prepared for a huge docks scheme and that Admiralty assent had been given for the whole area from Woodside Slip to Seacombe, an area of some 340 acres, to be enclosed. Consent from the Admiralty had been obtained to construct a tidal basin of some thirty acres, and, when damming up the Pool, a dock area of some 120 acres could be created. Mr William Jackson, who had brought forward the scheme, stated:

> This might take the public by surprise; and if it did, and they taxed them with moving so privately, he could only say that prudence induced them to keep their own counsel until such time as their plans were ripe and they received the assent of the authorities.

Mr John Nelson Wood who was one of the commissioners and also a member of the Liverpool Corporation voiced his concern and disquiet. He suggested that, had the corporation known the intended purpose for the land, then they, the corporation, would not have sold the land a so low a price. No sooner had the relevant agreements been signed than notices were issued for a bill to be introduced to parliament. The corporation naturally opposed the bill, but, having sold the land without any qualifying clauses as to the usage of the land, it was clear that there was an apparent inconsistency in their stance. As a result, the bill was passed into law.

All of the necessary plans had been submitted and approved by various authorities, and the matter now only required the consent of parliament. Needless to say, this development gave rise to extreme consternation on the part of Liverpool Corporation, who had sold the land on a lease—at a very modest sum—for a period of seventy-five years. Within the lease there was provision to construct docks.

The plans were placed before parliament virtually as soon as they were revealed. The corporation strongly objected to the plans, but were thwarted when the plans were passed without any difficulty—the battle lines had been drawn. Together with the granting of permission to build the docks, other powerful forces now came into play, such as the concentrated weight of Cheshire's most powerful nobility and land-owning classes. There was also a more insidious ally in the form of Manchester and a number of nearby manufacturing towns, who, always envious of Liverpool's dominant position, saw a dock system on the opposite side of the Mersey as an alternative port, thus thwarting further development in Liverpool's premier trading position. The primary objectives of seeking permission to build docks on the Birkenhead side of the Mersey was to offer better docking facilities on that side and also to curtail further dock development on the Liverpool side. The goals were aided by the fact that the ability of Liverpool to increase its borrowing requirement was severely limited, whilst the authorities on the Birkenhead side of the river were given almost unlimited access to further borrowing. However, although more than £5½ million was expended on dock buildings on the Birkenhead side, the returns on capital outlay barely showed a working profit.

In 1844, the Commissioners of Birkenhead docks were given authority to raise capital and build the planned docks and quays. They were given specific authority to 'form, maintain and repair a sea wall along the eastern limit of Wallasey Pool between Seacombe and Woodside ferries, and also construct an embankment from Bridge End in Birkenhead to the opposite side of the Pool, for penning up the water of the said Pool'.

Sir Philip Egerton laid the first stone that marked the commencement of the docks scheme at Birkenhead on 23 October, 1844. Although funds were limited and engineering difficulties were encountered—mainly due to Rendel's limited engineering knowledge—dock construction progressed rapidly, perhaps too rapidly, and the Morpeth and Egerton Docks were opened on 25 April 1847 by Viscount Morpeth. The original estimates for the building of the docks had been approximately £400,000, but the costs were a gross underestimation, the final construction costs being more in the region of £1,000,000. Capital for the building had been raised by the sale of bonds, similar to those that had been issued by the Liverpool Dock Trust. Sometime later, when further expansion was envisaged, another company was formed, the Birkenhead Dock Company. This company would be responsible for the financing of the dock construction and their associated warehousing facilities.

However, there were more surprises in store. In June 1847, new commissioners were appointed and a cursory glance at the accounts revealed that the company's former commissioners had already used all of the cash earmarked for further development work and that some work had proceeded without having first obtained the necessary permission. In desperation, the commissioners applied to Liverpool for financial assistance, but nothing was forthcoming. They then applied to Commissioners of Woods and Forests in order to complete the building of the dam and build the river wall. All building work came to an abrupt halt and many men became unemployed. Added to this, there was a significant downturn in shipbuilding orders at the Laird's works, which led to further unemployment in the town, with many of the former workforce leaving to seek employment elsewhere. The situation went from bad to worse and it was stated that 'Birkenhead was a splendid ruin'. In December of that year, a meeting of the shareholders of the Birkenhead Dock Company was held. It was agreed that, because of the parlous state of the company and the future trading prospects, the company should be dissolved. For various reasons, this decision was never implemented and in 1848, under a further Act of Parliament, it was agreed that the company would purchase the Herculaneum Dock on the Liverpool side of the river.

This development also met with innumerable problems and an approach was made to the Liverpool Dock Committee to assume responsibility for the undertaking, however, the Liverpool Dock Committee declined this overture. More funding was sought through yet another act, and the raising of an additional £50,000 was granted in order that the work could begin once again. Rendel had been the brunt of much bitter recrimination for his perceived failure to maintain the impetus of the initial construction work; he resigned his post in July 1847, but, following some political manoeuvring, he was reinstated in his former post and, working with the Commissioners of Crown Lands, they agreed the remove their interest in part of the lands that they owned there. They also agreed to meet the cost of the quay walls adjoining this land and other disbursements, which needed to be made. The provision made in the act also ensured that the Crown built a permanent road across the dam between Birkenhead and Seacombe, thus enabling the Birkenhead, Lancashire, and Cheshire Junction Railway to lay a track across the temporary dam. This line was extended to Warrington in the hope of attracting more trade to be diverted from Manchester.

The next few years, following the act that was passed in 1844, saw frenetic dock construction activity along the banks of the Mersey. The land upon which the docks were built, as far as Beacon's Gutter, was owned by the corporation, but, under the provisions in the act, the land was taken by the Dock Trust. Some 71 acres was sold at a price of £250,879. The land upon which the battery had been built by the government also had to be repurchased, and this cost another £27,850. To the north, a number of new docks were built including Salisbury Dock, Collingwood Dock, Stanley Dock, Nelson Dock, and Bramley-Moore Dock. Bramley-Moore Dock was named after the chairman of the Dock Committee, who had worked tirelessly to ensure that dock expansion continued at a rate which would, at least, keep pace with the still-rising volume of trade passing through the port. The new docks complex was opened by Mr John Bramley-Moore on 4 August 1848. Once again, Hartley employed techniques and principles that he had first used when building earlier docks, namely, the space immediately fronting the river was minimised and tidal basins, which had figured in the old docks system, were completely eliminated. Salisbury Dock itself had two direct entrances to the river, thus giving the opportunity for vessels to enter the dock system at times other than full flood tide. The fact that all five docks were connected gave significant commercial advantages, having a combined water surface area of in excess of 33 acres, and quayside access of over 2 miles in length. Stanley Dock was some distance from the other four docks, with large warehouses to both the north and south. There were also five basins, all connected by locks, which give access to the Leeds and Liverpool Canal. The other four docks in the immediate vicinity were covered by sheds to accommodate goods in transit.

It had long been recognised that there was a need for a central landing stage. Mr L. Cubitt was the commissioned engineer who oversaw the construction of the stage, which was off St George's Pier. The Dock Board paid the £60,000 that it cost to construct the stage, which was opened on 1 June 1847. The landing stage was 500 feet long and had a width of 80 feet.

In 1849, the last of the docks authorised under the act of 1844 was opened—the Wellington Dock and Half-Tide Basin. In total, there was a free water surface area of over 11 acres. However, even with this increase in docking facilities, it was clear that more accommodation was required to meet current and anticipated demand. In 1845, there had been 20,521 ships using the docks, having a gross tonnage of some 3,016,531 tons. It was also apparent that the size of ships using the port was also rapidly increasing.

Accordingly, on 19 January 1846, the chairman of the Dock Committee, Mr John Bramley-Moore, presented to the committee plans for even more extensions to the docks complex at Liverpool. The plan, as envisaged, required the Salthouse Dock to be enlarged; for a new dock, to be called the Wapping Dock, to be constructed to the east of the King's Dock and for a basin to be built behind Duke's Dock, which would connect Salthouse Dock and the new Wapping Dock. The development would not only cause considerable disruption during construction, as it necessitated Wapping to be relocated eastwards and several buildings in that vicinity being taken down, it would also mean a considerable financial outlay for the construction work itself and also for the purchase of the necessary properties and land. The works themselves would cost an estimated £154,386 and the purchase of the properties along Wapping would add another £377,000, giving a grand total of some £531,386. Due to the high costs involved, the Dock Committee was empowered under the act to extend their borrowing powers by an additional £1,000,000, increasing the bonded debt to £4,784,000. Perhaps because of the vast amount of work, together with various legal niceties having to be completed, the work took upwards of ten years to build—considerably longer than had originally been envisaged. In fact, the dock itself was not opened until 1858, almost at the end of Hartley's reign as dock engineer. The dock had a free water surface area of over 5 acres. There was provision under the act to build a new entrance basin between Canning Dock and George's Dock, but this development never happened.

The town and merchants of Liverpool continued to enjoy the wealth that was being created by the increasing number of ships that were using the port, while the expanding dock system was just about keeping pace.

Mr John Bramley-Moore negotiated a contract, on behalf of the committee, with the Earl of Derby. The original agreement was for 270,000 square yards of foreshore—extending to the township of Bootle—owned by the earl, to be given to the committee for the construction of new docks. In exchange, the spoil from the excavations would be used to in-fill other lands owned by the earl. In the event, however, the arrangement did not come to fruition and, instead, the lands were purchased for the sum of £90,000. The number of ships now using the docks had risen to 20,889, with an aggregate tonnage of 3,351,539 tons.

Work went ahead on the Sandon Dock, which had a free surface area over slightly more than 10 acres. The dock was opened in 1851 and was named after Lord Sandon, who had represented Liverpool in parliament from 1831 to 1842.

With the developing dock estate and the town itself gaining a degree of national importance, other considerations were now assuming greater significance. The Port of Liverpool was less than 3 miles distant from the open sea and was also located in a particularly wide estuary. Due to these two factors, it was now deemed necessary to erect a sea wall. The fundamental thinking behind this proposal was firstly, to ensure that shipping using the port was shielded from storms, thus allowing cargoes to be loaded and unloaded safely and securely, and secondly, to enable any minor repairs to vessels to be carried out. Jesse Hartley designed and built the sea walls in 'Cyclopean' granite from Scotland.

There were a number of constraints that had to be considered before the wall could be built. It was clear that, if the wall was to fulfil its designed function, then it would have to be built such that it traversed the whole length of the dock estate. Also, the foundations had to be deep enough to overcome any undermining effects caused by subterranean streams coming into the Mersey at that point. Similarly, the wall had to be strong enough to resist the frequent storms and withstand the notoriously fierce currents in the Mersey, and it should also be high enough to resist any squalls and waves in gale conditions from breaching it or overwhelming it at high tide. The wall that was built was nearly 5 miles in length and had an average width of some 11 feet. The wall was extremely robust, in that the average height from its foundations to its highest point was almost 40 feet.

Many obstacles had to be overcome when erecting the wall, most notable being that the wall had to be built on a solid foundation. This was particularly important near to Prince's Dock, as this was the narrowest section of the river and was thus subjected to some of the strongest currents. The depth for the foundations to be laid could only be accessed at two periods during the year, namely, when the tide reached its lowest ebb at the vernal and autumnal equinoxes. However, even then the builders often encountered difficulties because of unpredictable weather and river conditions. It was a painstaking and somewhat protracted process to lay the six courses of timber which were required for the foundations, but the importance of the task was never underrated, knowing that the wall would safeguard shipping and the port itself from violent storms and also the turbulent currents of the Mersey. Progress was made, however, with piles being driven to a great depth through the quicksand. A series of wooden piles were driven into the quicksand at the entrance to George's Basin and in front of the area by Albert Dock. It is reputed that a total of some 13,792 piles of beechwood timber was sunk along this area of the wall. Further difficulties were encountered at the entrance to Wellington Half-Tide Dock, and beech-wood timber was used once again and driven deep into the peat moss at that point.

On the far side of the Mersey, however, the docks at Birkenhead are very different in form from the docks on the Liverpool side of the Mersey. Whereas the docks at Liverpool run parallel to the river's edge, the docks at Birkenhead lie inland roughly following the line of the ancient Pool of Wallasey. The dock wall, in essence protecting the entrances to all of the docks, is less than half a mile wide, closing the mouth of the former pool.

It was also in 1851 that significant and far-reaching changes would occur in the management and ordinance of the docks system. After a number of disputes, it was considered that certain changes should be made to the constitution and the governance of the docks. It is also significant that the American Chamber of Commerce, now firmly established in the town, should be instrumental in bringing this bill forward in parliament. The draft proposal was that the Dock Committee should still consist of twenty-one members, but that the corporation, as trustees, should now have only five members to represent them, rather than, as formerly, thirteen members. Fifteen members were to be elected by the dock ratepayers, with the chairman being chosen by the committee from the ratepayers. The House of Commons proposed a compromise solution, whereby the new committee would have a total of twenty-four members; with twelve members being nominated by the council and the remaining twelve members were to be elected by the dock ratepayers. However, the chairman was to be elected by the committee from the council members, and the council was to retain their power of veto. After this new constitution was adopted, it continued in this form for a further seven years.

Dock construction continued apace, and in 1852 another new dock was opened, the Huskisson Dock. The original intention was for the dock to be used, primarily, as a timber dock, but, in the event, it tended to be used for the newer, larger ocean-going steamers. When built, the dock had a free surface area of 14 acres, but it was enlarged in 1860 by a cut, which extended eastwards, giving an additional 7 acres of dock space. Before that time, in 1854, a new fort and barracks was built by the government at the north-west corner of the dock. This was to compensate for the one that had to be demolished to accommodate the construction of Collingwood Dock.

Although the actual number of ships using the port appears to have plateaued, the gross tonnage of shipping continued to increase. By 1847, the gross tonnage had increased to 4,096,100 tons. Larger ships now required different docking facilities and powers were obtained to build more docks and also increase the number of dockside warehouses. Permission was granted to enable the committee to raise the additional capital required. However, never very far from the surface, politics once again began to play a part in the overall pattern of docks development. Companies on the Birkenhead side of the river had also submitted proposals for the development of their docks and dockside activities. They argued that, given a reasonable commercial chance, the provision on the Birkenhead side of the Mersey would obviate the need for further dock expansion on the Liverpool side. The argument met with a degree of success, in that the borrowing powers that had been requested by Liverpool were significantly reduced—from a borrowing requirement of £4,500,000 to a relatively modest sum of £850,000. The arrangement with the Earl of Derby, to extend the docks estate to the extremities of Bootle, was finally confirmed.

However, as things stood, the affairs of both the Birkenhead Dock Company and the trustees of the Birkenhead Docks were in such a parlous state of turmoil, bordering on insolvency, that it was considered prudent by members of Liverpool Corporation to repurchase the Birkenhead land, which had been so imprudently sold some twelve years previously, thus ameliorating any opposition from interested parties on that side of the river. The undertakings of the Birkenhead Dock Company and of the Birkenhead Docks were transferred to the mayor, aldermen, and burgesses of the Borough of Liverpool.

After being reinstated, Rendel was asked to give estimates of the total amount that had already been spent and that which needed to be spent to complete the work. Several other estimates were made, but finally it was agreed that there was a deficit of some £10,000. However, when this figure was compared with the docks construction activity, which was occurring on the other side of the river, it does not paint a particularly good picture for Birkenhead. In a little over three years, all that had been achieved was the construction of some 7½ acres of dock space, much of which had not been constructed to the exacting standards that were in place on the far side of the Mersey, and there was still a degree of financial uncertainty.

Sometime later, in 1850, Thomas Brassey agreed to finish the work according to Rendel's revised plan. It had been estimated that this work would cost an additional £500,000. This development marked a significant improvement in the fate of the docks at Birkenhead. With some government aid, an emigrant depot had been opened in Birkenhead and the numbers of sailings were on the increase. Discussions were also taking place with the South American and General Steam Navigation Company, with the idea of starting a trade route between Birkenhead and Brazil. Furthermore, the shipping dues, which were now coming into Birkenhead, also began to increase as companies gained confidence in the efficacy of the new docks complex.

Brassey had close connections with the town of Birkenhead, so it was perhaps understandable that he became the preferred contractor for the construction of a number of railways in the region. There was the Grand Junction in 1835; the Chester to Crewe line in 1839; the Lancashire to Carlisle line in 1844; and the Chester to Holyhead line in 1845. He had also had an interest in the Birkenhead and Chester Junction Railway in 1847, and for the Victoria Docks and Warehouses in 1852. Previously, Brassey had been the main contractor for Greenock Harbour in 1845 and, some years later, in 1863, was the contractor for

Barrow-in-Furness Docks. Brassey's approach to Birkenhead docks started with the tidal basin and graving docks to be constructed. Unfortunately, because of questionable production techniques, on 14 March 1854, the dam collapsed, just prior to completion. At this point, Brassey agreed to rebuild the dam at his own expense; however, it soon became apparent that the cost of rebuilding was way in excess of Brassey's budget. He gave backword on the project and insisted on receiving cash if the work was to continue. This situation was not acceptable and when the committee rejected his proposal, he withdrew from the contract.

Due to the many poor decisions taken with regards to the engineering and business decisions relating to the Birkenhead Dock project, an enmity developed between Birkenhead and neighbouring Liverpool. The estranged nature of the relationship also involved the city of Manchester in a purely political context. Manchester was intent on adopting free trade policies and resented the power exerted by the Liverpool Dock trustees. By deliberately fostering the poor relationships that were developing between Liverpool and Birkenhead, Manchester, in effect, put pressure on the Liverpool Corporation to adopt a more liberal approach to dock and town dues.

The next period in the history of Liverpool and its docks was an extremely critical one. Up until now, the corporation had been responsible for the construction, management, and development of the docks and the dock estate. However, it was considered by the legislature that this arrangement should be curtailed.

Following a lengthy legal system relating to the duties required on goods landed and shipped from Liverpool, it became established that the corporation would be in receipt of all of these dues. Initially, this was a relatively small amount, but as trade increased, so too did the dues payable to the corporation. As recent as 1830, there was no dispute as to the amount of dues payable and to whom they were to be paid.

However, there was much disquiet at both the amount of dues payable and also the rightful recipient—many were beginning to question the right of the corporation to collect and retain the dock dues. The case was taken to the courts, which, after a protracted period, found in favour of the corporation. There were still many misgivings pertaining to the case, so much so that a royal commission was established on 19 March 1853 in order 'to inquire into all local charges on shipping and goods in the ports and harbours of the United Kingdom'. Inquiries were conducted in all of the country's major ports. The four-man committee presided over by Mr Cardwell, formerly a MP for Liverpool, visited Liverpool and many other ports, holding an inquiry in every one. When they presented their report, the main recommendation resulting from their inquiries was that a new body should be appointed to take charge of the docks and harbour and, further, that all property and dock dues should be transferred. One of the more contentious recommendations was that the town dues should no longer be applied in payment of interest of any debts not contracted for strictly harbour purposes, and that such corporate debts should be, in future, a charge upon the inhabitants.

Accordingly, a bill was brought before parliament in 1856 in order to confer legal status on the recommendations. However, the bill met with much opposition and was withdrawn. Subsequent to that, on 14 March 1856, a select committee was set up 'to inquire into and report upon the several matters referred to the commissioners appointed by Her Majesty'.

The committee sat for a total of three months, at the end of which it concluded: 'that the committee do not find that there is sufficient reason to disturb the settlement of the question made by the Municipal Reform Bill'. The votes cast both for and against the adoption of the recommendation were equal. This outcome gave increased impetus to the opposition camp, whose members brought to the next session of parliament in 1857 a bill, which would transfer the dock estate to an entirely new body of trustees and managers and remove the town dues from the corporation. Significantly, the promoters of the bill were the Manchester Chamber of Commerce, the Manchester Commercial Association, and the Great Western Railway Company.

The matter was referred to a select committee, chaired by Sir James Graham. On 26 June that year, the committee announced its decisions:

1. The preamble was declared proved.
2. The Dock Trustees in future to be twenty-eight in number, of whom three were to be Government nominees, the remainder to be elected by the dock ratepayers. The chairman to be elected out of the general body.
3. The town dues to be taken from the corporation and made over to the dock trustees.
4. The Birkenhead Dock Estate to be made over to the new trustees, charged with the then existing debt of £1,400,000.
5. The bonded debt of the corporation at this time amounted to about £1,150,000. Of this sum it was proposed that £600,000, being the amount supposed to have been expended on harbour purposes, should be transferred to the dock trust; the remaining £550,000 to be a charge on the borough fund or provided for out of local taxation.

Before any agreement could be reached, other factors had to be taken into consideration. One of the main political contentions held by Manchester was the perceived privilege of the continuation of town dues, which were received by Liverpool due to the closed dock arrangement. It was seen by many people outside of the town that the so-called town dues were critical to the interests and continuing prosperity of Liverpool. With a more liberal attitude being adopted towards trade in general, there was little doubt that the activities of the Dock Committee were causing resentment. It was often cited that Liverpool's opposition to the Birkenhead Dock scheme was direct evidence of the town's determination to stifle competition. Manchester in particular strongly objected to the monopoly held by Liverpool with regards to the dues, which were levied as a tax on the import of raw materials and then a similar tax being levied on the finished products that were then exported through Liverpool. It was widely known that a proportion of the dock dues was paid on an annual basis to the corporation of Liverpool and was known as town dues. It was further argued that the town dues, which averaged £120,000 *per annum* at the time, were used to artificially reduce the local rates payable in Liverpool.

The Lords decreed that suitable compensation must be paid with regards to the transfer of the town dues. Following this, the other provisions of the bill were left unchanged.

The economic effects relating to the dues were given consideration in a number of parliamentary committees in 1855. The situation was also referred to in the Commission on Dock Charges in 1853 and the Select Committee on Local Charges in 1856. The culmination was that the whole of the dock system on the Mersey, which included both Birkenhead and Liverpool docks, were destined to come under a public body in 1858. The amalgamated docks of the Port of Liverpool were now under the control and overall management of the Mersey Docks and Harbour Board.

As a direct result of the Mersey Docks and Harbour Board being established in 1858, some of the more serious objections were overcome when the town dues were converted into a lump sum of £1,500,000 and paid, by way of compensation, to the corporation of Liverpool. As the board was now responsible for the management of the docks on both sides of the river, it was agreed, as part of the package, that Rendel's plans for rail links with Birkenhead would also be honoured. The result was not quite how the merchants of Manchester would have anticipated, in that the Dock Dues were not reduced to any great extent and now indeed was the rail access carried out as originally envisaged. Indeed, for the next twenty-five years the port charges continued to be paid. Sometime later, in the 1880s, a competitive alternative was embarked upon, when the city of Manchester became an inland port as a result of access from the sea being gained via the newly opened Manchester Ship Canal.

In addition to being responsible for the day-to-day running and development of the dock system, the Mersey Docks and Harbour Board also had some specific functions. For instance, the board was responsible for seeking sanctions under the Dock Acts to raise funds for further dock development. Equally, individual members of the board, many of whom were often ship-owners in their own right, were able to raise specific issues. It was an individual, T. H. Ismay, who initiated the dredging and deepening of the Mersey Bar at the mouth of the river. Similarly, Sir Richard Holt proposed the Langton entrances. The board ensured that not only new ideas for development were considered, but they were actively pursued.

The dock trustees had formerly been responsible for the conservancy of the river and estuary, but, under the new regime, the upper and lower reaches of the river would be under the control of different authorities. The estuary remained under the purview of the Mersey Docks and Harbour Board (MDHB) and the upper reaches were to be placed in the hands of a completely new trust, which would represent the many different interests concerned.

It was imperative that the work started at the Birkenhead docks should now be completed as expeditiously as possible. When the transfer to the new board took place in 1857, the bonded debt of Birkenhead Docks was £1,400,000. However, by the time that the remedial work had been completed in 1874, the debt amounted to £5,406,012. This was due, in the main, to the expenditure incurred because of having to reconstruct the works executed by James Meadows Rendel, the former dock engineer, and in deepening the Great Float. Due to the extensive remedial work that had become necessary on the Birkenhead side of the river since amalgamation, dock developments on the Liverpool side were necessarily reordered onto an extended programme.

The opening of the new landing stage opposite to the Prince's Pier occurred on 1 September 1857. It had been designed by Thomas Cubitt and built at a cost of £120,000. The structure had a length of 1,002 feet and was 81 feet wide. Called a floating landing stage, it was connected to the main land by three bridges that rose and fell with the tides.

The Queen's Dock, in the southern docks complex, was the original timber dock, but this was superseded by the Brunswick Dock. However, with the increasing amount of timber being imported into the country, storage in the southern docks was becoming somewhat problematical and expensive and it was clear that additional facilities were required at the docks. It was for this specific purpose that the Harrington dock estate was purchased in 1844. However, as was so often to prove the case, because of increasing trade and the need for more storage, this solution did not prove to be adequate. As time passed, it became evident that a specialist timber dock, built at the northern end, with adequate storage facilities, would be a worthwhile development, especially when the Mersey's adverse tidal and weather conditions were taken into account. This resulted in the building of Canada Dock in the northern dock complex. Canada Dock was constructed and opened on 16 September 1859; the first vessel to enter the dock being the Cunard steamship *Asia*. The large dock had a free surface area of over 17 acres, and lineal quayside access of some 1,272 yards. In order to take into account the special requirements relating to timber cargoes, there was an especially wide landing quay on the east side of the dock. The dock also gave direct access to the large timber yards that extended from the quayside to Regent Road and from there to the rail network. To accommodate the increasing berthing and storage needs of the expanding port, a half-tide dock was constructed to the north of Canada Dock, having three sets of lock gates giving access to the outer tidal basin. On the eastern side there were two more docks built extending to Regent Road. Timber imports continued to increase and between 1859 and 1862 much of the timber imports were transferred and handled in the northern docks, although some imports still came into the southern dock complex.

While it is undoubtedly true that the docks system had a monopoly on imports and exports to the region and the country as a whole, the town itself was constrained by some of the charges being levied by some of the canal companies for the carriage of goods. Coastal shipping was given some prominence to counteract this situation, but the real change came about during the middle years of the nineteenth century began to expand nationally.

The development of rail links into and out of Liverpool was contingent upon a number of factors, not least of which was capital from the town in order to build the rail links. Although there was some initial opposition voiced by leading landowners in the area regarding the prospect of introducing more rail links into the town and port, it soon became apparent that there was a high return investment on capital potential. Apart from anything else, by giving access to their estates, it was possible to solve many liquidity problems. For instance, John Shaw Leigh was in receipt of some £250,000 from the Liverpool and Bury Railway Company for passage rights over his estates in north Liverpool. Similarly, the Earl of Derby was in receipt of £500,000; the Earl of Sefton received almost £100,000; and the Marquis of Salisbury £170,000. In return for granting access rights, many landowners took railway stocks as part of the contract package, and, by 1850, it was estimated that £800,000 had been invested by Liverpool in railways that served the port. Many steam ship companies also bought into the emerging railway system and, by the last quarter of the nineteenth century, some fifteen of Liverpool's larger cargo companies had a combined holding in excess of £1,700,000, of which almost half was vested in companies in the United Kingdom.

With the improvements in rail communication, the freight carried between Liverpool and Manchester considerably increased. The two towns had become mutually dependent, although this fact did not ameliorate the rivalry that was held between them. In 1851, it was estimated that 125,000 tons of freight had been moved between Liverpool and Manchester during that year, this compared with 26,000 tons that was carried to Birmingham, 33,000 tons to the Black Country, 29,000 tons to Sheffield, and only 27,000 tons to London. It was clear that the market in Manchester was by far and away Liverpool's main trading partner. Most of the freight carried at this time was raw cotton, but, later, the railways carried an increasing amount of grain.

Several unforeseen difficulties were encountered when bringing rail tracks into the centre of Liverpool. The Liverpool and Manchester railway had planned to pierce the sandstone ridge on the eastern approach to the town. This, however, involved the costly construction of cuttings and tunnels. The line had its terminus at Crown Street, but this proved inconvenient as carriages had to be winched up a steep incline by means of a series of pulleys and cables to the Edgehill terminal. As Crown Street was not suitable for the purpose, a further tunnel was eventually constructed that linked with the more centrally positioned new terminus at Lime Street, which was opened in 1836. Competing lines were faced with either taking a route to the north of the town or, alternatively, to the south. The Liverpool and Bury Railway chose to follow the northern route, which involved a comparatively short length of tunnelling and ran across John Shaw Leigh's estate to its terminal at Exchange Station, which was opened in 1850. Meanwhile, during the 1860s, the Manchester, Sheffield, and Lincolnshire Railway, in conjunction with the Cheshire Lines Committee chose to take the southern approach from Garston and extended their line to the centre of Liverpool with a terminus at Central Station. This route, however, was dogged with difficulties and delays, which related to the purchase of land and a number of engineering difficulties that were encountered in the necessary tunnelling. The line to Central Station was not opened until 1874.

The county's rail links were being continually extended during the latter part of the nineteenth century. In 1837, the Grand Junction Railway linked Manchester and Birmingham via Crewe, Birmingham and Liverpool via Warrington, and Newton-le-Willows, and this was to start the transformation of the port's goods traffic. On the other side of the Mersey, the introduction of the Cheshire Lines Committee in the 1870s did not, as initially intended, deliver a competitive goods service; indeed, ship-owners, merchants, and shipping agents were becoming increasingly dependent upon one railway company for their transportation needs from the port. There was some controversy regarding the provision of facilities and, more importantly, the charging of excessive freight rates by the railway. Strong disagreement came about between the Dock Committee that predominantly represented the views of the ship-owners, merchants, and the railway's freight department. The confrontation became one of personalities, Bramley-Moore being the Chairman of the Dock Committee and Braithwaite Poole, who was the railway's goods manager. The newly formed Chamber of Commerce, which had been founded in 1850, suggested that the increasing trade through the port was in imminent danger of being constricted because of the exorbitant freight costs being levied by the railway companies and the inadequate provision of rolling stock in the dock area. Braithwaite Poole for the railway suggested that the lack of facilities was due to the short-sightedness of the docks' management, whereas Bramley-Moore for the Dock Committee countered by suggesting that the ship-owners were quite justified in complaining about the facilities that were being provided by the railway company. As an endnote, it was suggested that there were differential freight rates being charged by the company and if this could be rationalised then the port could indeed continue to expand, unhindered by the restrictions being placed upon them by the railway company.

The arguments relating to differential freight rates dragged on for many years. By the 1860s, imports into the town, especially grain imports, were increasing, but, coupled with this, the railways were also increasing their freight charges. In 1872, W. B. Forwood stated:

> By manipulating terminal charges and by using the leeway of maximum charges allowed under statute, railway companies were free to turn the steamer traffic over to such portions of their systems which they might elect.

This policy was obviously adopted since it was more in the interests of the railway's shareholders than the interests of the port and undoubtedly adversely affected the port's trade.

The fact that Liverpool did not have efficient rail links with the rest of the country needed to be analysed if the docks pre-eminent position in the import and export trade was not to be eroded. One factor was self-evident and that was the geographical position of the town, which, unlike either Manchester of Crewe, was not centrally located for national rail links to be established. Another factor that perhaps had a more significant bearing upon the argument was the fact that there was direct confrontation between the dock monopoly and the railway monopoly, with these two competing forces often operating in different directions for valid economic reasons. The docks estate not only had control of the import and export of goods, but also had a number of bonded warehouses that gave economic strength to the town. Even the building of the docks at Birkenhead was initially seen as a threat to the Port of Liverpool, the reality of the situation meant that any of the schemes, which were later proposed, including canal and railway schemes, bypassed the Port of Liverpool and seriously affected the expansion of overseas trade.

Jesse Hartley died in post on 29 August 1860. It is difficult to make a realistic estimate of his contribution to the development of Liverpool's dock system and, indeed, his immense contribution to the town of Liverpool itself during his tenure as dock engineer. During Hartley's time in Liverpool, from 1824 to 1860, there was indeed a massive rise in the total dock area in the town, with a total of some 140 acres of wet docks being added to the system through his design and oversight of the construction. He also added approximately 2 miles of quayside area. During Hartley's thirty-six-year tenure, he was responsible for almost doubling the docks area at Liverpool, and, when coupled with the fact that the cost of these developments only amounted to just over £5,000,000, it is truly a remarkable achievement by any standards and testament to his skill, ingenuity and initiative.

After Hartley's death, his son was appointed to the post, but his tenure in the role was short-lived, as, owing to failing health, he was forced to resign the position.

5

Wars

Before moving on to discuss the phenomenal development of the dock estate along the River Mersey, the background and context of that development must first be given some consideration. There were many political events as well as different trading practices and new markets that also informed and shaped change. Developments in civil and mechanical engineering technology were also hugely beneficial to the town. However, considerations outside of the town's direct control also impacted upon the town and port's development. Throughout much of this period, England was at war with many different adversaries. There was also privateering, which played a major role in the shaping and prosperity of the town.

England waged war for much of the eighteenth century with America, India, Africa, and other nations in Europe. During this prolonged period, there were many privateers on the high seas, so it was never safe for unarmed vessels, save when travelling in convoy. It was during this period that England lost her American colonies and the French Revolution was changing the political complexion in that country. The knock-on effects of these battles were severely felt in Liverpool, now England's second port. The fact that Britain was a maritime nation meant that the maritime ports were directly affected by any repercussions. Liverpool ships were engaged in all of these theatres of war, which meant that whenever ships were captured, men from Liverpool filled foreign prisons. Unfortunately for Liverpool and its people, when the Navy needed further recruits, they invariably started looking at the home ports. In 1795, the Navy needed to recruit 1,700 men from Liverpool. As a deterrent, no ships, for whatever reason, were allowed to sail from the Mersey until the target was achieved. Necessarily, this placed much stress on the town and also its sea-borne trading. Recognising these adverse conditions, the corporation offered cash incentives for men to volunteer for the Navy and, although the incentives were raised on a number of occasions, it became increasingly difficult to meet the targets. In the end, the Navy itself had to no alternative but to resort to other methods—the pressgang. The measures to which the Navy resorted to were nothing but incredible. When HMS *Vengeance* sailed into the Mersey in 1795, it was grossly under-manned. Shortly after the *Vengeance* dropped anchor, a whaler followed in her wake, returning from a long voyage to Greenland. Taking their opportunity, men from the *Vengeance* boarded the unsuspecting whaler and ordered her crew to board the short-handed naval ship. However, it was not going to be that easy for the men from the Navy. The whaler's crew refused to comply with their orders and promptly sailed on, hotly pursued by the *Vengeance*. The whaler's crew fled into the Custom House for refuge, but, still being pursued, they finally made their escape through back doors and windows. Undeterred, the crew of the *Vengeance* observed a slave ship returning from Jamaica. After a long chase, the slaver was eventually captured and all of the crew was pressed into the service of the Navy. Upon boarding, the pressed men were flogged—a regular occurrence. Pressgangs were forever roaming the streets and docks of Liverpool during this period. However, being taken by pressgangs was not the only threat to Liverpool sea-farers; the other was the possibility of being taken prisoner and languishing in one of France's dreaded dungeons—sometimes 40 feet deep or more—truly, a life sentence.

The Seven Years' War, which lasted from 1756 until 1763, caused complete disruption in trade coming from and going to Liverpool. In earlier conflicts, sailors from Liverpool could rely on the Irish Sea as being safe from enemy, but now a Frenchman, Thurot of Brest, had stationed himself off the Isle of Man, effectively stopping the passage of any vessels. England, at that time, ruled the waves, but now her own home waters were not secure. The loss in trade was causing consternation among Liverpool's ship owners and traders, encouraging them to mount a counterattack. However, it wasn't just Thurot who was wreaking havoc to Liverpool's trade, French warships and privateers were also inflicting damage and losses. As the waters around Africa and the West Indies were becoming increasingly unsafe for Liverpool ships, the speculative trade with Africa was not looking quite so attractive. Privateering moved to centre stage and Liverpool privateers brought many prizes back to the Mersey. Perhaps the best known and most successful of Liverpool's impressive list of privateers was Captain William Hutchinson. He captured many French ships and on his retirement from sea published a detailed manual giving specific instructions as to how to best fit-out a privateer. Over the period of the Seven Years' War, the exploits of Liverpool's privateers and prizes won more than compensated for the temporary dip in profits from the African trade. It was never a difficult task to find crews for privateer ships, as one third of any profits made during the voyage was divided among the seamen.

Towards the end of the Seven Years' War, the English fleet's dominance on the waves was restored, with both French and Spanish ships almost disappearing from the high seas. English ships were, once again, in a leading position with regards to trade with the West Indies. English vessels were now the principal purveyors of tropical produce to the whole of Europe, with ships from Liverpool capturing the vast majority of the trade. During the twelve-year period between the triumph of the Seven Years' War and the disaster of the American War, there was a massive expansion of trade through the Port of Liverpool. Another issue was also coming to prominence—that of political allegiance. Formerly, Liverpool had followed the Whig cause, but it was generally believed that the Whig Government's gross incompetence had been the main contributory factor in England's humiliations in the early years of the war. Pitt, forcing his way into power, had met with dazzling success.

Colonial administration was not a concept that figured highly in most people's minds, nor indeed was the question of the taxation, as it related to America, but these were issues that would soon be high on the government's agenda. Although Liverpool boasted strong commercial links with America, not much attention was being given to the unfolding argument. The passing of the Stamp Act sought to impose a money raising tax in the colonies without first gaining the approval of the colonial legislatures. It was then argued by the colonists that if the act was passed without any resistance, other taxes could be imposed without thought. Subsequently, trade with America plummeted and Americans pressed for the act to be repealed. However, even when the act was repealed, the situation continued to deteriorate, with Liverpool merchants continuing to lose trade. English armed forces were drawn into battle with the Americans and, according to a writer in *Gore's Advertiser* (1775): 'All commerce with America is at an end'. The writer went on to declare 'our once extensive trade to Africa is at a standstill; and the docks are a mournful sight, full of gallant ships laid up and useless'. In fact, during the seven-year period of the American War, Liverpool's population actually dropped as overseas trade declined—the actual tonnage through the port fell from 84,792 to 79,450 tons. As a direct result of the American War, riots broke out in Liverpool in 1775—a sad reflection of the frustration being experienced by many of the town's population. At that time, it was estimated that there were 3,000 unemployed sailors in the town. As there was also a marked turndown in African trade, merchants decided to reduce sailors' wages, in what they believed to be the certain knowledge that they could find as many men as they needed to crew the ships. This assumption was ill-founded. The trouble first started on a slave ship in the river, when the crew mutinied and cut the rigging to pieces. Crews from other ships were encouraged to mutiny. The authorities soon arrested nine of the ringleaders and imprisoned them. This action only led to further unrest, with a mob of 2,000 sailors marching with the intention of releasing the captives. The Riot Act was read to little avail and the authorities eventually took the sensible course and released eight of their prisoners. This action did not pacify the incensed rioters. They stormed the tower, where the prisoner was being held, and released the one remaining captive. However, by now, mob rule was in the ascendancy. The rioters, now joined by others who were unemployed, roamed the streets and demanded money from passing townsfolk. The destruction did not end there. The rioters then went on to loot shops, ransack private houses, and burst into public houses. Their final act was to lay siege to the town hall, which they threatened to burn down with cannon that they had brought from ships in the river. The rioters, effectively, held the town for over a week and it was only when troops were brought in from Manchester that the rioting ceased.

In 1771, the town council decided to appoint a police committee, which met on a daily basis. Among other edicts, this committee advised all law-abiding folk to stay in their houses at night, in order to avoid arrest. Throughout the period of the war, the situation on the domestic front was very tense, with more and more men becoming unemployed. When it seemed that the situation could not get any worse, France declared war on England in 1778, followed by Spain and Holland in 1779. The English Navy no longer ruled the waves and ships from the Mersey were daily facing adversaries in the form of foreign privateers and hostile warships.

With war being waged against both the French and the Americans, it was seen fit to build a large round fort on the north shore—where the Prince's Dock was built later. The barracks was designed for about 500 troops. Additionally, batteries were raised at the dock mouths. The newly formed regiment, numbering over 1,000 volunteers, became known as the Liverpool Blues and the corporation met much of their fitting-out costs. The regiment saw action out in Jamaica, but, because of the extremes of the climate, only returned with eighty-four men. Later, in 1782, when it looked as though a French invasion was imminent, the townsfolk raised and equipped a corps of volunteers, commanded entirely by local merchants.

With all of the negative factors besieging the town's wellbeing, the business of privateering soon gained momentum and many adherents. In the initial phases of the war with America, activity was limited in the extreme as it was considered that, because of the low level of trading with America, the returns would be too small to make any privateering proposition viable. However, when the French entered into war with England, privateering suddenly became a more lucrative proposal. It is recorded that more than 120 vessels were equipped as privateers within the first six months of commencement and, even within the first five or six weeks of privateers sailing from the Mersey, in excess of £100,000 had been returned to the town. The tales are legion of prizes being won. Perhaps one of the most famous being that of the captured French East Indiaman, the *Carnatic*, which was brought up the Mersey in October 1778. A box of diamonds and other precious stones was found on the ship; its value was reputed to be somewhere in the region of £135,000. Suddenly, everybody who was anybody in the town invested in the business of privateering. In his old age, Mr James Stonehouse recorded how, as a child, he had been taken along to be shown over a privateer ship of which he was, apparently, part proprietor. However, unfortunately, privateering was not always about winning. It was often the case that privateers limped home to Liverpool in a poor state of repair and with little to show for their endeavours.

The people of Liverpool could be justly proud of the town's contribution to the war effort. Over 3,000 local men were employed on Liverpool privateers during this war and there were the 1,100 men who had joined the regiment. Many Liverpool men also joined the Royal Navy and others were engaged upon allied duties ashore.

Although there was much to be said for the days of privateering, many Liverpool men were relieved when the war ended and life continued on a more even keel. The same could be said for the French prisoners who had been incarcerated in the tower or in the old powder magazine on Brownlow Hill.

Following the cessation of hostilities, life slowly returned to normal, with ships once again sailing from the Mersey on the lawful business and trade and prosperity returning to the town. As trade increased, so too did the population.

Politically speaking, a number of events changed the complexion of the town's allegiances. Both Whig members were defeated in the 1780 elections and, in spite of the privations suffered during the war, Liverpool supported the Tories, even though the Whigs opposed the war—nothing changed when it came to the elections of 1784. Colonel Tarleton, a popular local hero who had fought in the American War, stood as a Whig candidate, but failed in his attempt to secure election.

The elections themselves were not without riotous conduct; Mr James Gildart, a local merchant who caused bad feeling, had his house 'broke to pieces; all the windows, shutters, and even iron bars are broke; and they cut the window curtains with cutlasses all to bits, tore up and destroyed the palisades and wall before the house'. This was the dark side of returning heroes of privateering days.

The aftermath of the French Revolution was being felt across Europe in general and Liverpool in particular. The first tangible evidence of this was when Colonel Tarleton carried the election of 1790, a reversal in fortunes for the Tories. Liverpool Whigs, who included William Roscoe, Dr Currie, and William Rathbone, hoped for and worked towards amendments in the state of England and Liverpool; efforts that resulted directly from the lead taken by the French state. A direct 'knock-on' from the French Revolution was people in the town beginning to question the power held by the self-elected town council. An assembly of burgesses in the ancient manner was held. By-laws were passed, resulting in members being elected to vacant places in the council. A series of court cases followed, the objective being to subject the town's accounts to public scrutiny. Although the reformers won their case on three separate occasions, nothing much changed. During this time, the excesses of the revolutionary leaders in France were continually being brought into question and reformers in Liverpool became somewhat disenchanted. The town council retained its stranglehold on power, a situation that was to prevail until 1835.

Immediately following the French Revolution, there was much enthusiasm in England, but, just a few years after the revolution, the general attitudes had changed. They had changed so much that the town council sent a loyal address to the king, declaring that it 'observed with concern the prevalence of wild and delusive theories tending to weaken the sentiments of obedience to the laws'. Both Roscoe and Currie protested against the war, which they believed to be unnecessary and unjust. However, the majority of the people of Liverpool, like many people elsewhere, were convinced that anyone who desired reform was capable of executing the king. The government even passed a series of acts, which effectively repressed all public discussion. The general feeling seemed to be that, unless the French were annihilated, then civilisation as we know it would itself be destroyed. Liverpool, like so many other boroughs up and down the country, accommodated a new war, in a mood that was very different from any previous war. Tarleton managed to hold his seat in 1796, but it was his personal popularity that saved him rather than any allegiance to his political philosophy.

At the outbreak of war, many towns and boroughs (Liverpool included) were thrown into what amounted to commercial panic. Indeed, one of the town's three major banks ceased trading and that may well have been the future of the others had it not been for the confidence in the banks that the town's merchants placed in them. Merchants were prepared to accept trading in the private notes, which all provincial banks were allowed to trade in at the time. The town's corporation also helped by obtaining government approval to trade in their own notes— issued up to the value of £300,000 and secured against the corporation's estate. The imminent disaster having been averted, the private notes were called in and normal commercial trading continued as before.

However, as in previous conflicts, the people of Liverpool were anxious to play their part. A number of the town's merchants were invited to meet with Mr Pitt in London to discuss the means by which they could not only help with the war effort, but protect the port and its trade. Privateering once again took centre stage and, within a very short period from the outbreak of war (somewhat less than six months), sixty-seven Liverpool privateers were either at sea or being prepared for sea—and the number was rapidly increasing. A goodly number of French vessels and prisoners were brought into the Mersey and the prizes were very great. However, the practice was short-lived since French foreign commerce was virtually at an end and there was therefore very little profit to be made by English privateers. Liverpool privateers were extremely industrious during the American War and profits were never so high. There were, however, French privateers on the seas during this period and they were swift, well-armed, and had crews of well-experienced men. Liverpool's fleet had, by this time, reverted to more ordinary trading, but there were still skirmishes with the French fleet.

There are countless tales told of the heroic actions of Liverpool's sailors during this period. One such tells of the packet boat *Windsor Castle*, under the command of Captain Rogers. In 1807, the vessel had left Liverpool bound for the West Indies, when it was attacked by the French privateer, *Le Jeune Richard*. The French vessel was carrying 109 crew, whereas the Liverpool ship had a compliment of only twenty-seven men and boys. The first broadside from the French privateer inflicted ten deaths on the English boat. However, after remarkable resistance, by any standards, the seventeen remaining crew on the English boat managed to overcome and capture *Le Jeune Richard*. Some twenty-six men on the privateer were killed and a further sixty were taken prisoner. Another tale tells of the *Shaw*, another Liverpool ship. In 1808, the captain of the *Shaw*, Captain Hymers, reported to its owners that they had been attacked by a much larger French privateer. There ensued a mighty struggle, but the *Shaw* ran out of ammunition.

Being resourceful, the men were ordered to take off their stockings and fill them with nails and other scraps of iron. A final volley was fired, which, according to the story, drove off the assailant.

As in previous wars, many Liverpool sailors found themselves languishing in French prisons, but perhaps a far greater number of French prisoners were to be found in the old tower and also the powder magazine on Brownlow Hill. The new Borough Gaol, which had been built in Great Howard Street in 1786, but had not yet been used, was hired by the government in 1793 to contain the ever-increasing number of French prisoners. It was estimated that by 1799 there were over 4,000 French prisoners incarcerated in Liverpool jails.

As the number of men recruited to privateering declined, the numbers being pressganged into the Navy increased. The *Princess*, a permanent guard ship for pressed men and volunteers, was usually stationed opposite the George's Dock. From this base, pressgangs went out to a number of favoured locations in the town, including inns in Pool Lane and South Castle Street. However, sailors drinking in these inns had to be wary of their hostesses as well as pressgangs. Hostesses would hide sailors for a fee, but, once the sailors money ran out, they could be sold to the pressgang. Sailors from Liverpool lived in dread of being confronted by pressgangs. While at sea, ships were vulnerable to either French privateers or British warships eager to recruit more men. Even on their return to the Mersey, it was not unknown for sailors to leap into the river when they spotted the *Princess* and swim to the Cheshire shore to escape the gang. On the Cheshire side of the Mersey there was a well-known innkeeper, affectionately known as Mother Redcap. Her hostelry was on the Liscard shore and there were reputed to be subterranean passages that gave shelter to needy sailors.

During the war, huge numbers of troops were raised from Liverpool's men. At the start of the war, when France stood alone, there was little or no chance of invasion, so no elaborate precautions were taken. However, when, in 1796, Holland and Spain joined the war, the situation became far more serious. It was reported in 1797 that a French army had landed at the South Wales port of Fishguard. The call went out for volunteers and, within four days, more than 1,000 men had been enlisted. Fifty guns were mounted on the Liverpool fort, which was still standing, and several batteries were erected at a number of points along the coast and also at the entrance to the docks. Additionally, pilot boats were sent out to search for any signs of enemy action. In the event, however, the precautions turned out to be unnecessary as the French force, which had landed at Fishguard, was soon overwhelmed.

When a rebellion was threatened in Ireland and an invasion by the French of 35,000 men, the town of Liverpool raised another 2,000 volunteers; these men remained under arms until after the signing of the Peace of Amiens in 1802. Perhaps this disarmament was a little premature as, the following year, Napoleon recommended war on an even larger scale and the whole of England was turned into an army of volunteers. In 1804, a review was held in Liverpool where 3,686 volunteers together with 180 officers paraded through the town. There was also at this parade a regiment of artillery, which had been recruited from the boatmen on the Mersey. At the same time, one of Liverpool's wealthiest merchants, Mr John Bolton, raised and equipped at his own expense a regiment of 800 men of Liverpool. As these were unpredictable times, all men between the ages of sixteen and sixty were registered on a reserve list, ready to be called upon as and when required. Prince William was sent to Liverpool to command these men.

During the night of 2 January 1804, firing was heard from the guard ship, *Princess*, which was permanently moored in the river. At the time it was believed that this firing was a signal alerting the town to an imminent invasion. Forces were alerted and cavalry assembled, but when morning dawned it became evident that the firing had been to signal that the vessel had slipped her mooring—but the alert proved to be a useful exercise. After the Battle of Trafalgar the following year, any perceived danger from invasion was completely removed and hence many of the forces were disbanded. The final years of the war saw the English Navy completely ruling the seas, with the result that overseas trade continued completely unhindered and unmolested. However, although Napoleon had lost battles at sea, his resourcefulness and ingenuity were used to greater effect by ensuring that English vessels were excluded from continental ports. In this way, it was believed that the whole basis of England's commerce could be completely undermined. England's response was swift, debarring all neutral vessels from trading with Napoleon's subjects or allies or run the risk of confiscation of their cargoes. This action resulted in more restrictions in trade and had a great adverse effect on Liverpool's further development and prosperity. A significant proportion of Liverpool's trade consisted of the export of textiles from Manchester and the importation of sugar and tobacco. One of the avenues, which many traders were forced to take, was that of smuggling and this activity took place on a very large scale. The rewards were great, assuming that the smuggling was successful, but, for those ventures that failed (and there were many) cargoes were confiscated, which often meant complete financial ruin for the merchant. Overall, the effects of this situation were quite disastrous for the town and its people. By the year 1807, trade passing through the port had declined by more than a quarter and there was much unemployment in the town. Almost inevitably, this was accompanied by rising prices.

The situation became so acute that £10,000 was raised for the purchase of potatoes to help alleviate the plight of the destitute in the town. A further £20,000 was raised for the purchase of other necessities. Householders were implored to exercise frugality in their use of potatoes and to practice utmost economy when giving fodder to horses.

The government appeared to be completely unaware of some of the destitution it was, perhaps unwittingly, inflicting upon its people. Many merchants insisted that trade could have been continued through neutral ports and trade with America and the West Indies could have been continued and, similarly, the looms of Lancashire would have been kept in business. Many of the town's leading merchants protested against the British Orders in Council. After many protracted protests, the Orders in Council were withdrawn, but by this time Britain was involved in a needless and disastrous war with the America—a war that did immense damage to Liverpool's economy and increasing prosperity.

Due to England's supremacy on the oceans and Napoleon's command on land, America's trade was fast dwindling to nought and America protested, but in vain—the only answer was to declare war. This had a profound effect upon Liverpool's trade. In 1810, the number of ships entering Liverpool's docks was 6,729, but, only two years later, in 1812, that figure had dropped to 4,599.

Being debarred from peaceful trade, many American ships turned to privateering at this point and were extremely successful. American ships were soon hunting quarry in the West Indies, the African coast, and some even successfully entered British waters. One American privateer, the *True-Blooded Yankee*, patrolling in the Irish Sea, is reputed to have captured twenty-seven vessels in a voyage only totalling thirty-seven days.

The war with America caused much consternation, which was accompanied by a significant loss in trade. However, those in Liverpool who had the vote held to the party in power, as was demonstrated in the general election of 1812. The Whigs fielded Brougham and Creevey, while the Tory's protagonists were Canning and General Gascoyne; however, in effect, the battle lines had been drawn between Brougham and Canning—both brilliant orators. Brougham had his election headquarters in Clayton Square, while Canning's campaign centre of operations was conducted from the home of Sir John Gladstone in Rodney Street. Brougham's main election argument was focused on his opposition to the pernicious Orders in Council, which had done so much damage to the town. He had in fact been instrumental in having them repealed—a strong argument, especially in Liverpool, and, with William Roscoe as an ally, the prospects were looking good for Brougham. However, the town's electorate were so deeply rooted in Tory philosophies and practices that Canning returned with a large majority. He held the seat until 1823.

The war lasted for twenty-two long years and throughout that period Liverpool's trade and Liverpool's townspeople had suffered many deprivations. At the cessation of hostilities, church bells were rung, there were firework displays, and many balls and dinners held in celebration. Festivities lasted for a week. The end of the war with France heralded almost a century of unbroken peace. The Crimean War was still raging and there were still border skirmishes in the more remote parts of the British Empire, but, in essence, the country was at peace and stability was re-established. Trade also began to develop once again and Liverpool docks were playing a full part in the recovery. Slave ships were no longer sailing and the number of privateers was also rapidly diminishing. As peace was declared, Liverpool welcomed the very first steamboat to sail into the Mersey. There was change in prospect—a sea-going revolution was about to begin. The age of war, in which Liverpool had not only played her full part, but had also seen many deprivations to its townsfolk, was now on the cusp of imminent change and gain. England not only, unquestionably, ruled the waves, but her trading investments and holdings were spread throughout Europe and the wider world. Liverpool ships and shipping were in in a prime position to capitalise on the opportunities being presented.

6

Industrial Revolution

In a little more than thirty years, the population of Liverpool had trebled, with many of the new inhabitants arriving from outlying rural districts; although, there was also a great influx of people coming from Wales and Ireland. Following the rebellion in 1798, many people from Ireland crossed the Irish Sea in the hope of finding a better life in England. Upon landing on English shores, many remained in Liverpool; a situation that was to continue until crossing to America appeared to offer better prospects. The Welsh and the Irish far outnumbered the immigrants from Scotland coming to Liverpool. In 1793, the first Scottish Presbyterian church was consecrated in Liverpool and, from that time, Liverpool became the most Presbyterian town south of the border. Many of the town's leading merchants hailed from Scotland, as did a number of captains from slavers and privateers.

An impression of the remarkable progress that was being made in Liverpool can soon be ascertained by comparing ships passing through the port and the number of men employed in servicing the ships and the port itself. In 1751, 220 ships were owned by Liverpool merchants, having a total tonnage of some 19,175 tons. These vessels were worked by 3,319 men. Fifty years later, the number of ships owned was 821 and the number of men employed was 12,315. The tonnage had dramatically risen during that time to some 129,470 tons. However, for a more accurate reflection of the port's development, it is necessary to consider the total tonnage passing through the port and not merely the ships owned by local ship-owners. In 1751, the total tonnage of British and foreign ships passing through the port amounted to 65,406; but, by 1791, just before the beginning of the war with France, the tonnage was 539,676 tons. By 1835, the figure had leapt to an incredible 1,768,426 tons. There were other indicators that reflected the phenomenal rise in the port's activity. In 1780, the customs collector is reputed to have stated: 'How happy I should be if the customs of Liverpool amounted to over £100,000!' Yet, by 1823, the duties that were collected in the port amounted to £1,808,402. During this period, it had been essential that the docks in the town expanded to keep pace with the shipping passing through the port. However, up until 1825, the docks were both owned and directed by the town council. Even as late as 1760, Liverpool could only boast the Old Dock together with its tidal basin, and the Salthouse Dock, which had been opened in 1753, and the combined free surface area of these docks amounted to little more than 8 acres. During the war years, which lasted from 1756 until 1815, another four new docks were opened with an area of over 21 acres and this did not include the tidal basins. Then, with the cessation of hostilities and the fervour of Jesse Hartley, the docks network developed at an unprecedented rate between 1815 and 1835, with the opening of eight new docks, having a total surface area in excess of 45 acres. Remarkably, in an unprecedented time of war, Liverpool's port and docks benefitted rather than suffered. While many foreign ships were being destroyed, Liverpool's ships and merchants were quick to fill the void, but wars themselves were not the sole reason why Liverpool was experiencing a time of almost unbridled expansion.

However, there was a mixed picture with regards to Liverpool's other industries. The Herculaneum pottery, which had been one of the leading employers in the area, was now in terminal decline, with many of its key workers migrating to the developing potteries in Staffordshire. The Herculaneum pottery had opened in 1796, but, for a number of reasons, it had never realised its full potential. In contrast, along the banks of the Mersey there were many thriving shipbuilding businesses—both to the north and the south of the docks. Shipbuilding had been at its zenith during the slaving days, when clippers designed and built in Liverpool were renowned for their speed and ergonomic efficiency—they could cram more slaves into smaller spaces. Liverpool shipyards also built ships for the Royal Navy, building no less than twenty-one Royal Navy vessels between 1778 and 1811. Indeed, the need for local wood was so great during this intense period of ship building that every single tree on Lord Sefton's estate was felled. The industry was short-lived as, shortly after this expansive period, the shipbuilding industry on the Liverpool side of the Mersey fell into decline. However, as is often the case, as industries fall into decline other new markets are found; whale fishing and the associated whale oil refineries were being developed in Liverpool. The Greenland whale fishing enterprise started in 1764, with three whaling vessels, and, by 1788, there was a total of twenty-one vessels, having an aggregate tonnage of 6,485 tons sailing out of Liverpool. The rise in the industry had been rapid, but so too was its decline, and in 1823 the last whaler made her final voyage out of Liverpool. The aptly named Greenland Street, near to the Queen's Dock, was the site of the large whale oil refining factory that gave employment to many townspeople. Also employing large numbers of workers were the herring curing houses, whose products were exported, mainly to ports along the Mediterranean. By 1835, however, most of this business had migrated to the east coast ports as ease of access made them economically more viable—a factor that would be detrimental to Liverpool right through to the twentieth and twenty-first centuries.

It was self-evident that Liverpool's industry was predominantly based upon its sea trade, although other embryonic industries did survive for a little while. Sugar-baking and rope-making were two of the earliest of industries based in Liverpool, and there was also a thriving watchmaking industry, employing upwards of 2,000 men. Over 150 watches were made in the town every week, with many being exported to America and Geneva. Meanwhile, the trade through Liverpool's port continued to increase unabated. The rise in trade can be largely attributed to the strides being made in engineering, with mechanical engineering transforming the manufacturing base of the country in general and the north of England in particular. Liverpool's port, with its integrated and developing docks system, was the obvious choice for exporting the products being manufactured as a direct result of the Industrial Revolution.

Great strides were being made in the field of textile manufacture. Hargreaves' spinning jenny, Arkwright's spinning frame, and Crompton's spinning mule completely transformed the industry. Formerly, hand labour at a spinning wheel could not produce a yarn fine enough to form the weft of cloth. Consequently, a linen weft always had to be combined with a cotton warp, but the spinner could not produce yarn fast enough to keep pace with the demands of the weaver. The new inventions meant that yarn could now be spun so fine that it was no longer necessary to use linen yarn. Furthermore, the product was much cheaper to produce, which in turn gave rise to greater demand. Following Cartwright's invention of the power loom, the process was transformed yet again, with one man now able to weave as much as ten men had previously. A further development, Watt's application of steam to the process, meant that greater volumes of cloth could be produced at even lower costs. Lancashire provided an abundance of coal to raise the steam and factories became established throughout the region, with all of their products being exported through Liverpool's port.

Other developing industries were playing a pivotal point in Liverpool's continuing rise in economic prosperity. As well as the cotton industry of Lancashire profiting from the Industrial Revolution, Yorkshire's cotton industry was also a recipient of the new methods of production, and again more of their products were finding their way to Liverpool to be exported. While these developments were prospering, Britain's iron trade was in decline due to the paucity of wood; however, Smeaton developed a method of smelting iron using coal instead of wood, which rejuvenated the west Midlands, and, similar to Lancashire's and Yorkshire's export trade, meant that yet more products were now passing through Liverpool for export. Liverpool docks also benefitted from the growth of the pottery industry in Staffordshire and the glass manufacturing industry in and around south Lancashire and St Helens.

With the coming of the Industrial Revolution, counties blessed with having coal seams were well-placed to benefit financially from emerging industrialisation. Within the time of a single generation, an economic shift had occurred, transferring much wealth from the southern counties to the Midlands and the northern counties. Indeed, it would not be an exaggeration to suggest that much of the nation's economic wellbeing was derived from the industrial centres in the north and midlands. A 100-mile radius from Liverpool encompassed the vast majority of these industrial centres, making Liverpool the logical centre both to import necessary raw materials and also export finished products. Furthermore, because of the continuing development of the docking facilities at the Port of Liverpool, no other docks complex in the country could compete with the amenities and services offered at the port.

However, the port's development was not governed solely by the economic benefits that the Industrial Revolution was yielding. There was much economic development occurring in the United States of America and, as Britain's trade with both Africa and the West Indies began to decline, new markets for both the importation of raw materials and the export of finished products were being found in America. With the abolition of the slave trade in 1807, commerce through the Port of Liverpool undoubtedly suffered, but much of this loss in trade was compensated for with the growth in trade with America.

Liverpool was also an unwitting and unexpected beneficiary of a territorial deal that occurred at the end of the Napoleonic Wars. In a blatant political manoeuvre in 1803, aimed to ingratiate France to the leaders of a fledgling western nation, Napoleon sold the French colony of Louisiana to the United States of America. The territory included a vast swathe of the uninhabited Mississippi valley. In a very short space of time, the valley became the greatest cotton-producing area in the world and this new, massive cotton field coincided with England's need for all the raw cotton that it could import.

In purely economic terms, there were other benefits that accrued to Liverpool as a result of the sale of Louisiana. Labourers were required in large numbers to work in the cotton fields and many destitute emigrants from England were soon making their way from Liverpool across the Atlantic to a new future. America became a land of promise.

Trading with America increased steadily, but, as soon as the Erie Canal was opened in 1825, joining the Hudson River with the great lakes, a new era in trading relations was born. Products were brought from the central plain to the then relatively minor port of New York, establishing shipping links between Liverpool and New York. The trade route became one of the busiest and most prosperous in the world.

During this intense period of economic activity, other markets were being opened to Liverpool merchants—markets that had previously been closed to them because of vested legislation. Prior to 1813, no ships from Liverpool had ventured round the Cape of Good Hope to the Far East, as, under legislation enacted in 1600, any trade with the Far East was protected by the monopoly held by the East India Company based in London. Although, during the age of war, the company had effectively been transformed from a trading operation into the controlling power of the country. During the fifty-year period from 1757, when Clive made the conquest of India, until 1804 at the close of Wellesley's governorship, the East India Company had become all powerful in the country. Many considered that any organisation maintaining a trade monopoly while continuing to be the ruling company was both dangerous and undesirable. In 1813, trading with India became open to any English trader. The East India Company did, however, hold a monopoly on trade with China until 1833, when that barrier was also broken. With the entrepreneurial spirit that was becoming a hallmark of Liverpool ship-owners, vessels from the Mersey were soon taking advantage of the new markets, exporting manufactured cotton goods from Lancashire and importing abundant supplies of raw cotton. March 1814 saw the first ship from Liverpool, the *Kingsmill*, owned by Mr John Gladstone, set sail for India. The trading links grew at such a rate that, within a very short period, business with India was only second in importance and volume to trade with America.

Other trading benefits were to come as a result of the Napoleonic Wars. Portuguese and Spanish colonies in South America had been a closed market because of the home government's policies; however, when Napoleon was dominant in Spain and Portugal, the situation changed completely. Firstly, the Portuguese royal family exiled themselves to Brazil and opened up their markets to England; similarly, the Spanish colonies in South America refused to acknowledge the new ruling power in Spain and lifted all trading restrictions. This continued to be the case when the colonies were returned to their former rulers. There was more than a passing interest in Liverpool with the *contretemps* between Spain and her colonies in South America. Many merchants and even the town council appealed to the government to recognise the legitimacy of the South American states. It is no coincidence that it was Canning, in 1825, who was the architect of this key change in policy. England's trade with South America grew rapidly, and Liverpool ships dominated that trade.

With transportation of goods for both import and export becoming easier through improvements in road, rail, and canal infrastructure—thanks, largely, to progress in civil and mechanical engineering technology—manufacturers and merchants were now benefitting from the easier access, as indeed was the town and Port of Liverpool. One of the many problems that constantly beset merchants wishing to transport their products to the docks at Liverpool was the difficulties encountered in the actual transportation of goods; to say that the physical barriers that made effective transportation difficult would be somewhat of an understatement. Some modest attempts had been made to widen and deepen many of the shallow streams near to the Mersey estuary, but they were proving to be totally inadequate to meet the needs of the multitude of manufactured products, which were now transported to Liverpool for export. The same problem was experienced in reverse when raw products were being imported through Liverpool to satisfy the ever-increasing needs of Lancashire's mills. Right up until the close of the eighteenth century, most goods for import or export were still being transported to and from Manchester by packhorse. As late as 1788, some seventy pack-horses were leaving Dale Street in Manchester every single day and transporting manufactured goods to Liverpool for export—an extremely costly and inefficient means of conducting business. In order to maintain any trading advantage over other ports and indeed over other countries, developing more efficient means of transportation was rapidly becoming one of the major economic problems to be conquered.

During the second half of the eighteenth century, a number of important canals were being constructed. The Sankey Brook, which was opened in 1755, was a river-deepening project and opened an easy and direct route from Wigan to the Mersey. Brindley had achieved a resounding success using his ingenuity and experience, and his work was being closely watched by many others including the Duke of Bridgewater. Wishing to emulate such a magnificent achievement, the duke immediately engaged Brindley, charging him with designing and constructing a canal between Liverpool and Manchester—destined to be the first great canal to be built in England. Work started in 1758 and the Bridgewater Canal was opened in 1776. In building the canal, the duke had one primary purpose in mind: to reduce the cost of transporting coal from his mines in and around Manchester through to Liverpool. Transporting the coal overland cost in the region of £2 a ton, whereas when the Irwell was deepened the cost was reduced to 12*s* a ton (60p), but, with the new canal being opened, the cost was a mere 6*s* a ton (30p).

With the impetus and obvious advantages gained from the opening of the Bridgewater Canal, other similar projects soon followed—the rewards in cost-savings alone were too great for eighteenth-century entrepreneurs to ignore, and soon canals were being constructed in every part of England, but by far the greatest activity was occurring in the north of England, with merchants often bearing much of the construction costs.

The canals that added most to Liverpool's continuing prosperity were the Grand Trunk Canal, or, as it is sometimes called, the Trent and Mersey Canal, which was started in 1765; the Mersey and Calder Canal, started just one year later, which directly connected Liverpool with Hull; the Leeds and Liverpool Canal, which was started in 1767; the Mersey and Severn Canal, which was started in 1792; and, finally, the Grand Junction Canal, which, in effect, linked the whole northern canal system with the southern system. From that time it was possible to travel by barge to the Thames, thus giving direct water communication between Liverpool and London.

The town council took an active interest in promoting canal development. When construction of the Trent and Mersey Canal was under consideration by parliament, a letter was sent on behalf of the council to every MP representing either a Cheshire or Lancashire constituency, asking them vote in favour of the development. The council also contributed towards the costs of the preliminary parliamentary expenses. It was certainly in the interests of the town council to promote developments of this kind, as Liverpool was fast becoming a focal point for the export and import business of England's new manufacturing centres.

The importance of the canals to the increase in trade through Liverpool should not be underestimated, but another development brought about by the need for faster, more efficient and more economic transportation of goods was soon to appear—the railway. Stephenson had long experimented with the concept of steam-powered engines running along on rail tracks. In 1830, his dreams came to fruition with the opening of the world's first railway. It is no coincidence that the railway's termini were Liverpool and Manchester. Just like the canal system had extended and spread to the whole of the country, so did the advent of the railway system. Liverpool was now in a prime position to garner even more of the export trade by virtue of the emerging rail network.

Although the steam-driven railway engines had made a tremendous impact in 1830, sometime before that, in 1815, steamboats were already making their first appearance on the Mersey. At that time, steamboats were regularly seen on the Mersey, plying between Liverpool and Runcorn. However, it was not until 1819 that Liverpool entertained the first steamboat to cross the Atlantic from America. The steamboat was on its way from New York to St Petersburg, where it was to be presented to the Emperor of Russia.

The latter part of the eighteenth century saw some amazing developments in Liverpool. The Industrial Revolution was certainly leaving its mark upon the town of Liverpool and its wellbeing. Some of the greatest benefits came about as a result of developments in textile machinery, but coal was also being used more, especially in the smelting of iron. It was also of significance that many of these developments were taking place within less than 100 miles from Liverpool. With much-improved transportation of goods through better-quality roadways, the emerging canal system, and the development of a national railway system, Liverpool was in a prime position to take advantage of the overseas markets that were being developed in Spanish America and India and also the fast-developing markets in America, with special reference to the growing strategic importance of New York.

When Manchester began large-scale production of cotton goods, most of the raw materials necessary were imported through London rather than Liverpool. Even as late as 1758, only a small amount of cotton was being imported through Liverpool; in that year, twenty-five bags were imported from Jamaica. However, trade did increase, and by 1770 5,521 bags are recorded as being imported from the West Indies. Up until that time, America was not exporting cotton in any great quantities. However, shortly after that (at the start of the nineteenth century), America moved into large-scale production of cotton and this did much to satisfy the apparently insatiable demands of the Lancashire mills. However, the supply came to an abrupt end when, on 18 June 1812, America declared war on Britain and, although the war only lasted for about two and a half years, it caused much disruption both to the Lancashire mills and also the Port of Liverpool; it is easy to appreciate just why the American war was so unpopular with the townsfolk of Liverpool. By 1835, the situation had completely changed, with America now producing and exporting far more cotton than any other of the cotton-producing nations.

However, with trade through the port increasing at such a phenomenal rate, many of the town's merchants found themselves hampered by some of the trade regulations that were impeding progress and were under the direct control of the forty-one-strong, self-elected town council. What made matters worse was that many on the council were completely out of touch with the everyday concerns and aspirations of the town's merchants and traders. It was the responsibility of the town council to administer the corporate estate and collect town dues—payable by all, except freemen—on merchandise brought into the port. The town council, previously responsible for docks construction, collected the dock-dues that were part of the town's revenue.

In 1800, the dock dues were £23,380, but by 1835 the figure was nudging £200,000. It was deemed to be necessary to place the administration of the docks into the hands of a sub-committee of the town council. The Docks Committee had its own budget, but the town council could still overrule any decisions of the Docks Committee, and, significantly, could appropriate any of the dock dues coming to the Dock Committee. This last provision was not acceptable to many of the town's merchants who used the docks, as they asserted that specialist knowledge was required to administer the docks and the dock estate.

Eventually, in 1825, a compromise was reached and a new constitution for the Docks Committee was established via an Act of Parliament. The new committee had thirteen members drawn from the council and eight members who were directly elected from merchant ratepayers who used the docks. The council were still in the majority, but at least some degree of direct governance was established. Unfortunately, because of this new constitution, there was almost constant conflict between the merchant members on the committee and those who were directly co-opted from the town council. One of the provisions in the Reform Bill of 1832 was to set up a commission that would examine arrangements such as occurred in Liverpool.

One aspect of the collection of Dock Dues, which was deeply resented, was the exemption for freemen from the imposition of having to pay any dues, whereas non-freemen had to pay Dock Dues. In 1830, with resentment running high, a number of the town's merchants decided to have the principle tested in the courts. They lost, with the court ruling that, historically, freemen were exempt from the dues, whereas all others were bound to pay. Liverpool, as a town, had always voted Tory, but now voted for reform and the Reform Bill of 1832. The Reform Bill opened the parliamentary franchise, not only to the town's freemen, but also to all qualified residents. In this instance, 'qualified residents' also meant those living within the limits of the borough, which included the suburbs of Everton, Kirkdale, Toxteth, and part of West Derby. A royal commission was charged with investigating the constitution and proceedings of closed corporations, which at that time meant most of the boroughs of England. During the commission, it soon became clear that in prosperous and developing towns (such as Liverpool), many townsfolk took exception to the arbitrary power that councils often irresponsibly exercised. It was obvious to most members of the council that legislation would soon be enacted in order to reform municipal corporations. In fact, the indications were so strong that the town council did not raise any opposition to the bill, which was introduced by the Whig Government. The Municipal Reform Act was passed in 1835 and ended the close corporation, which had been in existence since 1580. Under the old system of town governance, trading through the Port of Liverpool was seriously restricted. The town council, as it existed before the

Reform Act, was not coping with either the new-found prosperity or the influx of new inhabitants. During the great enquiry of 1833, Liverpool's town council emerged almost unscathed, as opposed to many councils who were charged with using council funds for private advantage or for improper purposes. The main distinguishing mark that separated Liverpool from other councils was that, during the period under question, Liverpool had constructed a whole system of docks, streets had been widened, and public buildings erected, and all of this had been achieved without recourse to adding further rates onto the town's inhabitants.

Much of this progress had been made possible due to the foresight of many of the town's leading merchants, who had borrowed funds against the security of the town's estate, thus making it possible for the town to embark upon the ambitious programme of dock development. It has to be conceded, however, that not all of the decisions made by the council, *vis-à-vis* land sales, were sound business propositions. In general, the council had acted in a judicious manner, owning or having control over more than half of the area of the original township. When the reformed council came into power in 1835, it was faced with a series of problems that had been caused by the previous council being somewhat lax in their attention to elementary matters of administration. On the other hand, the new council did inherit a significantly sized corporation estate, which yielded a good revenue—much larger in fact that many other similar provincial boroughs.

7

Consolidation

Towards the end of the nineteenth century and the beginning of the twentieth, there were still many sailing ships using the port, on both sides of the river, but they were now vying with steamships for harbour space. As different markets opened, sailing ships tended to operate in the more specialist areas of carrying grain and other bulk cargoes to Australasia and the west coast of North America. Shipping companies such as the British & African Steam Navigation Company and T&J Harrison tended to use sailing ships on their outward voyage and utilised steam on the return journey. By now, sail was fighting a losing battle, with steam proving to be more efficient, but it was another twenty to thirty years before Liverpool welcomed the last sailing ship into the port. However, it was another event in 1869, far from Liverpool's shores, that marked a further stage in the ultimate demise of sail and that was the opening of the Suez Canal. With the canal's obvious advantage of providing a much shorter route for British vessels to the Far East and India, Liverpool's ship-owners soon recognised that it was also proving to be a much better economic proposition for steam ships. Indeed, for many years, at least 75 per cent of all traffic passing through the canal sailed under the British flag.

With the establishment of the Mersey Docks and Harbour Board in 1858, there was a significant increase in the net registered tonnage of cargo passing through the port. In 1858, the tonnage was recorded as 4,400,000 tons, whereas, by the outbreak of the First World War in 1914, the recorded net registered tonnage passing through the port had now risen to 19,000,000 tons. Throughout this period, however, there were a number of plateaux in trade and also some significant downturns. During the Civil War in America, there was a marked decline in cotton exports from that country. As a counterbalance, new routes and markets were constantly being developed by enterprising merchants from Liverpool. Trade was being promoted with China, Brazil, Malaya, India, and other hitherto undeveloped and underdeveloped markets. With some fluctuations in world trade being experienced during the 1880s, there was rapid growth in

Trans-Atlantic lines always docked at the far end of the landing stage. The *Aquitania*, seen here in 1920, was a regular visitor to the port.

A typical dock scene in Liverpool in 1895, showing masted barques in port.

Another Cunard liner being brought alongside Liverpool's landing stage by one of the Mersey's experienced pilots.

trade during the following decade. It was during this time that, coincidentally, many ship-owners in Liverpool were renewing and rebuilding their fleets.

In the early part of the twentieth century, up until the outbreak of the First World War, Liverpool's throughput of cargo increased by in excess of 50 per cent, but, since 1857, when Liverpool's share of the export trade amounted to 45 per cent of the UK total, the port's ranking had dropped such that, by 1914, Liverpool's share of the export trade only amounted to 25 per cent.

Cotton was the main commodity passing through Liverpool during the late nineteenth century and the early part of the twentieth. It was brought into the new city from countries around the world, then stored in the huge warehouses that had been erected adjacent to many of Hartley's new docks. Liverpool's cotton exchange had the dual functions of both regulating the price of cotton and ensuring that there was a ready supply of raw materials reaching the port. The cycle was completed when ships leaving the port carried the finished articles to all parts of the world. From the start of the nineteenth century, cotton had been the most important import to the town. In 1820, more than 111,000 tons of cotton were imported into Liverpool and, by 1850, the amount being imported had risen to 360,000 tons per year. In most years, Liverpool's imports of cotton accounted for at least 80 per cent of the total imports of cotton into the country and very often that figure reached 90 per cent. With demand being almost insatiable, when supplies failed in one part of the world, market knowledge was such that alternative supplies were soon secured. Cotton from America continued to dominate the market for some time, but imports from East India and Egypt were becoming more significant.

However, there was now a marked change in the composition of cargoes and trade passing through the port. In the middle of the nineteenth century, cotton imports into Liverpool accounted for over 40 per cent of the total value, whereas, by 1914, the proportionate figure had dropped to 30 per cent, although Liverpool was still importing, on a national basis, in excess of 70 per cent of all of the cotton being brought into the United Kingdom. The volume of sugar and tobacco being imported through Liverpool's docks also rose in absolute terms, but fell in terms of overall percentage of total imports. Tobacco was also another import that continued to rise in volume, from 7,000 tons in 1850 to 422,000 tons in 1914. The changes in composition can to a large extent be accounted for by the increase in the importation of grain. Wheat, barley, and maize imports were now increasing as indeed was rubber from Malaya. Another import that was growing in volume was the importation of rice from the Far East. Timber imports through Liverpool continued to account for approximately 2.5 per cent of the total imports in value. During this period, the export trade from Liverpool consisted largely of cotton yarn, piece-goods, and cotton textiles. These commodities alone amounted to almost half of the total exports at the beginning of the twentieth century, however, the proportion was beginning to decline and, immediately before the outbreak of the First World War, the figure had dropped to 40 per cent. England's dominance of manufactured goods, during and subsequent to the Industrial Revolution, was now being reflected in cargoes leaving the port. Much heavy engineering and rail equipment was now being exported to South Africa, India, South America, and Mexico. For instance, at the turn of the century, engineering exports through the port amounted to £15,000,000, whereas, by 1913, that figure had more than doubled.

One significant factor needs to be taken into account at this juncture, and that is from the middle of the nineteenth century until the early years of the twentieth century the volume of imports coming through the port actually trebled; similarly, the value of exports leaving the port increased five-fold in terms of volume. These figures would more than justify the massive investments that were being made to the dock estate in terms of docks, warehouses, port facilities, and, significantly, the smooth flow of goods to and from the city. Liverpool was indeed coping with the vast increase of both imports and exports, which reflected, in no small measure, the tenacity and foresight of both its shipping company owners and the members of the Mersey Docks and Harbour Board.

While freight charges were dropping year by year, technical innovations were ensuring that a balance was maintained between profit margins and freight costs. Generally speaking, the average size of ships was now increasing, from 2,500 to 3,000 tons during the latter half of the nineteenth century, to almost 10,000 tons by the beginning of the twentieth century. Economies of scale played a significant part in reducing Holt's cost per ton-mile by as much as 50 per cent, and T&J Harrison boasted a reduction in costs per ton-mile of some 55 per cent.

Prior to 1858, the Liverpool Dock Estate had seen an investment of over £5,000,000, which had been invested mainly in the building of dock facilities and adjacent warehouses. However, following the establishment of the MDHB, investment in the dock estate came from three principal sources: directly through the channels of the MDHB; via private investment; and, to a lesser extent, through railway companies. With the advent of both new shipping companies operating from the port and new markets, there was a need for improved dock facilities and better warehousing accommodation. There was also an emerging divergence of opinion as regards the direction in which the port should be developing in order to meet future needs. Whereas the passenger liner companies required larger docks, longer quays, and wider dock entrances to accommodate the larger trans-Atlantic liners, many of the purely cargo companies, Alfred Holt included, considered that the vessels in their fleets had reached the optimum size, so they were quite content to see the dock estate remain much the way it was at the turn of the century. The main board of the MDHB was in an invidious position, having to act as arbiter and decision maker on many occasions.

As a consequence of turn-around time becoming a factor in shipping economics, as indeed was shorter voyage time, improved dock and associated facilities were required. Therefore, in addition to building new docks and warehouses, more investment was made in hydraulic and electrical cargo handling equipment.

The first ten years after the creation of the Mersey Docks and Harbour Board saw a total investment of £6,400,000 in the dock estate, £1,900,000 being spent on the

Liverpool side of the river, and £4,500,000 being spent on the Birkenhead side. This figure accounted for 35 per cent of the total spending on ports nationally during that period. However, it was after 1870 that there was a massive extension to the dock estate, with seven new docks being built at Liverpool and a new dock also being built at Garston, on the Liverpool side of the Mersey—although docks development at Garston was a separate enterprise and did not fall within the purview of the MDHB. On the Birkenhead side of the river, there was a new dock built at Wallasey.

A significant act was passed in 1899 whereby the MDHB was given powers to create redeemable capital stock 'in such amounts and manner and at such prices and times and at such terms and subject to such conditions and to be entitled to such interest as they think fit'. Through the different clauses in the act, there was now a number of ways in which the board could raise capital to resource new developments in the dock estate.

Although resources for dock construction were, generally speaking, readily available, there still existed the enmity and rivalry for the allocation of funding between interests on the Liverpool side of the Mersey and vested interests on the Birkenhead side. It was this tension between rival factions that in fact dictated the future 'shape' of the dock estate. On the Liverpool side of the river, consideration had to be given to the modifications necessary to existing docks and also to new docks to be built to both the north and south of the docks, which had been built during Hartley's tenure as dock engineer. On the Birkenhead side of the river, the Morpeth and Egerton systems had to be completed, together with further construction work necessary for associated docks and basins.

After the death of Jesse Hartley and the relatively short tenure of his son John Bernard Hartley, George Fosbery Lyster was appointed as the dock engineer. Lyster's tenure in that role was lengthy, lasting from 1861 until 1897, when he too was succeeded by his son Anthony George Lyster, who held the post until 1913. George Fosbery Lyster carried out extensive dock improvements and extensions, mainly on the Liverpool side at the north end of the dock estate. He also proposed additional docks at the north end of the estate following pressure being exerted by the ship-owners. He also proposed a central group of new works east of Sandon Dock, but this development never materialised.

A very definite pattern of berthing was now becoming established, with Cunard and Inman's trans-Atlantic lines and Bibby's Mediterranean ships all berthing in northern docks; Bramley-Moore Dock tended to be used by American packet ships, whereas East Indiamen tended to discharge their cargoes in Albert Dock, but then loaded in the adjoining Salthouse Dock. Alfred Holt's Far Eastern fleet tended to discharge cargo in Liverpool, but then took on cargo on the Birkenhead side. South American-bound boats tended to use the west side of Prince's Dock for discharging cargo, but then loaded the export cargo on the eastern side of the dock. Lyster's problems were compounded by the several different and conflicting demands placed upon him by the different shipping companies, while still attempting to maintain a balance between usage of dock facilities in Birkenhead and Liverpool.

George's dock in 1890, which was opened in 1771. Due to increased usage and the increasing size and weight of ships, the dock had to be enlarged in 1825. At the beginning of the twentieth century, the dock was filled-in and became the area that is now known as the Pier Head.

The Gorée Piazzas, as seen from Mann Island in 1890. The Gorée warehouses were rebuilt after a fire in 1802.

By the start of the nineteenth century, the Old Dock in Liverpool was rapidly becoming redundant because of its inadequate size. In 1811, an Act of Parliament was passed that gave authorisation for the dock to be filled-in.

George's Dock and Gorée Piazza looking from Mann Island. The Gorée warehouses in the background survived until 1958.

Several tug boats near George's Dock in 1906.

In the mid-twentieth century, the Port of Liverpool still had a considerable cargo throughput.

During the 1860s, a number of acts ensured that resources were always available for dock improvements and extensions. In 1862, the Canada Half-Tide Dock was built east of the Canada Basin and renamed Brocklebank Dock. The following year, parliamentary approval was obtained to raise the sum of £450,000 to finance a number of projects including the construction of the north river wall and to build the Waterloo grain warehouses and part of the Herculaneum Dock system. Lyster built another dock to the east of Huskisson Dock, which was to be known as Huskisson Branch Dock 2. Then, in 1864, another act was passed that was designed to transform Huskisson into a system of docks, but when the act passed through the Lords, a clause was inserted that forbade any monies to be spent on the enterprise until the northern entrances at Alfred Dock in Birkenhead were completed. Nevertheless, because of an upturn in both imports and exports, more expansion was envisaged and, in 1866, permission was granted to alter and enlarge Birkenhead's Morpeth Dock system and to convert the low-water basin, which had previously been the river entrance, into a wet dock. There was still tension between the Liverpool side and the Birkenhead side over the allocation of resources, with Birkenhead gaining a greater allocation of resources than Liverpool during the first ten years of the MDHB.

The dock extension at the northern end of the system was to be Lyster's first major project. Parliament had authorised a sum of £4,100,000 for the work, but stipulated that no more than £500,000 could be borrowed in any one financial year. This stipulation had the effect of slowing down to some extent the expedition of the work. There was much disagreement with regards to the need for dock extensions.

The great 1873 building programme was very ambitious, starting with a sea wall that was to be built north from Canada Dock Basin to Rimrose Brook, with a return wall ending close to Gladstone Graving Dock. Following this, and within this shelter, Langton Dock, together with its branch dock and graving docks, was to be built. The grand project also included the building of the Alexandra Dock with its three branch docks and the Hornby Dock. However, Lyster also had plans for the south end docks. Work on the Toxteth and Harrington dock systems was completed, as was some additional work on the Herculaneum Dock.

Although the Langton Dock was partially opened in 1879, the whole of the system did not come into full use until the entrances were finally completed in 1881. The dock was named in honour of William Langton, a member of the old Dock Committee and later a member of the MDHB when it was established. William Langton was elected chairman of the MDHB on the retirement of Ralph Brocklebank in 1870.

The Hornby Dock was opened in 1884. The dock was named in honour of Thomas Dyson Hornby, chairman of the MDHB from 1876 until his death in 1889. By this date, shipping entering the Liverpool dock estate, operating under the auspices of the MDHB, was now in excess of 7.8 million tons.

With the steadily increasing tonnage of shipping using the port, Lyster was faced with a complex dilemma of where to site dock entrances. With the Mersey's prevailing winds, the strong tide race, and the heavy surge of water, entering or leaving the dock system could often be a hazardous operation and the problem was now further compounded by the ever-increasing size of ships using the port. Through a series of acts in the 1890s, approval was given for the dock entrance to the new dock system at the north end to be constructed and also for already existing systems, including the Birkenhead docks system, to be modified in accordance with Lyster's plans.

June 1892 saw further decisions taken, relating to the widening of the Canada–Huskisson passage, and also to make the southern entrance to the Sandon Half-Tide Dock 100 feet wide instead of 80 feet. Later, when the two new trans-Atlantic liners, RMS *Lusitania* and RMS *Mauretania* were built, this decision proved to be the correct one, as both liners had to use the widened southern entrance. More modifications needed to be made to accommodate the expanding trans-Atlantic liner trade. In 1893, Prince's landing stage was strengthened and the channel deepened so that large liners could berth alongside the landing stage, whatever the state of the tide or weather. A station was also built giving direct access to the main railway line.

Yet further modifications to the system, as a whole, were deemed to be necessary. An act was passed in 1898, which was wide-ranging in its scope. In 1896, Canada-branch Dock Number 1 had already been opened, then, three years later, in 1899, Canada Graving Dock was opened. Canada Dock itself, which opened in 1859, had been Jesse Hartley's last and most ambitious dock and was built to provide specialist discharge and storage berths for timber imports. The dock facility had been designed to relieve the berthing congestion at the Brunswick Dock to the south, which was also a timber importing dock. The location of the new dock at the farthest northern end of the dock system had been especially chosen because of the risk of fire. Indeed, in 1893 there had been a massive timber fire, which resulted in damage in excess of £50,000. Canada half-tide basin, which later became Brocklebank Dock, was added in 1862 by G. F. Lyster. The entrance, which was via the tidal basin, had been designed specifically for shallow paddle steamers, but, as the draft of vessels increased, dock engineers were faced with a number of unforeseen problems.

The year 1901 saw the opening of Queen's Branch Dock Number 1, with the widening of the entrances to Sandon Half Tide-Dock being completed in 1901–02. Building continued apace, with Huskisson Branch Dock Number 1 opening in 1902 on the site of the old Sandon Graving Docks. This was followed by Canada Branch Dock Number 2 opening in 1903; the year 1905 saw the deepening of the Brunswick Dock river entrances completed, and in the same year Queens Branch Dock Number 2 was also completed. In the following year, Queens Graving Dock was built, partly on the site of an existing half-tide entrance and the Queen's Branch Docks Numbers 1 and 2. In 1906, there were alterations to Sandon Dock and also King's Docks Numbers 1 and 2 were built on the site of the old King's Dock and King's Dock tobacco warehouse.

There were further dock extensions planned to the north of the existing dock estate and, with the increase in passenger liners using the port, the passenger-

The docks system was considered to be complete in 1927, when the king performed the opening ceremony for the Gladstone Dock system. The vast bulk of Liverpool's economy was focused on its waterfront.

An image of St George's landing stage and Prince's landing stage in 1905.

The *Aquitania* in Gladstone Dock in 1914.

The floating landing stage was a feature on the Liverpool waterfront for many years. It was not until 1934 that the first Mersey Tunnel was opened, so there was always a queue for the goods ferry.

The Benedictine monks of the Birkenhead Priory were granted the right of ferry to Liverpool in 1330 by Edward III. There has been a ferry across the Mersey ever since.

Vehicles waiting to catch the ferry over to the Birkenhead side of the river. The first Mersey Tunnel was not opened until 1934.

carrying companies were also seeking additional berths. In 1903, permission was sought from parliament to acquire land to the north of the existing dock estate. This land, together with earlier acquisitions, enabled plans to be brought forward to construct docks near to Seaforth. Later, in 1906, permission was sought to build a half-tide dock with direct entrances from the river. It was also envisaged that there would be a lock connecting with the Hornby Dock; this would include two branch docks and river walls extending to Cambridge Street in Waterloo. This scheme would eventually become known as the Gladstone system. There were also extensions planned on the Birkenhead side of the river, with the building of Vittoria Dock in the East Float.

The building of the Gladstone Dock system was not started until 1908. The Graving Dock was the first part of the new system and was opened in 1913, but the system was not actually completed until 1927. The final configuration of the Gladstone system included a turning dock, together with two branch docks, and there was a total water area in excess of 58 acres. The construction of the docks also included some 3 miles of quays, with a number of single, double, and treble-storey transit sheds. There was a river entrance lock, which, in itself, was over 1,000 feet long and had a width of 130 feet. The design was such that it could accommodate the largest ships entering the port. The dock estate was now nearing completion, with continuous docking facilities reaching from the Gladstone docking system in the north of the estate to the Dingle end of the docks in the south; in fact, a continuous line of docks stretching for almost 7 miles. However, not all of the companies using the docks were convinced that the new dock complex catered for their needs. Timber importers often found that it was difficult to obtain berthing facilities at peak times and complained that more timber cargoes were now bypassing Liverpool and using the Manchester Ship Canal.

The original system over at Birkenhead, which consisted of the Morpeth and Egerton Docks and the East and West Floats, had now been enlarged by the construction of the Alfred and Wallasey Docks. Although the total of the docks on the Birkenhead side was now nearing 150 acres of free water surface area, there was increasing pressure that called for new docking facilities to be constructed. The MDHB took affirmative action and acquired Tranmere Pool. The Vittoria Dock was built and greatly added to the facilities now being offered on that side of the river.

Significant changes were about to happen at the docks. With the constant tensions between the cargo vessels and the passenger-carrying liners both constantly vying for docking facilities, something had to give. In 1907, the White Star Line moved the centre of their operations from Liverpool to Southampton. This move inflicted severe adverse economic effects on the docks in particular and the city of Liverpool in general. As a result of this devastating blow, it became tacitly agreed that the port, on both sides of the river, should firmly concentrate on the cargo trade, with little or no emphasis being given to the passenger trade. A settled pattern was becoming established, with Hornby Dock being principally used by the timber trade; Alexandra Dock tended to berth boats engaged in the South American trade; Langton Dock was used by ships serving the Mediterranean ports; and Cunard, White Star, and Canadian pacific liners used a combination of Canada Dock, Sandon Dock, and Huskisson Dock. These docks were also used by the Dominion and Leyland Lines. Other docks, such as the Wellington Dock and the Bramley-Moore Dock, were used by the Stotts and Curries Lines. Towards the southern end of the docks estate, Queen's Dock was used by British & Continental, Booths, and the Larrinaga Line. Queen's North Dock Number 2 was used by Holts for discharging cargo, but they then tended to use Birkenhead docks for loading for their outward voyages. T&J Harrison Lines used Brunswick and Toxteth Docks, while Elder Dempster's used Toxteth and Harrington Docks. The docks over at Birkenhead were used, almost exclusively, by ships plying on Far Eastern routes. At this time, just before the outbreak of the First World War, ships sailing from Liverpool were carrying almost 36 per cent of the total of Britain's export trade and approximately 23 per cent of her total import trade. The cargo trade was definitely where Liverpool's strength as a port lay.

With the plethora of activity being directed towards the extension and improvement of the dock estate, Liverpool—and the dock system in particular—was fast becoming a victim of its own success. As a consequence of the increasing tonnage of shipping moving through the port, with the accompanying increase in the volume of imports and exports, traffic (both by road and rail along the dockside) was rapidly becoming totally congested, to say nothing of the problems that it was causing to people who had legitimate business along the length of the dock estate. It was all too obvious that, if total gridlock of the system was to be avoided, something had to be done and rapidly. Improving transportation systems was the key issue, coupled with the obvious need to separate vehicular traffic from the transportation of people. The question resolved to one of simply asking, what could be done? Change, and indeed rapid change, was happening. Not only was the volume of trade reaching record levels, but, as has already been seen, the types of ships taking their cargoes to and from Liverpool were also changing. Sailing ships, which had for so many years dominated the skyline of the river and the docks, were now gradually being superseded and replaced by steam-driven ships.

Towards the middle of the nineteenth century, the dock estate already extended over an impressive length of in excess of 3 miles, from Brunswick Dock to the south of the Pier Head, to Wellington Dock, which had been constructed to the north. All of the docks in-between housed their own accompanying warehouses, sheds, and workstations, together with countless railway lines for access. Now, at the end of the century, the dock estate covered a much greater area and would soon stretch for an impressive, uninterrupted 7 miles in length along the waterfront. Although it was possible to access the docks by rail, wagons were hauled through the dock area by horses; with so many canvas sails filling the quayside, the dock authorities, understandably, were particularly vigilant and fearful of fire breaking out. If fire did break out, it was feared that there would be a distinct possibility that it might spread to the adjacent warehouses and destroy any goods stored

Canadian Pacific's SS *Montrose* leaving the Liverpool landing stage, with many of the passengers seeking a different life in the new world.

The Liverpool fire ship, *William Gregson*, seen here in front of the Liver Building.

With so many boats coming and going along the Mersey, a boatman's skills were always in demand.

A photograph of George's Dock in October 1901. Being past its useful life, the dock was in-filled and later became the site of the Liver Building.

Construction work started on the Liver Building in 1908. A new building system of reinforced concrete and a steel framework was used. The building was one of the first in the world to adopt this technique.

inside. Now, with the development of yet more docks along the waterfront, it was essential that the problem should be addressed and solutions found. Local people were not the only ones who realised that the whole transportation system in and around the docks area needed a radical overhaul; a certain Mr W. H. Curtiss on a visit from London also witnessed the desperate need for improvement. His solution entailed utilising and modifying existing resources—namely the rail track system that ran throughout the docks. His revolutionary idea was to modify omnibuses such that they could be converted for use on rails. This was achieved by using a series of retractable flanges, which were operated by a simple lever action. Curtiss then went on to gain a concession from the port authorities, which enabled him to operate the new passenger service that was introduced in 1859— the problem was solved. Indeed, the service proved to be so popular that the port authorities realised that there was revenue to be gained and promptly started to levy a toll on Curtiss's omnibuses. He was forced to abandon the service, but other operators soon filled the void. The service was proving to be so popular, with a frequency of one omnibus every five minutes during the day, that the Mersey Docks and Harbour Board was forced to introduce tighter regulations. One of the more significant regulations forbade omnibuses from coming within 300 yards of one another—a regulation that proved difficult to enforce. Later still, as cargo traffic through the port increased yet again and congestion returned, the MDHB increased the tolls payable in an effort to deter omnibus operators, but the service continued unabated, that is until the ultimate solution was found—the Liverpool Overhead Railway.

Although the Curtis omnibus service was proving to be a great success and alleviating, to some extent, the problem of traffic congestion along the length of the dockland waterfront, alternative schemes had been proposed. As early as 1852, John Grantham, a respected engineer, had forwarded plans to build an elevated railway from the newly opened Huskisson Dock to the Mersey Forge at Toxteth, a distance of some 4 miles. Grantham's plan envisaged an elevated rail track system some 20 feet above road level. Another advantage of his proposal was that it created even more storage and warehouse space underneath the tracks; although generating considerable interest, no positive moves were made to turn the concept into reality. It was many years later, in 1877, that the port authority—the Mersey Docks and Harbour Board—gave further detailed consideration to the now acute problem of traffic and cargo congestion. Many different schemes were deliberated upon, including excavating in order to build an underground rail system. This proposal was ultimately rejected, mainly because of the prohibitive costs and complexity of the excavation work itself. After further discussion, the board despatched Mr George Lyster to New York, where there was an overhead rail system already in operation. The main objectives of his visit were to make a detailed assessment of the system and also to form an opinion as to whether the system could be adapted to suit the dockside transportation needs of Liverpool. On his return, Lyster drew plans for an elevated railway, similar in many respects to the New York system, to run along the Mersey waterfront.

When Lyster presented his plans, which was for a twin-track system, many prominent members of the board, including Alfred Holt the ship owner and leading merchant in the town, objected to his proposals, favouring a single-track system with passing places at each station. Following much discussion on the pros and cons of the competing systems, the single-track system won the approval of the board. Parliamentary approval was sought and granted in 1878 for a single-track railway to be constructed. One major problem remained, however, and that related to the motive power to haul the trains. It was originally proposed that the Liverpool system would be similar to the New York Railway, in that the motive power would be steam driven, but there were concerns about the risk of fire as a result of sparks coming from the engine. However, even with parliament's approval, there were still many problems to be overcome by the Overhead Railway. When the scheme came under consideration by the Board of Trade, the plans for the single-track system were rejected on the grounds that, as rail traffic increased, a single-track system would not be able to meet the passenger numbers demand. The rejection added to the problems and plans were shelved for some considerable time.

The Mersey Docks and Harbour Board then instructed Lyster to make specific proposals with regards to the route and, more particularly, the possible effects on the docks and dock traffic that the construction would have. After Lyster's report was accepted by the board, a modified scheme was presented to parliament for approval, which was duly given. However, during the intervening period, the board's policies with regards to passenger transportation was modified, which, in effect, meant that the proposals were shelved. Not being satisfied with this outcome, a number of Liverpool's prominent businessmen, including Sir William B. Forwood, established the Liverpool Overhead Railway Company. On 24 July 1888, the powers formerly held by the Mersey Docks and Harbour Board were transferred to the new company and construction work was all set to start. By this time, the dock estate ran from Alexandra Dock in the north of the city to Toxteth Dock at the southern end.

The first problems with the building of the overhead railway soon manifested themselves, when it was realised that many existing buildings along the proposed route of the railway would have to be re-sited. This in itself led to the construction costs being considerably increased. A further complication was that, during construction, there was to be no impediment to the dock traffic; this, for obvious reasons, was a stipulation laid down by the MDHB. As a direct result of all of these complicating factors, the construction time went well outside of the period specified in the original act of 1888. Another act was sought and obtained, which gave the company an additional three years to complete the mammoth project. As construction went ahead, albeit slowly, motive power technology was fast changing. For instance, when a tube line was opened in London by the City & South London Railway, the motive power used was electricity. Similarly, many of the rail lines now being built in America were also being driven by electricity. The decision to power the new railway by electricity was not taken likely, although

The Overhead Railway's Pier Head station in the 1920s, a popular boarding point for city dwellers and workers.

View of the Overhead Railway looking towards the Canning Dock station. The Overhead Railway was originally conceived to alleviate increasing traffic congestion along the whole of the dock estate.

A view of the 'Overhead' along the Dock Road near to Water Street. The railway was 16 feet above the roadway and was colloquially referred to as the docker's umbrella.

A number of advertisements, similar to this one, were a constant feature on advertising boards all over the city and beyond.

Liverpool's Overhead Railway did much to boost its passenger numbers outside of work travelling times.

some people still had misgivings. It was largely due to the efforts of Messrs Lyster and Forward that the final decision was taken. The initial concerns that were felt by some people were soon dispelled.

The overall design of the railway was led by two of the most prominent engineers of the day; namely Sir Charles Douglas Fox and James Henry Greathead. Greathead was well-known for his revolutionary and pioneering work on the London Underground system, whereas Fox's main area of expertise was the design of railway viaducts and bridges. J. W. Willans of Manchester was the company that won the contract to build the overhead track.

Progress was such that rolling stock began to arrive by the start of 1893, ready for the official opening of the railway by the Leader of the Opposition, the Marquis of Salisbury, on 4 February that year. Public services started on 6 March 1893. Shortly after the Liverpool Overhead Railway (LOR) was opened to the public, it acquired the local colloquialism of 'the Dockers' Umbrella'; a title bestowed upon the railway because of the shelter it provided underneath the tracks for people walking along the Dock Road when it was raining. Also, it was not unknown for men in need of a night's rest, but without the resources to pay for accommodation, to sleep in the shelter afforded under the railway's structure.

The 'Overhead' was proving to be very popular and was very effective in achieving its primary objective of separating vehicular traffic from the transportation of people, but the line was virtually 'dead' after the end of the working day—a detail which the directors of the company had not overlooked. The route of the track undoubtedly served the dock estate, but it did not reach any significant residential areas. However, by gaining permission to extend the line at both the northern and southern terminals, it was possible to reach some of the city's outer suburbs. The northern extension of the line opened on 30 April 1894, thus giving access to Crosby, Litherland, Seaforth, and Waterloo. The southern extension, which came into operation on 21 December 1896, took the line from Herculaneum Dock to the district of Dingle; it was a more complex engineering challenge than the short northern extension had been.

Much as the Overhead had proved to be an inspirational development along Liverpool's waterfront, the true benefit of the railway became apparent during the dark days of the war years.

In order to ensure that vessels entered and sailed from the port in complete safety, a number of pilots were trained and engaged—a body of men who were well-experienced and thoroughly acquainted with the tides, currents, channels, and approaches of the Mersey. The pilots had to be competent to guide ships through the waters in and around the Mersey at whatever time of day or night they were either approaching or leaving the port as, immediately upon boarding, the master and officers of the vessel passed complete control and responsibility to the pilot and acted under his direction until the vessel was brought into dock.

With the continuing of the rise in volume of shipping passing through the docks, safety and security, in addition to the ambitious docks building programme, was not neglected. When the Mersey Docks and Harbour Board was established in

1858, the act that incorporated the board also stipulated that 'it should have the whole and sole regulation and management of pilots, and of pilot boats, in the Port of Liverpool'. It also stipulated that the committee was to be appointed by the board, that it should number not less than twelve persons, and that it should be known as the Pilotage Committee. The act went on to state that at least one third of the members of the committee should be composed of persons familiar with the duties and qualifications of pilots and that they must not be members of the Mersey Docks and Harbour Board. For some reason, the act also stipulated that the committee should be appointed in the month of January every year. The Pilotage Committee was a committee of the Mersey Docks and Harbour Board.

The act did make some concessions, granting licenses to those already holding a pilot's license, but decreeing that anyone wishing to obtain a license in the future must be over the age of eighteen, have served an apprenticeship of at least three years in any of the Liverpool pilot boats, have the consent of their master, and, finally, be examined by the board. There was, however, an escape clause, in that the act also stated that any other person could be examined by the board and, if found to be acceptable, could also be granted a pilot's license. There were severe penalties imposed upon pilots refusing to take command of either an incoming or outgoing vessel that had called for the assistance of a pilot. Licenses could be revoked if pilots failed in their duty.

When taking charge of a vessel, either entering or leaving the port, there were definitive and prescribed limits relating to the pilot's responsibilities. If leaving the port through the Queen's Channel, the limit was set at the Formby Northwest Buoy. Similarly, if sailing through the Rock Channel, the limit to the westward was marked as the Northwest Buoy of Hoyle.

The provisions in the act relating to where pilots were to board inward-coming vessels were totally explicit. The act stated that if any vessel did not have a pilot on board before reaching the House and Telegraph Station on Hilbre Island, then they were to bear south-south-west or, alternatively, be piloted from the road of Hoylake. There were reduced rates for such pilotage. The act further stated that if no pilot was on board before the vessel passed the Brazil Buoy in the Rock Channel, or the Crosby Lightship in the Formby Channel, then the rate charged should be fixed by the Mersey Docks and Harbour Board.

In addition to pilot's having to be licenced, the pilot boats themselves also had to be licensed by the board. Among other conditions of securing a license, the boats had to be owned by the same person who had owned the boat when the license had been granted and the boat had to be in good repair and sea-worthy. There were severe penalties if these conditions were not adhered to.

On the subject of pilotage, it is recorded in a parliamentary return (dated 12 April 1858) that the total number of persons engaged in this perilous occupation in the Port of Liverpool numbered 306, of whom thirty-six were classed as master pilots, 168 were known as journeyman pilots, fifty-four were licensed apprentices, and fifty-three were unlicensed apprentices. At the time, there were twelve pilot boats operating out of the Port of Liverpool. During the year 1857, Liverpool pilots attended 18,719 vessels and the total fees earned by the twelve pilot boats amounted to almost £61,000.

In his report of January 1858, the acting conservator, Rear Admiral George Evans, stated:

> Owing to the skill and meritorious conduct of the Liverpool pilots, a prodigious number of vessels was safely conducted through the channels and quicksands of the port, with the loss of only one vessel, under their charge.

Before leaving the topic of safety and security, mention must be made of the Liverpool's many lifeboats. The first lifeboats were stationed at the Point of Ayr, which was on the Welsh side of the River Dee. This location was particularly appropriate as directly opposite was the West Hoyle Bank, a perilous bank of sand that is exposed at low water. Being one of the most dangerous points on the coast, the MDHB maintained two lifeboats on this station; a truth that was proved on 4 January 1857, when one of the lifeboats went down and all of the crew perished. Further along the coast, there is a lifeboat station on Hilbre Island and another at Hoylake, opposite to the East Hoyle Bank and the Horse Channel. The passage through the Horse Channel is particularly narrow. In the river itself, there are always four lifeboats available, a precaution that was very necessary considering the volume of traffic coming into and sailing from the Mersey. Two of the boats are kept on the Liverpool side of the river and the other two are stationed at the magazines on the Cheshire side. The final boat is stationed at Formby on the Lancashire coast, Formby being the nearest point on the coast to the Queen's Channel, the Victoria Channel, and the old Formby Channel. Although the total number of lifeboats being deployed by the MDHB might at first sight appear to be somewhat excessive, given the number of vessels entering and leaving the port by day and night, it was a small price to pay for security of passage. Indeed, in his report of 1858, Rear Admiral Evans states that 'the crews of the Liverpool lifeboats, during the year 1857, with their usual intrepidity, assisted twenty-two vessels in distress, and saved the lives of forty persons'.

Although the docks expansion and the facilities were now firmly in the control of the MDHB, the matter of labour relations throughout the estate was causing some concern on a number of fronts. Since the end of the Boer War, the wages of seamen and dockworkers had fallen in real terms, also, the working conditions of dockers were not good, and the casual nature of employment continued to cause friction and hostility between various work gangs in different parts of the system. There was a seamen's strike in 1911, which brought matters to a head. As the situation deteriorated, with the ship-owners and the MDHB refusing to recognise any unions, the dock workers showed sympathy and supported the seamen by refusing to handle ships that were 'tainted'. As the situation fell to a new low, the dock workers themselves went on strike on 28 June, seeking to obtain better working conditions and remuneration. As there was fragmentation along the dock, there was no overall settlement found. The strike spread to tugboat men and also railway men working at the port. The port came to a complete standstill and the dispute dragged on throughout the summer, with a number of localised riots breaking out, causing the military to be sent in. Home Secretary Winston Churchill used his powers for the maintenance of law and order. On the other side, this prompted one of the strike leaders, Tom Mann, to call all transport workers in Liverpool out on strike. Lord Derby, who was then Lord Mayor of Liverpool, used his influence to bring the two sides together, although this initiative did not meet with too much success; however, there was some movement with regards to conditions of employment and a new plan was being proposed for the de-casualisation of labour. The prolonged dispute did, in many respects, mark a turning point in the history of labour relations in the port.

Towards the end of the nineteenth century, it was self-evident that competing internal forces, as represented by ship-owners, organised labour, railway companies, and factions within the Dock Board itself, were creating unnecessary obstacles to the port's future development and wellbeing. However, there were more insidious forces at work that would have far-reaching and deleterious effects upon the port's competitive edge. Firstly, there was the competition being faced from other competitive docks that were being established and financed by the railway companies; and secondly, there was the major challenge being waged by the building of the ship canal linking Manchester with the open sea—effectively turning Manchester into a port in its own right.

There was a widely held belief that many of these problems had been caused by the monopoly that the docks undoubtedly had on the export and import trade. Also to be taken into account was the monopoly that the railway companies held and the fact that, within reason, they could charge exorbitant freight rates, which merchants wishing to export or import goods had no alternative but to accept. It was these two principal monopolies that created so much tension between the Dock Board and railway companies on one side and the ship-owners and merchants on the other.

From 1850 onwards, coal became one of the biggest exports from the north of England. As charges increased at Liverpool and Birkenhead, railway companies built their own docks and, although more modest than the dock facilities at either Liverpool or Birkenhead, they served a useful purpose. For instance, Garston Dock, on the Mersey to the south of the Liverpool dock complex, was built by the St Helens Canal and Railway Company. The primary purpose for building the dock had been to give direct access to the Mersey, so that coal could be supplied to the salt fields of Cheshire and that St Helens coal could also be supplied to markets further afield. In a similar development, two docks had been built at Widnes further down the river, but these were not capable of dealing with the volume of traffic, so the St Helens Railway Company had extended the line as far as Garston and built a dock there. The dock, which was opened on 21 June 1853 and had a free surface area of in excess of 6 acres, gave direct access to the River Mersey and had a capacity to load coal at the rate of 250 tons in two and a half hours—much faster than any dock in the Liverpool complex. In building

WHITE STAR

EX-ROYAL MAIL LINE OF
AUSTRALIAN PACKETS.

These Magnificent Clippers, which have been so long and successfully employed in the conveyance of Her Majesty's Mails between Liverpool and the Australian Colonies, are despatched from

LIVERPOOL TO MELBOURNE,

On the 20th and 27th of every Month,

FORWARDING PASSENGERS, BY STEAM, AT THROUGH RATES, TO

GEELONG, SYDNEY, HOBART TOWN, LAUNCESTON,

AND ALL PARTS OF AUSTRALIA.

STEAM IS TAKEN TO CLEAR THE CHANNEL, IF NECESSARY.

RED JACKET, O'Halloran . .	4,500	SHALIMAR, I. R. Brown . . .	3,500
WHITE STAR, — Kerr . . .	5,000	ARABIAN, W. Balmano	2,500
GOLDEN ERA, H. A. Brown .	3,500	ANNIE WILSON, — Duckett.	3,500
MERMAID, Devey	3,200	TITAN, — Sears	5,000

The Ships of this Line are known to the World as the LARGEST and FASTEST afloat, and are fitted up regardless of expense, to suit the various means of every class of Emigrants. From the Saloon to the Steerage every article of dietary is put on board under the careful inspection of Her Majesty's Officers of Emigration, who likewise superintend the proper disposal of the necessary light and ventilation. The Saloons are elegant and roomy. The Second Cabins are fitted up with unusual care, and Passengers in this class have Stewards appointed to wait on them. The Intermediate and Steerage berths are exceedingly lofty, and the sexes are thoroughly separated. A properly qualified Surgeon is attached to each Ship.

RATES OF PASSAGE.

Saloon	£45 to £60
Second Cabin	£25 to £30
Intermediate, according to Rooms . .	£17 to £20
Steerage	£14

As Conveyances for Fine Goods, these Ships have long had a preference, having uniformly discharged their cargoes in first-rate order, and goods sent out by them can be Insured at the Lowest Rates of the day. For particulars of Freight or Passage, apply to the Owners,

H. T. WILSON & CHAMBERS,
21, WATER STREET, LIVERPOOL.

Agents in Melbourne . . . . H. T WILSON & Co., 41, King Street.

A steerage passage to Australia could cost as little as £14, but the passage was very basic to say the least.

Being half conventional lorry and half railway engine, the Sentinel was a familiar sight around the dock estate, right up until the late 1960s. The United Africa Company Limited owned many such vehicles.

Looking over to the parish church of Liverpool, the Church of Our Lady and Saint Nicholas. The site has been a place of worship since 1257.

Canning Dock in the late nineteenth century.

Langton Dock in its heyday.

Mann Island looks very different now from what it looked like at the turn of the last century.

the dock, the company had hoped that coal exports could rival those from the Wigan coalfields. The strategy did not meet with the anticipated success, as large ocean-going vessels had difficulty in entering the dock. Later, in 1875, a second dock was opened at Garston and, because of improved navigational systems, the docks became a serious rival to Liverpool when handling certain specialised cargoes. By the turn of the nineteenth century, it was estimated that over 50 per cent of Liverpool's exports of coal were now being diverted via Garston. This was due to both improved handling at the docks and preferential rail freight rates. Also, as much as 10 per cent of Liverpool's trade in grain was now being diverted through the newly emerging port. Liverpool's position as the premier port in the north-west was taking some unwelcome knocks.

It soon became apparent that the emergence of Garston as a dock facility posed little or no threat to Liverpool's apparently unassailable position. Nevertheless, there were other complications that would have a bearing upon the docks monopoly, which Liverpool had for so long enjoyed. As the tensions grew between Manchester merchants and opposing forces in Liverpool, an attempt was made to bypass Liverpool docks. A rail link from Manchester to Birkenhead was established, but this development was thwarted when the docks on both sides of the river came under the auspices of the Mersey Docks and Harbour Board. Prior to the establishment of the board and following the completion of the rail link, Manchester merchants enjoyed reduced freight rates and favourable dock dues. As this initiative was destined to failure, another ingenious solution was found; the construction of a canal between Manchester and the Mersey—the Manchester Ship Canal.

MDHB took a somewhat complacent view of activities in that arena, until a bill was brought before parliament in 1883 seeking permission to build such a canal. At the time, many observers considered that the Manchester Canal development was somewhat more than just an instrument for ending the monopoly that the Port of Liverpool had held for so long, it was seen as a direct attempt to finally break the power held by the Liverpool ship-owners and, by extension, the structures that underpinned Liverpool's economic strength. The canal did have the effect of reducing costs in two distinct ways. Firstly, by loading cargoes in Manchester, rail freight charges were completely eliminated; and secondly, reduced port fees enabled substantial saving to be made. It soon became clear that there were undoubted benefits to be gained by using Manchester as a port.

As the effects of the canal were being assessed by the Liverpool shipping companies, it was generally agreed that loading ships at Manchester did not offer that many benefits, although T&J Harrison did send some ships up the canal for loading. Other companies, such as Holt's, decided that there was little to gain when the overall costs were fully analysed. There was also the matter of apportionment of cargoes to be taken into account. This was a system agreed between London, Liverpool, and Glasgow, whereby cargoes were allotted to these three major ports and that any deviation from this established practice could have untold repercussions. In fact, the perceived threat from the construction of the Manchester Ship Canal never materialised as shipping companies found that manufacturers were completely indifferent as to where their cargoes were loaded, be it in Liverpool, Birkenhead, or Manchester. The main point of contention between the merchants and the shipping companies was the freight rates that the shipping companies were continuing to charge.

Liverpool ship-owners did, however, agree to send some vessels through to Manchester for loading, when it emerged that the Canal Company had entered into an agreement that would have allowed other ships to enter the docks at Manchester.

When the Manchester Ship Canal opened in 1894, a number of ships from Liverpool did in fact sail as far as Manchester to load their cargoes, but this practice was very soon brought to an end by the merchants themselves. Although the costs of transporting cargoes to either Birkenhead or Liverpool was proving costly because of the high rail freight costs, it was often more costly to send large ocean-going vessels through the canal to Manchester, as the Canal Company were charging, in many cases, prohibitively high transit charges.

The period from 1860 right up until the beginning of the First World War could still be classed as boom years for the port, as much wealth and prosperity was still in evidence and there continued to be vast resources being invested in docks and dockside developments, but it was apparent that the era of continuous growth was now beginning to draw to an end. Although there continued to be investment in the dock estate, Liverpool's share of the country's total export trade had been steadily declining since the 1850s, although almost 25 per cent of the country's imports still came in through the port.

As a general statement, the Port of Liverpool saw steady and sustained growth from 1860 to the outbreak of war in 1914, with the dock estate benefitting from cash injections for new docks, quayside facilities, and modern handling equipment, but the actual tonnage of shipping passing through the port increased at relatively slow rate. There were also repercussions from the First World War, with a marked trade recession during the interwar years. Foreign shipping companies were now posing more of a competitive threat to the traditional stronghold of British shipping companies, which also had knock-on effects for the port, as did labour unrest that surfaced on occasions. It was beginning to appear that the Port of Liverpool and the city itself were destined for a bleak economic future.

8

The War Years

When the First World War started in 1914, many changes occurred in and around the Port of Liverpool. By way of preparation, Liverpool had taken the precaution of forming a committee in 1912, whose main brief was to look into the possible steps that might have to be taken in order to secure the nation's supply of food and raw materials. It had been anticipated that Liverpool, together with ports on the south coast, would have to shoulder a greater volume of traffic should ports on the east coast be closed to shipping. During the period of the war, the MDHB were severely curtailed in the progress they were able to make as regards dock expansion and efficiency. Many problems had arisen, such as labour shortages, rising costs, falling revenues, and continuing congestion in the port. Also, and for perhaps obvious reasons, there was significantly more government intervention in the working and administration of the port.

During the four-year period of the war, the revenue accruing to the board remained relatively stable, being £1,560,000 in 1914 and £1,660,000 in 1918. The income from cargo increased during this period, while there was a slight decrease in the income gained from ships using the port. However, a stable income was not enough for port expansion to continue; interest rates were high when borrowing money, materials charges were increasing after the war, and labour costs had also increased as a direct result of the war. Expansion was severely curtailed, with major projects, such as the completion of the Gladstone system, held in abeyance.

A Port Labour Committee had been established in 1916, mainly due to the severe shortage of dock labour since most able-bodied men had been enlisted for war service. During the hostilities, it was central government rather than individual dock authorities that set wage rates. After June 1916, dock workers were included in the act that regulated the employment of munitions workers, so, from that time, the wages of both dock workers and warehouse men increased.

Cargo handling and cargo-handling equipment along the dock was becoming totally inadequate, but, because dock revenue was not increasing, the board was forced to manage on existing equipment, knowing that cranage along the dock was totally inadequate.

As the war progressed, more and more ships were being lost to enemy action, especially due to the intensification of submarine warfare. In an effort to reduce these losses, Joseph Maclay was appointed as shipping controller in 1917. Given wide-ranging powers, he decreed that there should be a convoy system of ships leaving the port. This strategy proved to be very successful, in that it reduced the number of ships being lost to enemy action, but there were negative knock-on effects for the port. As a consequence of the large number of ships either entering or leaving the port at any one time, dock space was severely limited. Furthermore, when the Americans joined the war effort on 6 April 1917, Liverpool was the disembarkation port for most of the troops, with over 700,000 passing through the port in 1918. At the outbreak of war, President Woodrow Wilson had pledged neutrality, which chimed with the general sentiment of most Americans at the time. However, early in 1915, a private American vessel, the *William P. Frye*, was sunk by a German cruiser. This caused some shift in American opinion, but this violation was eclipsed later in the year. On 1 May 1915 the Cunard liner, RMS *Lusitania*, had left New York bound for Liverpool; on Friday 7 May, the ship was torpedoed by a German U-boat, *U-20*, 11 miles off the coast of Ireland with the loss of 1,198 lives—785 passengers and 413 crew. At the time of sailing, fierce battles were being waged in the Atlantic, with waters around the British coast being declared as a war zone by Germany. The German embassy in New York had even gone as far as placing advertisements in local newspapers informing prospective passengers of the dangers being faced when sailing on the ship. Following the initial strike on the liner, there was a second internal explosion, which caused the ship to sink in just eighteen minutes. As the vessel was a non-military ship, it was evident that the U-boat had flagrantly chosen to ignore the internationally agreed laws known as Cruiser Rules. The Germans did, however, have some grounds for targeting the ship as she was carrying an amount of munitions for the British government, who themselves were guilty of contravening the Cruiser Rules. A total of 128 Americans lost their lives on the *Lusitania*, causing a shift in public opinion that helped lead America to ultimately join the war in April 1917.

Germans nationals living and working in Liverpool had become accepted members of local communities and were not seen as posing any threat. For much of the early part of the war, life went on just the same for most of them, although some were interned over in the Isle of Man. However, after the events of 7 May 1915, that acceptance and forbearance changed, as many of *Lusitania*'s crew hailed from Liverpool. The following day, with anti-German feelings running high, a number of riots broke out on the streets of Liverpool. A store in Walton Lane, owned by Mr Fischer, a German, was targeted, with windows being smashed and foodstuffs thrown around the outlying area. Another shop, Dimler's in County Road, was also attacked. Before the day was over, three more shops had been ransacked. The riots spread to other parts of the country and became known as the anti-German riots or the *Lusitania* riots.

Before the war was over, the Mersey was given further honour when two of the river's ferryboats, the *Iris* and the *Daffodil*, were requisitioned by the Royal Navy. A commando raid on the Belgian harbour of Zeebrugge was planned as the German Navy was using the port as a submarine base. Both boats had draughts of less than 9 feet, which made them ideal for sailing over the deeper-set minefields at the mouth of the port. However, on the night of the assault, 23 April 1918, they met with a number of unforeseen mishaps, which resulted in many of the volunteers on board being killed or badly injured. The *Iris* was badly damaged, but she did manage to get back to England under her own power, and the *Daffodil* had to be taken in tow and repatriated to Dover. After repairs had been carried out, both ships returned to the Mersey on 17 May 1918 to a rapturous welcome. In recognition of the role that they had played, they were given the appellation 'Royal', and were henceforth known as the *Royal Iris* and the *Royal Daffodil*.

As the war was drawing to a close, a spirit of rejuvenation was apparent throughout the dock estate, with electrification being introduced at the north end of the dock estate and then later at the southern end. Railway haulage also increased, with additional rails, sidings, and locomotives being introduced on the estate. Work on the Gladstone system was restarted, albeit with the aid of German prisoners of war. A cold storage facility was built at the east end of the Alexandra Branch Dock No. 3 by the Union Cold Storage Company; this new facility significantly increased the cold storage capacity of the port.

The war had had many deleterious effects on the nation's shipping companies. At the start of the war, almost 40 per cent of the total world tonnage was trading under the British flag, but that figure had been reduced to 33 per cent at the end of the hostilities. Countries such as France, Japan, and the United States had all increased their trading fleets, with much of this trade coming about because, during the war, British ships were unable to trade with certain countries. This downturn impacted upon Liverpool's shipping and its port, coupled with the fact that, during the war, Liverpool-based companies had lost in excess of 1,500,000 tons of shipping. Much effort would be needed to re-establish the port's standing in a changed and changing world trading economy. It was estimated by the Liverpool Steam Ship Owners' Association that the replacement costs for ships lost during the war amounted to in excess of £280 million, whereas the figure received from war-risk insurance only amounted to £140 million; shipping company reserves were needed to make up the shortfall.

In order to regain their competitive effectiveness, Liverpool's ship-owners had, first of all, to replace lost tonnage. This was much easier said than done as shipyards were still being overburdened with ship orders from the Admiralty. From this situation there arose a frenzy of company acquisitions, with companies with free tonnage being vulnerable. By 1922, shipyards were becoming less congested with orders and many of Liverpool's ship-owners took advantage of the situation by embarking on planned building programmes. During this period, many companies amalgamated, thus reducing overhead costs and gaining from economies of scale.

Although shipping and trade recovery after the war was somewhat protracted, many of the shipping companies had anticipated stiffer competition well before the war broke out. As early as 1902, Holts took over the China Mutual and then, in 1906, Brocklebanks re-entered the China trade when they bought an interest in the Shire Line. In another similar acquisition, Glen Line was incorporated into the Elder Dempster Line. The early part of the twentieth century also saw some changes in the motive power of many of the newer ships sliding down the slipway. Glen Line took delivery of four new motor ships in 1920. The ships were designed to be fast cargo liners, weighing 9,500 gross tons. The high cost of the new ships stretched the limited financial resources of the company, which ultimately led to it being absorbed into Alfred Holt's.

The competition for different trade routes was becoming more intense, with P&O entering the Far Eastern trade. Like a number of other companies at that time, expansion often meant absorption of other shipping companies. P&O acquired Blue Anchor Line in 1910 and later amalgamated with the British India Steam Navigation Company in 1914. This was a logical business decision as British India had strong business links in Australia, India, and the Far East.

It was because of many of the astute business moves, which Liverpool ship-owners took both before and after the First World War that trade did show some signs of recovery after the cessation of hostilities, only to be dashed again when trade plummeted in 1929 as a result of the worldwide depression.

Greater efficiency was seen as one of the most important factors in maintaining a competitive edge in the shipping industry. After 1924, Holt's fleet was re-equipped with oil-burners and motor ships. Although it had been difficult to anticipate the world trade depression that was to follow, the Darwinian maxim 'survival of the fittest' still held true, and, while many companies failed in the severe economic times, companies such as Holts managed to maintain trading links, albeit on a much reduced scale.

Liverpool's port, like others throughout the country, was feeling the draught from the economic recession. Not only had the Far Eastern markets seen a huge downturn, the effects were also being manifested in the Gulf, Indian, Central American, Brazilian, and West Indian markets. Traditional imports of tobacco, sugar, wool, rubber, timber, and cotton were all much reduced in volume. Similarly, exports of finished goods such as engineering equipment, coal, and cotton piece-goods were also adversely affected by the recession. Liverpool's ship-owners approached the situation as they had always done, by seeking new markets, new commodities to trade in, and new shipping routes.

The war had undoubtedly had disastrous effects upon the shipping lines and also on the port itself. Booth Line ended the war with eighteen ships, only half of the fleet that they had before the start of hostilities. Harrison Line lost 25,000 tons of shipping during the war, ending with a remaining fleet of forty-nine vessels. The companies adopted different strategies to re-equip their respective fleets; Booth's chartered ships, whereas Harrisons purchased ships from other fleets. Unfortunately, unlike many of their continental rivals, neither Booths nor Harrisons had invested in motor ships, even though both companies had embarked upon extensive rebuilding programmes in the 1920s and 1930s. Booths sold many of their older ships and focused on using their newer, faster ships. They also discontinued many of their traditional passenger services and operated out of ports where dock charges were less onerous.

Sir Thomas Harrison Hughes, now Harrison's Director of Policy, focused on delivering the most efficient services on the most profitable routes. Leyland Line was purchased, not for the additional tonnage, but because of the profitable routes on which it had the monopoly. Harrisons were in direct competition with Union Castle Line on the South African route. They bought four oil-fired steam ships from Prince Line and immediately returned a working profit. The company also had built new ships specifically for the West Indian trade. Under Hughes' guidance, the Harrison Line was well-placed to face any further competition.

Mention must be made of the fact that Owen Philipps had taken over the shipping interests of Alfred Jones. These interests were subsequently absorbed into the Royal Mail Group, which was controlled by Owen Philipps under his title of Lord Kylsant. Kylsant had vision and ambition, hoping to create a conglomerate that could match the strength of Pierpont Morgan's operation in America. Kylsant's scheme involved many of Liverpool's leading shipping companies, including Lamport & Holt, Elder Dempsters, the Pacific Steam Navigation Co., Coast Lines, the White Star Line, the Moss Line, and a number of other smaller shipping companies. It was therefore understandable that the port suffered considerable economic difficulties when Kylsant encountered financial difficulties. Also resulting from Kylsant's downfall was the demise of a number of Liverpool's shipping companies, including Elder Dempsters. Elder Dempsters did, however, recover under the direction of Richard Holt. The company reorganised under the name of Elder Dempster Lines Ltd and, by the outbreak of the Second World War in 1939, its gross tonnage amounted to 213,000 tons and the company had a working capital of £3 million. Liverpool's trading connections with West Africa were maintained and strengthened, not least because of the addition of a number of diesel-driven ships. However, the Kylsant crash had severe repercussions on the Port of Liverpool and this was at a time when many traditional skills and trades were in decline.

It was not just cargo companies that suffered during the war, passenger-carrying liner companies also ended the war with depleted fleets. Both the White Star Line and Cunard were anxious to strengthen their services out of Liverpool. White Star built new motor ships, while Cunard continued their sailings to St Lawrence after acquiring the Thompson Line. There was intense competition to be faced with the French, Italian, and Germans, who were all intent on gaining a segment of the lucrative trans-Atlantic passenger trade. It was time for Cunard and White Star to reassess their strategy. White Star's share capital changed on a number of occasions, being taken over by the Morgan group in 1902 and again in 1927 when it passed into Kylsant's Royal Mail Group. However, when that group ran to economic difficulties, White Star turned to the Cunard Line, which was also experiencing severe economic pressures. Following some central government intervention and financial assistance to complete the building of the RMS *Queen Mary*, the two companies merged in 1934. The arrangement continued until 1949, when the White Star title was dropped and Cunard carried all of the trans-Atlantic passenger trade.

There were many changes that affected Liverpool's shipping companies during the interwar years. To start with, because of a recession in world trade, fierce competition from foreign shipping companies and the uncertainties following the Royal Mail Lines crash, many of the city's independent shipping lines had been forced to regroup or amalgamate. In fact, the demise of Royal Mail Lines affected seven of the city's major shipping lines, involving a total of 1,500,000 gross tons of shipping and an estimated capital of £20 million. It is debatable as to whether many other ports could have survived such an onslaught. However, over the years, the city's ship-owners had become well-versed in seeking and developing new markets. Most of Liverpool's shipping was kept afloat during the interwar years, which did much to maintain relatively high levels of employment in the city. The Port of Liverpool continued to be a lifeline for the importation of foodstuffs and other raw materials. Although it cannot be denied that, because of the disruption caused by the war and the subsequent marked depression in worldwide trade, usage of the port system considerably fell in both the need for cargo and passenger provision.

Directly after the end of the First World War, the government placed pressure upon authorities to develop and institute a public works authority in an effort to combat the rising rates of unemployment. The Mersey Docks and Harbour Board responded to this request by proposing to erect five bascule bridges to replace the swing bridges at Birkenhead and Stanley Dock. There was also to be an extension of the West Float at Bidston and some replacement of equipment at the Langton Graving Docks. Other improvements included some modifications at Clarence Dock. There was also a number of other initiatives that were taken locally by committee members of the MDHB. After a prolonged absence, Richard Holt had rejoined the board as chairman in 1931. One of his first decisions was to reduce the charges on goods coming into the port. This was by way of an effort to increase trade coming into the port. However, he and the board in general also took steps to reduce the interest charges, which the board had incurred on its loans; this was achieved by judicious dealings in war loan stock. Then, as there had been a general upturn in trade towards the end of the 1930s, the board made plans to upgrade facilities at the port. As the coasting trade was still important to the port, emphasis was placed upon turnaround time. In this regard, a new entrance lock at the west side of Waterloo Dock was constructed, enabling vessels drawing up to 17 feet to enter and leave the port at any state of the tide. Ambitious plans were also made for the reconstruction of the Langton Dock entrances, which became known as the Langton-Canada Improvement Scheme. However, the outbreak of the Second World War in 1939 caused these plans to be held in abeyance until after the war ended.

During the years of depression in the 1920s and 1930s, the monetary value of cargoes passing through the port was subject to wide fluctuations, but the volume of trade, in tonnage terms, remained fairly constant, which in itself enabled employment levels to be maintained.

During the 1930s, the board's income was depleted due to trade bypassing both Liverpool and Birkenhead and sailing on to Manchester through its ship canal. In 1914, this represented 21 per cent of all shipping entering the Mersey, but by 1937 this figure had risen to 28.4 per cent—a worrying trend for members of the board.

Many economic analyses have shown that during the interwar years the Port of Liverpool had a zero growth rate. The period from 1860 to 1914 showed that total tonnage entering the Mersey increased by an average of 2.8 per cent and that shipping using berthing and other services of the Dock Board increased by 2.1 per cent. However, during the period from 1920 to 1939, the corresponding figures were 0.7 per cent and 0.03 per cent respectively; in effect, virtually no growth during this period. During this period, the Port of Liverpool lost trade to other ports, which was aggravated by a general recession in world trade. However, plans had been put in place that would both increase the port's capacity and its efficiency. During the interwar years of depression, Liverpool's problems were exacerbated by the fact that employment within the dock estate was falling, there was no increase in growth of local industry, and nor were there any new industries being introduced into the region. Unemployment rates during these times never dropped below 18 per cent, which lead to unrest and a degree of labour militancy. There were protest marches organised on a daily basis, with groups of unemployed men marching through the city's streets.

In 1921, the Transport and General Workers Union came into being. This development did much to overcome the sectionalism that had previously existed in the trade union movement in Liverpool. It was also significant that, within the city, the Labour Party and the Trades Council amalgamated. Resulting from these and other amalgamations within the city, Merseyside's unions were prepared for the general strike, which occurred in 1926. The mechanics of strike activity were well-coordinated by the different unions and quickly mobilised for effective action. Having said that, the impact of the general strike did begin to weaken on Merseyside, as the tramway men—an important grouping—went back to work relatively quickly. One of the governing factors in any strike being the ability of striking men to provide for their families and in reality, by the time that the general strike was called off, many men in Liverpool had begun to drift back to work. The net result was that little was achieved that would enhance the power of organised labour within the country in general or Liverpool in particular.

Although there was some increase in numbers of men employed in the manufacturing industries on Merseyside from 1924 to 1939, there was a far greater rise in men employed in service trades during the same period. Indeed, there was becoming an overdependence in the service trades within the area, which lead to weaknesses in the local economy. Many resources were also channelled into the services side of the port, which lead to a certain vulnerability when there were changes in demand within the port. Acknowledging this weakness, the city council sought to redress this imbalance at the end of the Second World War and began to develop and promote a number of trading estates on the periphery of the city, much of which was encouraged and promoted by central government, who recognised the need to develop industry in the north-west region. The central aim was to avoid replication of the economic difficulties, which had beset the city during the interwar years. Nonetheless, the unemployment figures in Merseyside were still significantly higher (almost double) than those being experienced in other parts of the country.

During the period from 1920 to 1939 there was, nationally, a general stagnation in trade, employment, and capital growth. However, the impact upon the docks and Merseyside in general was somewhat less than in other parts of the country, although the port did lose trade to London and other places. Nevertheless, the dock estate did manage to contain the impact resulting from the Royal Mail Lines crash, and again, although there was a long-term drop in trade, the dock estate was actually enlarged by 18 per cent during the interwar years.

During the Second World War, the port of London was the Luftwaffe's major bombing target, causing it to become occasionally inoperative, which necessitated Liverpool becoming the primary port for supply and despatch. The port was subjected to the most intense and unrelenting attacks from the air. In this respect, the role of the Mersey Docks and Harbour Board was pivotal in securing the daily operational efficacy of the port. By the outbreak of war, the docks on the Liverpool side of the river stretched for some 7 miles along the waterfront, whereas, on the Birkenhead side of the river, there were another 182 acres of docks to be maintained and guarded from attack. Another of the Luftwaffe's targets on the Mersey was the busy shipbuilding yard of Cammell Laird and Co. and, although the city and the port on both sides of the river were prime targets for enemy aircraft, national security was such that little information relating to bombardment was ever broadcast on national radio.

Hitler adopted a large number of changing tactics during the Second World War, all geared to the overall strategy of invading Britain, ending the war, and ensuring that Germany was victorious. The capitulation of France in 1940 saw Hitler's focus turn to England. Initial attacks were concentrated on London, but very soon after Liverpool became a prime target for the Luftwaffe bombers due to its importance in maintaining supply lines from its docks. When German planes failed to achieve their declared objective in the Battle of Britain, Hitler modified his approach and concentrated on starving Britain into submission. The plan adopted was essentially a two-pronged strategy: firstly, his navy would destroy the Atlantic convoys, thus cutting off vital supplies to the country; and secondly, Luftwaffe bombers would paralyse Liverpool docks by intense and sustained bombing raids—the blitzkrieg.

The first Luftwaffe attack on the Liverpool area was on 12 August 1940, when German planes bombed Birkenhead docks. After that first foray, the raids continued unabated, with more raids following just a few days later when bombs were dropped near to the grain silos at Brunswick Dock. Throughout the intense period of bombardment, the damage to the board's property was considerable, with repair bills running into millions of pounds. In total, 91 acres of dock sheds and warehouses were totally destroyed and a further 90 acres of sheds were deemed to be out of commission. There was also much plant and machinery either lost or damaged during the bombing raids. Ten dock gates were damaged and needed remedial attention, but none of the river entrances were seriously damaged. A number of dock locomotives sustained damage, as did seventy-four railway wagons. Damage was also inflicted on some of the pumping stations and many of the quayside cranes. The burden of responsibility for effecting all of the repairs that were caused by bomb damage on the dock estate was the responsibility of the engineer's department.

Most of the bombing raids on Liverpool occurred between September 1940 and May 1941, but the bombing of the docks became heavier after July 1940 and reached its zenith in May 1941. During this intense period of sustained bombing, the docks themselves and the dockside warehouses suffered great losses, as did the area of central Liverpool. The areas around Lord Street, Ranelagh Street, and Scotland Road were virtually demolished. There was also much devastation along the whole length of the dock estate from the northern end in Bootle, to the southern end of the docks complex at Garston. Liverpool was seen as an easy target for German pilots to find, as they knew the contours of the Welsh coast and they also knew the shape of the Liver Building; a landmark, right in the centre of the dock estate. The Liver Building never took a direct hit during the war and many attribute this to the fact that, because the Liver Building was such a recognisable landmark, German pilots were instructed to leave it intact, so that other pilots could use the landmark as a navigational aid. The Christmas Raids, which lasted for three consecutive nights from 20 December 1940, killed 365 people in Liverpool. The 'sailor's church', St Nicholas, was also damaged during these raids.

There was some reduction in raids during the early part of 1941; this was due to poor weather conditions, which made for difficult flying. However, as the weather improved and the situation became more critical, Liverpool was bombarded with more intense raids, culminating in the May Blitz of that year, which lasted for eight consecutive nights from the night of 1 May. During that time, some 681 Luftwaffe Heinkel and Dornier bombers dropped a total of 2,315 high-explosive bombs, 119 land mines, and many other incendiaries on the city's docks, warehouses, ships, and private dwellings, ensuring that almost half of the docks were effectively out of action. During the sustained onslaught, a total of some 1,746 Merseysiders lost their lives—1,453 from within the city boundary itself. Another 1,154 people were seriously injured during that time. Consequently, due to the devastation that was caused during the intense raids, over 41,000 people had to be found alternative accommodation, upwards of 10,000 in neighbouring towns—a staggering feat that was achieved in less than a week. During the totality of the bombing raids, 3,966 people living in the Merseyside region lost their lives and a further 3,812 suffered serious injuries. The damage to property during that time was also immense, with 10,000 homes being completely destroyed and a further 184,000 sustaining damage to a greater or lesser extent.

Just before midnight on 2 May, the blitz started again. Along with many other buildings in Liverpool city centre, the Dock Board office was damaged. There were also many docks damaged during the May blitzkrieg, including South Queens Dock, Coburg Dock, and Wapping Dock amongst others. Then, on the night of 3–4 May 1941, Liverpool was subjected to yet another sustained and intense bombardment from the German Luftwaffe. A dockside shed in Huskisson Dock No. 2 was on fire. Two police constables, PCs Fredrick Spicer and Percy Green, fought to put the blaze out, knowing that the shed contained high explosives. Rapidly running out of water, they changed tactics and pulled the explosive materials away from the burning shed and away from a cargo ship, the *Pinto*, which contained over 500 tons of explosives. In light of the imminent danger, they also advised the *Pinto*'s captain to move to a safer berth. Both men later received the George Medal from King George VI.

There was also a cargo liner that had been specially converted into a munitions carrier in the dock on that fateful night, the SS *Malakand*, and it was also on the same night that the most devastating single damage caused by enemy action occurred; this was on the Brocklebank ship, Huskisson Dock, and the dock estate itself. The *Malakand* was berthed at the south-west side of the dock and had in her holds 1,000 tons of bombs and shells destined for the war theatre in the Middle East. There was a particularly heavy air raid on the port that night, with several incendiaries falling around the vessel, but these were being dealt with. Then, just as the operation was being completed, a partly deflated barrage balloon, which had become loose from her moorings, got entangled in the boat's rigging. When

A great amount of damage was inflicted to the docks during the Second World War—the Overhead Railway, running along the whole length of the dock estate, could not avoid the carnage. Canada Dock station, seen here, was just one of the many victims of the May Blitz in 1941.

During the Second World War, many aircraft were imported through the Port of Liverpool.

The scene of utter devastation in Huskisson Dock immediately after the SS *Malakand* exploded; this was during the May Blitz of 1941.

the balloon eventually landed on the ship's weather deck, it immediately burst into flames and the fire quickly spread to the ship's bridge and upper decks. The captain and his crew tackled the fire and somehow managed to put it out, but, while they were attending to the fire on the ship, falling incendiaries had set alight some adjacent cargo sheds. Within minutes, the flames had spread to the ship once again and soon the whole ship was ablaze. By this time, many other firefighters had been called to attend the blazing ship, but there were other fires raging throughout the dock estate and resources were limited. At the height of the bombing, the fires were so numerous and so intense that Liverpool's many fire tenders along the dockside could not cope with the onslaught. Fire tenders from as far away as Halifax, Scunthorpe, and Hartlepool were drafted in to assist. During the whole of the time that the fire was raging on the *Malakand*, the ship was being dive-bombed by enemy aircraft. The blaze had started late at night, at about 11.15 p.m., and after several hours of heroic efforts the blaze was still not under control by 3 a.m. Being fully aware of the danger to everyone on board and also to those in the near vicinity, the ship's commander, Captain Kinley, together with his crew and aided by personnel from the Auxiliary Fire Service (AFS), under the command of Officer John Lappin, continued in their endeavour to save the ship's dangerous cargo from exploding.

Oxy-acetylene equipment was called for, in the hope that a hole could be cut into the side of the ship so that she could be scuttled in an attempt to avert a catastrophic explosion. Their gallant efforts were, however, in vain—time had run out. The first massive explosion occurred before the equipment could be put to use. The whole of the munitions cargo then blew up in a series of huge explosions; an unfolding catastrophe that continued for almost three days. Some of the buckled plates from the ship were found almost 2½ miles away and one of her 4-ton anchors was located 100 yards from where the ship had been berthed. Resulting from the destruction caused by the explosions, there was much damage caused to many of the docks in the vicinity. Out of shear necessity, the clear up started almost straight away and, because of the magnitude of the devastation, it was considered necessary to bring in troops to help with the operation as well as the thousands of dock workers and other volunteers. Although the disaster had been the worst that Merseyside had suffered, miraculously only four people lost their lives; two of the men who had valiantly tried to scuttle the vessel when they became aware of the impending disaster, and a young, newly married couple who were returning home along the Dock Road, when part of one of the ship's plates landed on their car causing instant death.

The devastation and damage caused by the explosion resulted in major disruption to the workings of the docks—a total of sixty-nine berths out of 144 were temporarily decommissioned. Supply lines were also severely disrupted, with losses of ships and much-needed fuel and food. Huskisson Dock was completely wrecked and the falling debris caused damage to many nearby quayside sheds and buildings. There was also damage to the Overhead Railway, which ran very close to the dock. With so many docks effectively out of action, it took a colossal effort to clear the damage and bring the dock system back into normal working.

The speed at which the port recovered is testament to the heroic efforts made by all those involved, working day and night under extremely difficult circumstances. An indication of the speed of recovery can be gained by considering the volume of imports during the time immediately before and immediately after the *Malakand* disaster:

Week ending	Imports (tons)
19 April 1941	85,187
26 April 1941	181,562
3 May 1941	145,596
10 May1941	35,026
17 May 1941	85,678
24 May 1941	84,032
31 May 1941	93,285
7 June 1941	108,773
14 June 1941	126,936

The debris from the raids took some considerable time to completely clear. During that time, upwards of 200 lorries had to be used, many coming from as far as Derbyshire and Yorkshire. There were well over 1,000 men engaged in the operation.

The May Blitz on Liverpool had been Hitler's last ditch attempt to completely disable the port and hence cripple the effectiveness of the Atlantic convoys. The sustained bombardment failed, thanks largely due to the heroic efforts of many of Liverpool's men and women, who combined to thwart the onslaught. Following the Luftwaffe's failure, air attacks over Liverpool were scaled down, as Hitler's attention was now turning to the Invasion of Russia and all of the Luftwaffe's resources were needed in that theatre of war. Hitler's main objective in bombing Liverpool with such sustained intensity had been to ensure that this vital lifeline was, effectively, severed; that did not happen. The convoys continued to arrive and the port continued to receive, unload, and distribute vital supplies throughout the length and breadth of the country and beyond.

While the bombs were raining down over the docks and wreaking their havoc, especially during the May Blitz, a dedicated band of many volunteers were risking their lives to save the docks and the country it was serving—they were known, for obvious reasons, as suicide squads. The group was made up of people having various skills, all of whom were familiar with different aspects of dock and ship operation—merchant seamen, dock workers, firefighters, officers of the Home Guard, Royal Naval personnel, and others. When bombing raids were occurring, it was often necessary to move ships at short notice or to ensure that cargoes were removed into secure locations—it was in circumstances such as these that the suicide squads came into action. Their work was extremely hazardous, not only requiring much skill and expertise, but also much bravery—knowing the risks involved.

Although the Germans parachuted mines into the Mersey at the port approaches in an attempt to disrupt shipping, Liverpool still managed to accommodate and welcome more than 12,000 ships during the sixty-eight months of conflict, which translated into 75,150,100 tons of cargo passing through the port—56,494,800 tons of which were imported goods and provisions. The port also received 73,782 gliders and aircraft during the war. Also, upwards of 5,000,000 troops passed through the port, including 1,200,000 American troops.

The working of the port in a time of hostilities needed to be somewhat different from the normal practices and systems that operated in peacetime. Recognising this fact, the Committee of Imperial Defence set up the Port Emergency Committee in August 1936. In the event of war, this committee would have complete authority as to the strategic and day-to-day operation of the port and all that that role entailed. The committee's work began almost immediately, given the knowledge that, in all probability, shipping imports and exports would be transferred from ports on the east coast of England to ports on the west coast. Up until the outbreak of war, the committee had operated on an informal basis, but, on 23 August 1939, the Port Emergency Committee was formally appointed by the Minister of War

Transport and had authority to deal with the movement of ships in and out of the port and other associated functions. However, they could not override existing by-laws relating to the dock estate without first referring to the Minister for War Transport. The committee consisted of members from all interested parties, including members from the MDHB itself as the port authority; shipping interests, both coastal and international; and dock labour, both employers and employees. Also represented were warehousing, railway, and canal companies. Indeed, every interest pertaining to the efficient working of the docks was represented on the Emergency Committee. The committee's main functions were to determine port priorities with regards to berthing allocation, warehouse space, allocation of labour, etc., and also to establish port policy in general. The committee met on a regular basis throughout the war as it was of paramount importance that cargoes were discharged as soon as possible and were then distributed, rather than being stored in sheds or on the quayside, as had often happened during the First World War. A Regional Port Director was appointed who would take any major decisions on behalf of the Minister of War Transport when and where necessary. To say that the dock estate was a hive of activity during the war would be a gross understatement. The fact that upwards of 50,000 men were involved at any one time along the dockside gives some indication as to the magnitude of the tasks involved. Not only were ships being loaded and unloaded, their cargoes were then being distributed around the country or despatched to different theatres of war. There were also many men working on the dock estate who were engaged in ship repair.

Due to the imminent threat posed by fire from bombing raids, the board built a series of fifteen fire stations, strategically placed along the length of the dock estate and three more at the Birkenhead docks. In addition to this, thirteen fire boats were stationed at various points about the docks and many of the board's employees were trained in different aspects of civil defence work.

On 7 February 1941, the headquarters of the Western Approaches, which was the responsibility of Combined Operations, was transferred to Derby House in Liverpool. The Western Approaches Command had total responsibility for the safety of the entire convoy system of merchant vessels, all of which were protected by accompanying Royal Navy ships. The convoys normally sailed across the Atlantic from Canada and America into the Port of Liverpool. The command had initially been established at Plymouth, but as Liverpool was strategically in a better location, and as the Battle of the Atlantic increased in intensity, it was logical to transfer the nerve centre to Liverpool. Derby House, which was just behind the town hall, became the Area Combined Headquarters for the RAF and Royal Navy. It was from this base that all Atlantic operations were masterminded. The operations room, which was located in the building's basement, was both bombproof and gas proof, having 3-foot thick walls and a 7-foot thick ceiling. From this heavily guarded and secret location, spread over 100 rooms that covered an area of 50,000 square feet, the Royal Navy, Royal Air Force, and Royal Marines combined their collective knowledge, expertise, and resources to ultimately win the Battle of the Atlantic—the longest battle fought during the Second World War. As a precaution against bomb damage, a duplicate facility was built at Lord Derby's estate at Knowsley. One of the group's main roles was to monitor the movement of enemy submarines, known as 'wolf packs', which roamed throughout the Atlantic, hoping to attack convoys of vessels bringing much-needed supplies to Britain. Rather than attacking Royal Navy ships with any real conviction, Germany's strategy was to focus attention on Britain's merchant fleet, much of which used Liverpool as its home port. During the war, more than 2,000 merchant ships, both British and Allied vessels, were lost in the North Atlantic.

Just a few hundred yards away from Derby House, the Western Approaches Tactical Unit (WATU) had their headquarters at Exchange Buildings. It was from here that naval officers were trained in anti-U-boat tactics; training that helped to turn the Battle of the Atlantic in Britain's favour. It was essential that Britain not only survived during the Battle of the Atlantic, but was actually victorious; if Liverpool had not been able to receive the munitions and other supplies that were being sent to the port, then the invasion of Europe in 1944 could not have been mounted. As Britain's main convoy port, most of the country's wartime foodstuffs, munitions, fuel, and other materials necessary to sustain the war effort were imported through Liverpool. The port was able to maintain the vital link with Canada and America and thus help secure the ultimate Allied victory—literally becoming a lifeline during the wartime economy.

The convoy system, which had been instituted at an early stage during the war, proved very beneficial and many ships were shielded from enemy action. The system did, however, call for a high degree of resourcefulness from the harbour master, as upwards of sixty ships could at any one time be waiting to berth, discharge their cargoes, be repaired where necessary, and then return to convoy duties. A total of 1,285 convoys sailed into Liverpool during the war. The port accommodated, on average, three or four convoys every week. Due to the numbers involved, there was a very definite procedure that was meticulously followed. The Liverpool harbour master was in daily contact with the Shipping Diversion Room based in London. With many ships being diverted from London and the east coast ports, it was essential for the harbour master to be informed of vessel locations and cargoes. The problems faced and overcome were numerous, as ships carrying certain cargoes could only be berthed in particular docks. Consideration had also to be given to the large number of Royal Naval vessels that were berthed in the docks at any one time. There were always many ships in the docks in need of repair facilities, hence the pressures on the graving docks were another major consideration. A total of 5,513 vessels used the Liverpool graving docks during the war.

After the war ended, Admiral Sir Max Horton, who was the last of the three officers to hold the position of Commander-in-Chief for Western Approaches Command, was given the Freedom of the City of Liverpool. His leadership helped secure the final defeat of the U-boat threat.

In a time of war, many procedures have to be modified in light of circumstances. For instance, there was so much pressure to bring fuel into the country that fully laden oil tankers were often left in the middle of the river while waiting to discharge their cargo. This situation obviously posed a safety hazard. After some debate, a solution was found; pipes were taken along the river bed from Bromborough and then flexible piping was connected to the tankers in the middle of the river. This eased the problem of congestion and also placated safety officials. Another safety issue was the loading of live munitions directly onto the quayside. This was always carried out under strict supervision by armed forces, but remained a constant concern for safety officers.

It was perhaps understandable with so many vessels using the port that some would suffer damage or sinking due to either bombing or colliding with mines, many of which had been parachuted around the mouth of the Mersey, near to the Mersey Bar. Therefore, one of the major tasks facing the specialist teams was to salvage vessels that had been sunk in the docks and to clear channels for other vessels to enter and leave the port. One factor that undoubtedly helped in the in the continuing operation of the dock system was the robust construction of the docks that Jesse Hartley had built. The board's salvage service was devolved to its Marine Department, who attended to no fewer than 202 vessels, with a total tonnage of over half a million tons. One of the most important salvage operations that was undertaken was to attend the board's floating crane, *Mammoth*. The crane, which had a lifting capacity of 200 tons, had been damaged twice at the start of the war, but then in March 1941 she was bombed again, receiving two direct hits, which caused her to sink stern first. At the time, she was engaged in work on the West Float on the Birkenhead side of the Mersey and was one of the most important vessels operating in the dock estate and on the river. Being such a valued asset to the operation of the port, salvage work was immediately started, but it was some seventeen months later before the crane was able to go back into service. The operation of refloating and restoring the crane amounted to £21,500. One of the other floating cranes, *Hercules*, was also sunk after receiving a direct hit. Again, the crane was refloated and repaired, which cost both time and effort. Another of the board's floating cranes, *Samson*, was near to the *Malakand* when she was blown up. *Samson* received little damage, however, apart from a railway line from the Overhead Railway striking the crane, but this superficial damage was soon repaired.

The floating cranes were often deployed in offloading the many planes being shipped into Liverpool. However, as the numbers being imported increased, the cranes were unable to cope with the volume. A ferry steamer was equipped with special derricks that enabled the planes to be offloaded in mid-river. Later on, a second ferry was modified for this purpose. Additional tugs were also brought over from America as the number of ships coming into the port increased by the day.

Innovation and adaption to changing circumstances were key factors in the wartime success of the port. As enemy bombers inflicted more destruction and

1 Built between 1847 and 1848 to celebrate the opening of Salisbury Dock, the Victoria Tower (designed by Jesse Hartley) was colloquially known as the Dockers' clock. The tower was constructed from Kirkcudbright granite and, since 1975, has been designated as a Grade II listed building.

2 Port of Liverpool Building; for many years, this building was the home of the Mersey Docks and Harbour Board.

3 The *Stena Lagan* leaving Birkenhead, bound for her home port of Belfast.

4 The 29,735-gross-ton oil-products tanker *Excelsior Bay* unloading cargo at Tranmere Oil terminal on 12 August 2015. The coastal tanker *Stott Puffin* can be seen in the foreground on her way to Eastham.

5 The cruise liner *Mein Schiff 1* berthed at Liverpool's landing stage on Saturday 25 July 2015. The liner, built in 1996 and refitted in 2009, is operated by TUI Cruises.

6 With the assistance of painters from Cammell Lairds, the artist Carlos Cruz-Diez created a dazzle ship using the *Edmund Gardner* pilot ship berthed in Canning Graving Dock. The work's title is 'Cromatique à Double Fréquence pour l'*Edmund Gardner* Ship/Liverpool. Paris 2014'.

7 Now a major tourist attraction. Looking towards the city centre through Jesse Hartley's iconic gable arch at what was the vehicular entrance to Salthouse Dock.

8 Albert Dock, opened in 1845, one of Jesse Hartley's many iconic docks at Liverpool.

9 Salthouse Dock is now the Liverpool terminal of the Leeds and Liverpool Canal.

10 Seen leaving the Mersey, the trailing suction hopper dredger UKD *Orca*. The dredger, built in 2010 and owned by UK Dredging, is fitted with twin suction pipes, which makes it ideal for maintenance dredging.

11 One of the speedy pilot cutters returning to port.

12 The New Brighton lighthouse stands next to Perch Rock. It was first lit in 1830 and was finally deactivated in 1973.

13 Quayside cranes at the Royal Seaforth Container Terminal.

14 The *Sea Jack* or the *Jumping Jack* as some prefer to call it is owned and operated by A2Sea AS. The vessel, which sails under the Danish flag, was built in 2003 and is classed as a self-elevating platform. It is currently helping to build the new sea wall for Liverpool2.

15 Liverpool has been exporting huge quantities of scrap metal since 1982.

16 The 2,967-gross-ton Netherlands-registered MV *Moseldijk* discharging cargo at West Float, Birkenhead.

17 HSC *Manannan* at Liverpool landing stage. Built in 1998 and now owned and operated by the Isle of Man Steam Packet Company, the HSC *Manannan* made her maiden voyage in company colours on 11 May 2009 from Douglas to Liverpool.

18 Looking towards the old Customs House and the Pumphouse.

19 Built at Cammell Lairds, MV *Royal Daffodil* was withdrawn from regular service in December 2012 and returned to the ferries berth at East Float, Birkenhead.

20 Currently laid up in West Float Birkenhead, the Royal Fleet Auxiliary Service support tanker RFA *Orangeleaf*.

21 RMS *Queen Elizabeth* shown against a backdrop of Liverpool's Anglican Cathedral, 25 May 2015. (*Courtesy of Martin Unwin*)

22 The 'Three Queens' visited Liverpool on 25 May 2015 to celebrate the 175th anniversary of Cunard and its association with Liverpool. (*Courtesy of Martin Unwin*)

23 RFA *Wave Knight* in Cammell Lairds shipyard, undergoing routine maintenance on 12 August 2015.

24 The iconic Liverpool waterfront, showing the 'Three Graces', the Liver Building, the Cunard Building, and the Port of Liverpool Building. (*Courtesy of Martin Unwin*)

25 Henry Tate first established his sugar refinery in Liverpool in 1872. In 1955, construction work started on Tate & Lyle's concrete sugar silo.

26 The Waterloo Corn Warehouse, a Grade II listed building, dates back to 1868, when there were three warehouses on the site. The north block was destroyed during the May Blitz in 1941 and the west warehouse was demolished in 1969. The remaining building has now been converted into a number of luxury apartments.

27 The Liverpool Marina has berths in both the Brunswick Dock and the Coburg Dock.

28 The tugs *Smit Sandon* and *Zeebrugge* seen here in Sandon Dock on 12 August 2015.

29 An image of the ever-changing mountains of scrap metal being exported to destinations around the world.

devastation to the port, it was decided that, in order to minimise the risk of imported cargoes being damaged or lost, as soon as cargoes were unloaded they should be immediately transported to warehouses some distance from the docks, where they would be stored and sorted for onward despatch. A 97-acre depot, with four large storage sheds, was established at Kirby, some 11 miles inland from the dock estate. The work on building the facility started in September 1941 and was fully operational just twelve months later—a remarkable achievement. During its four years of operation, over half a million tons of goods passed through the depot.

Many children were evacuated from Liverpool, both as part of official and private schemes, going mainly to Canada and America. The liners that transported these children normally carried less than 300 passengers, but, in war-torn Britain, the passenger totals often exceeded 2,000 on some of these ships. Coming in the other direction, from 1942 onwards, American troops began to arrive at the port and were transported from Riverside Station, the branch station that adjoined Liverpool's landing stage. On many occasions, with trains leaving every hour, it was not unusual for upwards of thirty trains to depart.

Almost inevitably, during the whole of the war, the costs of maintaining the port in a viable working condition meant that there needed to be a significant rise in port dues. Dues were increased by some 60 per cent and this figure proved to be sufficient for the remainder of the war, but financial management was difficult during the war years due to the unpredictable nature of damage to both docks and warehouse facilities. The board did, however, receive permission from the Capital Issues Committee to renew and replace bonds, which, by 1945, enabled it to proceed with the new northern entrance to the Langton Dock system.

As D-Day approached, a large amount of munitions and other necessary stores were delivered to the port, ultimately to be loaded and conveyed to the Normandy beaches. It was imperative during this time, as indeed it was throughout the whole period of the war, that the dock quays were not cluttered with imported cargo. In that respect, much planning was the key to success and the board's traffic department successfully managed this aspect of the port's role.

The last of the air raids on Liverpool occurred in 1942, but it was not until many years later that the Liverpool cityscape and many of its buildings were restored. The city's ship-owners also suffered economically, with over 3,000,000 tons of Liverpool shipping being lost during the conflict.

Towards the end of the war, there were many heart-rending scenes played out at the landing stage, as troops were repatriated from prisoner of war camps in Germany and Japan. In October 1943, 800 wounded officers and men—the first to be repatriated—sailed into Liverpool on the *Atlantis*. As the ship tied up at the landing stage, it was given the traditional Liverpool welcome, with every vessel on the Mersey sounding its siren in salute.

Before leaving the role that the port played in the Second World War, mention must be made of a naval commander, Captain Frederic John Walker CB DSO and three bars. In the spring of 1942, Captain Walker was given command of the

Second Support Group; the striking force's role, which operated outside of normal escort duties, was to seek out and destroy enemy U-boats. Under his command were HMS *Woodpecker*, HMS *Cygnet*, HMS *Wild Goose*, HMS *Kite*, HMS *Wren*, and HMS *Starling* (his own sloop). They sailed out of Gladstone Dock, as did the Navy's minesweepers and Atlantic escort fleet. It is a matter of record that on many of his patrols Captain Walker and his flotilla were responsible for sinking large numbers of U-boats. Sadly, and mainly due to overwork and battle fatigue, Captain Walker died on 9 July 1944 and was buried at sea. Some very fitting words were spoken at the service that preceded his burial: 'Not dust, nor the light weight of a stone, but all the sea of the Western Approaches shall be his tomb'.

Immediately after the cessation of hostilities, the board was seeking to increase dues, but the situation was compromised by a dock strike that occurred at the end of 1945. The other major factor that needed to be taken into consideration was the settlement of the claims associated with war damage. Discussions in this area were protracted, mainly because of the sheer magnitude of the amount of financial restitution involved. Agreement was eventually reached in 1948 and the final payment, which amounted to almost £11 million, was made in June 1949. In actual fact, much of the reconstruction and renovation work did not begin until the 1950s and even then there was much dislocation in and around the dock estate, with many berths still being out of commission and reconstruction and repair work being extremely slow because of a shortage of skilled labour. Matters were not helped by three disastrous fires that occurred on the dock estate; the first being in 1945, when much cargo (which had been stored in sheds adjacent to Gladstone south dock No. 2) caught fire, and then in August, the following year, sheds were completely destroyed in Canada south dock No. 3. Finally, and perhaps most disastrously, the sinking on 25 January 1953 of the Canadian Pacific Steamship's liner *Empress of Canada* due to fire, when she was berthed on the north side of Gladstone branch dock No. 1. The fire occurred when the ship was being refurbished to take dignitaries from Canada across to England for the coronation of Queen Elizabeth II.

The enormity of the reconstruction necessary to the docks was difficult to envisage and was not helped by lethargy of central government. Trade pressures also played a part, as did the fires already made reference to. The new Langton Dock entrances were one of the new major works that had been sanctioned, but there was much preliminary work to be completed before work on the entrance itself could be started. There had been much war damage to the Gladstone-Hornby Dock and this had to be completed before the Langton entrances could be started. The Waterloo entrance also needed to be completed and there was remedial work necessary to the gates at Sandon Dock. The Langton–Canada Improvement Scheme was started in 1949 and encompassed the new river entrance at Langton; the widening of the Canada–Brocklebank passage and further work on the old Canada entrance and the Canada Basin. The work was of such magnitude that it was not completed until 1962. There was also much activity on the Birkenhead side of the river, with Vittoria Dock being extended at its western end, thus providing improved facilities for ships trading in the Far East. Also, because of the changing nature of materials being imported, Bidston Dock was converted to an iron-ore berth, and more sheds were erected to cater for the needs of the improving export market to the East and to Africa.

Although, in purely physical terms, the dock estate had been restored to its former state, there was still significant dislocation in trade through the port. Immediately before the war, in 1939, more than almost 22,000,000 tons of cargo had entered the port, but, with the exception of 1945, it was not until after 1953 that there would be any marked growth in trade.

9

Looking to the Future

After the war, there was little doubt that the work of rebuilding the port and redeveloping the port's shipping fleets and trade would be immense, but, looking back over the chequered history of the port, right from the beginning of the fourteenth century to the start of the twentieth century it is interesting to note that, after significant changes, not only the volume of trade increased, but also the composition of the cargoes changed over time to meet the changing needs of the market. Historically, two of the most important commodities, as far as the Port of Liverpool was concerned, during the whole of that period were the importation of sugar and tobacco. Almost without exception, the increase in the importation of sugar since the sixteenth century had, on average, been 2.9 per cent *per annum*, while the corresponding figure for tobacco was 1.6 per cent *per annum*. Raw cotton imports also increased for a while, from 1770 to 1850, but then dropped off, right up to the start of the twentieth century. Supply was greater than the demand at the time; also, there was a cotton famine during the 1860s and then, to cap it all, there was the opening of the Manchester Ship Canal, which gave cotton merchants direct access to their raw materials. The diminution of trade passing through the port after 1850 can, in part, be accounted for by the changing demand for cotton and also the obvious advantages of unloading at a more accessible port—Manchester. It was after this time that there was significant diversification in the composition of commodities entering the port. Cocoa imports dramatically rose between 1785 and 1810, 13.5 per cent *per annum*, coffee and rum imports also showed some increase during the same period, 5.2 per cent *per annum* and 2.3 per cent *per annum* respectively; however, it was cereal imports, mainly from America, that illustrated the changing nature of the raw materials being imported through Liverpool, with wheat, barley, and oats all showing increases.

Turning to the composition of exports from Liverpool, before the impact of the Industrial Revolution, the main exports from the port were coal and salt, but, with the coming of the Industrial Revolution, more and more manufactured goods were being exported through the port. Cotton piece-goods accounted for 40 per cent *per annum* of Liverpool's exports from 1840 right up until the beginning of the twentieth century, when exports to India declined. In the wake of this shifting demand, a changing pattern began to emerge, with increases in the exportation of chemicals, road vehicles, manufacturing machinery, and other metal products.

If consideration is now given to the tonnage entering the port, it is clear that between the years 1716 and 1744, although there was some growth in tonnage, it was relatively modest at 0.7 per cent *per annum*; however, then there was a marked increase in tonnage between the years 1744 and 1851, when growth in tonnage increased by almost 5 per cent annually. It was during this period that trade with India was opened up to Liverpool shipping, and later, in 1833, trading links were forged with China and the Far East. As has already been seen, it was also during this period that Liverpool's road, rail, and canal networks were improved, thus ensuring a better supply of goods both to and from the port. However, with the coming of more steamships after the 1850s, and the frequency and reduced voyage times of cargo liners, the rate of growth fell away. This was due to a number of factors, not least of which was competition from other ports, both in Britain and also on the continent of Europe. It could be argued that, until the outbreak of the First World War, Liverpool's position as a major trading port had remained unassailable.

There is a marked contrast in the port's fortunes after the Second World War. Immediately after the end of the war, there was some growth in trade (5.4 per cent *per annum*), mainly due to the post-war recovery, but the increase in trade came to an end in 1955, with growth between 1955 and 1963 being a very much more modest 2 per cent *per annum*.

Another indicator as to the development of the port can be gauged by the amount of capital being expended in order to improve the port's competitiveness, both in terms of new docks being built and also in the number of quayside transit sheds that were being erected.

Between the years 1860 and 1909, the amount of investment expended on the port was considerably more than the pressure on demand for dock space. Although tonnage through the port during this period increased by some three-fold, capital expenditure showed a four-fold increase. However, just because there was a marked rise in capital expenditure does not mean that there was a corresponding rise in dock space; in fact, it was quite the contrary. During Jesse Hartley's time as dock engineer, the general design and construction of docks and associated dock facilities was far less complex, as most of the docks that he designed and built were for sailing ships, but, with the introduction of steam vessels and later motor ships, dock installations and berthing facilities needed, of necessity, to be more complex; thus, increasing unit costs. There was a degree of vision shown by the collective efforts of the Mersey Docks and Harbour Board, in that between the years 1858 and 1914, the board raised £31.5 million in anticipation of any future expansion in the dock estate.

It was undoubtedly the case, whether deserved or not, that industrial relations on the dock estate were tarnishing the image of the Port of Liverpool and also affecting its economic viability, with more shipping companies transferring their business to other, more competitive ports such as Rotterdam and Antwerp. One conclusion that was generally agreed was that, if the port was to remain in competition with other ports, then cargo handling needed to be much more efficient; this, in turn, meant new methods of handling being brought into the port and by implication, a reduced workforce. One of the newer handling technologies being considered was the introduction of containerisation to the port, whereby a small number of operators could unload a large number of containers using a computer-controlled automated system. After a lengthy gestation period, it was decided to opt for a purpose-built dock north of Gladstone Dock.

However, the resolution of the current issues were, to some extent, outside the control of the port authority due to a number of factors. As had always been the case, there was the question of the geographical position of the port and where the cargoes were coming from and going to. The question as to whether ships were destined for continental Europe as well as Britain had to be taken into consideration; ships bound for Europe would tend not to stop at docks in the Mersey. However, Liverpool would be ideally placed when considering trade with North America. A critical consideration was the question of land transportation and communication. Motorways and a second Mersey tunnel were under active consideration, but the question remained as to whether these infrastructure improvements would be adequate to cope with the anticipated changes. Finally, there was the overarching question as to whether the cost structure in the newly emerging port, as it related to the effectiveness of the local government authority to institute, regulate, and control services, would be adequate to deliver a profitable operation. There was another factor that was sometimes overlooked, and that was the difference between the driving forces within the port as it was in the late nineteenth century and the difference in the port's development in the post-war period. Formerly, it had been the merchants and ship-owners (Liverpool families such as the Rathbones, Booths, Holts, and Harrisons), based in Liverpool, who had the interests of their Liverpool-based companies and, by association, the interests of the port and the town itself at heart; whereas, in the twentieth century, the structure of shipping companies and industry in the environs of Liverpool, more often than not, had their headquarters based in other centres such as London with some being global corporations. It often appeared that the impetus to drive the dock estate forward was almost becoming of secondary importance. It was undoubtedly a period of transition, with different consortia aiming to secure the optimum bases for their trade. For instance, the Far Eastern container trade had moved its operational base from Liverpool to Southampton and others were to follow. Also, with the development of larger, specialised air freighters, a number of companies moved some high value cargoes to this form of transport, although the amount was relatively small in volume terms.

It was becoming obvious that the recovery in the port's trade might take some considerable time, as, not only was there need for much remedial work on the port estate itself, the shipping companies who used the port also had to recover from the ravages of war. Many Liverpool shipping companies, including Holts, Harrisons, and Elder Dempsters, had lost significant tonnage and it would clearly take time to replace their depleted fleets and for lost markets to be re-established. As in previous times, Liverpool countered the change by searching for and finding different markets. With increasing imports of crude oil, the MDHB constructed an oil jetty at Dingle, towards the southern end of the dock estate. A number of storage tanks were also built nearby. However, the development was soon to become overwhelmed by further increases in imports and two, much larger, jetties were constructed on the Birkenhead side of the river. The terminal, known as the Tranmere Oil Terminal, came on-line in 1960, having been under construction since 1958. The facility handled almost 6 million tons of crude oil in its first year of operation. Similarly, when the iron-ore berth at Bidston Dock opened, the first full year of operation, 1961, saw almost 1.5 million tons being landed at the dock. Most of the iron ore landed at Bidston was directly transported to the John Summers works at Shotton.

In 1964, Rendel, Palmer & Tritton, a firm of consulting engineers, were commissioned to undertake a feasibility study looking into the possibility of making extensions to the dock estate. The study was carried out working in conjunction with the MDHB's Engineer in Chief. In 1965, the board also authorised a survey, which would examine the economic factors that needed to be taken into account if a new dock was to be built. Central government approved the board's plans in 1967. The work, which was being conducted on the feasibility study, also happened to unfortunately coincide with labour disputes on the docks, which led to a number of strikes and unofficial stoppages. As a consequence of this disruption, many shipping companies diverted cargoes bound for Liverpool to other ports. Initially this was seen as a temporary expedient, but, as labour relations did not improve to any marked degree, what had been a temporary measure became more permanent, with other ports demonstrating better labour relations and a more stable workforce. These companies, many of which had trading links going back a long way with the port, never returned to Liverpool.

Following the criticism that many British ports, including Liverpool, had been subjected to after the war, the Rochdale Committee was convened to look into the state of British ports. Many factors had influenced the commissioning of the Rochdale Committee, not least of which was the fact that a number of continental ports such as Rotterdam and Hamburg had already made huge investments in rebuilding their war-damaged docks, and, perhaps of more concern, these new docks were now attracting some of the cargoes that traditionally passed through British ports. In addition to the vast resources that were being expended upon of these continental ports, there was also another major factor that improved their competitiveness—the geographical difference between these ports and the predominantly estuary located British ports. Many of the continental ports were much more accessible to shipping. One way or another, it was clear that some action was needed if British ports were not to become totally redundant. The Rochdale Report included a number of general statements that were applicable to most ports:

> Ports should be regarded as commercial undertakings. The present financial condition of the major ports is generally unsatisfactory and a comprehensive overhaul of their financial and accounting arrangements is needed.

Another of the report's definitive statements suggested:

> Government financial assistance for ports would not in general be desirable though there may be cases where Government loans, at normal interest rates, would be justified and a very limited number of cases where entirely exceptional circumstances would justify Government grants.

The report also focused on the question of de-casualisation, and, when considering the question of the control of port development, recommended that a National Ports Authority should be established. Resulting from the Rochdale Report, the Harbours Act of 1964 passed through parliament, but the National Ports Authority was transmogrified into the National Ports Council by the Minister of Transport and would only function in a purely advisory capacity. The main role of the council was to develop a centralised organisation that would collect and disseminate information and good practice relating to port working and development. Although Rochdale had advocated decasualisation of labour in the docks, this recommendation had not been implemented. The only positive outcome in that regard being a further inquiry into dock labour, which resulted in the Devlin Report being published. The main recommendation of that report was to reinforce the stance taken by Rochdale—the decasualisation of labour. The introduction of decasualisation on the dock estate came about in September 1967, when decasualisation was achieved and men no longer had to suffer the indignity of waiting at the hiring stand to offer their labour; however, this did not occur before there had been a six-week national strike regarding the terms of its implementation. With the increasing volume of trade passing through the port, the dock labour force was reaching a total of almost 14,000 workers, all of whom now worked for the National Dock Labour Board. The new terms of employment also brought a number of improvements to the men's working conditions, as had been recommended in the report. One of the most sought-after improvements was the provision of washrooms with hot and cold running water.

As a direct response to the report, the Mersey Docks and Harbour Board established a Cargo Handling Division, based at West Langton Dock, and companies whose vessels used the port on a regular basis were allocated specific docks in which to discharge and load their cargoes.

Trade through the port totalled almost 30 million tons during 1966, which represented an increase of almost 5 per cent over the previous year and in excess of 18 per cent higher when compared with 1964. Perhaps the trade might have been somewhat higher than this, had it not been for the National Seamen's dispute that year and also the fact that there were some government restrictions placed upon imports during that period. However, even though trade was increasing, it was a fast-changing market at that time; a concept that the Mersey Docks and Harbour Board recognised. The board took the view that it was critical to join the growing group of ports that were moving towards the container trade. A bill was passed through parliament that sanctioned the work being proposed for the Seaforth Container Dock. Accepting the urgency of converting to containerisation, Gladstone Container Berth was used a temporary expedient until the Royal Seaforth Dock was brought into commission. The company, realising that the market was changing very rapidly, also converted Gladstone Graving Dock into a wet dock for additional container traffic and developed a container berth at Hornby Dock. A number of other changes were being made along the dock estate, all of which were designed to aid the operational efficiency of the port and thus maintain its competitive edge. A specialist refrigerated transit shed was being built at North Alexandra Dock No. 2 and, in south dock system, new transit sheds were being built at East Harrington Dock, King's Dock, and Queen's Dock. South Vittoria Dock on the Birkenhead side was also being modernised for the Ocean Fleets group. Over at North Canada Dock No. 3, a new timber berth was being developed, which boasted four 10-ton quayside cranes. With the links between the mainland of England and Northern Ireland being strengthened, a Ro-Ro berth was being constructed for crossings to Belfast at South West Princes Dock. As ship sizes increased, river channel depths were increased to accommodate oil tankers that were now using the port more frequently, and the bar channel itself was realigned.

In the emerging post-war economy, ease of communication and transportation were becoming key factors in sustained profitability. Most of the dock estate, on both sides of the river, was well-served with a number of goods yards, so, once cargo had been transferred from the quayside to the depots, it could be despatched to destinations around the country. As time issues were also becoming more critical, the MDHB opened a Port Information Centre, with the specific objective of ensuring that haulage companies were made aware of any delays on the dock, thus helping to alleviate any unnecessary waiting time and congestion.

As methods of cargo handling changed and improved, palletisation became widely used as it improved cargo loading and unloading and also reduced the risk of damage to cargo. To facilitate this revolutionary approach to cargo handling, many docks, such as West Langton Dock, now had wider quays between the transit sheds and the ships themselves.

The wider quays were now well-equipped with modern roof rail-mounted quayside cranes, used for unloading and loading cargo directly into ships' holds. Most of these cranes were capable of lifting up to 4 or 5 tons, but, should there be

A photograph of the fire at Gladstone Dock in 1949 that caused much damage and disruption to the docks for many months.

The *Reina del Mar*, the flagship of the Pacific Steam Navigation Company for many years.

Since the new Canal Link was formally opened on 25 March 2009, narrow boats now have access to many of Liverpool's south docks.

a need for greater capacity, there was available a number of floating cranes, owned by the MDHB, which had lifting capacities ranging from 25 tons up to 200 tons.

It was now becoming self-evident that the southern docks, a dock expanse roughly stretching from the Pier Head to the Herculaneum Dock at the southern extremity, were not fit for purpose, with a number of companies, such as Elder Dempster Lines, relocating to the northern dock system. B&I Line, who operated a car ferry service between Liverpool and Dublin from Carriers Dock, also relocated to Waterloo Dock. In general, larger operators tended to use Gladstone Dock, whereas smaller carriers, such as Ellerman Line, normally used North Hornby Dock. The MDHB was faced with the problem of having to find buyers for the redundant dock area, in order to mitigate the financial burden that would have to be carried because of the development plans at Seaforth. The original plans for Seaforth made provision for improved access to the river. However, because of the prohibitive costs involved, the plans were modified and the Gladstone Lock was used to serve as the entrance to the new Seaforth Dock. There were other benefits, apart from the obvious savings in construction costs; the completion date for the scheme was brought forward and, without the new river access, there was increased tonnage capacity available in the dock. When work on the Langton–Canada Improvement Scheme was completed—the biggest dock improvement scheme in post-war Britain—it was officially opened on 14 December 1962 by Queen Elizabeth II.

Many of the new transit sheds being built, such as those in Canada Dock and Huskisson Dock, were two-storey, but some docks retained the single-storey buildings. The newly refurbished Canada Dock now had a number of transit sheds in its three branch docks, and, although the dock was still being used to load and unload general cargo, it was now being used, to an increasing extent, for the importation of timber. T&J Harrison also used Canada Dock as a main base, taking cargoes to and from the West Indies and South and East Africa.

The Gladstone Container Terminal was opened in 1968, and was operated on a strictly cash-limited budget. Containers were packed and unpacked some distance away from the terminal at East Hornby Dock. Containers were handled by Lancer Boss side loaders and Clark straddle carriers. After a faltering start, business began to pick up in the following year. To accommodate the new trade, the MDHB invested in two ship-to-shore container cranes and augmented the fleet of straddle carriers.

It was also at this point that many of the world's major shipping lines were ready to transfer their cargo handling methods to the potentially more efficient container approach to shipping, and embrace this new and more profitable system of cargo transportation and handling.

The two main consortia that were then operating were Overseas Containers and Associated Container Transportation. The Ocean Group was a member of Overseas Containers Limited, whereas Harrisons was a member of Associated Container Transportation. A clause in the consortia agreements stipulated that, when any cargo was being transported in containers, the control of the cargo passed from the responsibility of the individual shipping company to that of the consortium. Sir John Nicholson, chairman of Ocean Group, was quick to observe that, should any mishap befall the containers during the land transportation of the cargo, then the whole operation could become unviable; due emphasis was therefore placed on this aspect of the operation. At the time, the Ocean Group, which had over 100 ships, operated container services to Australia and the Far East. Nicholson was proud to declare:

> I would think that during the next decade, containers look like being the most economic vehicle for the vast majority of manufactured goods. However, it is a precision operation which depends on the ability to rely on precise port operations not yet found in the less developed parts of the world. I do not think that it will extend in a hurry to Africa or, for the same reason, to parts of Asia.

Companies like Cunard Lines were in the container consortium Atlantic Container Lines (ACL), together with other companies such as the Holland America Line, Wallenius Lines, and the French line CGT. The consortium operated a number of new Ro-Ro container ships and Cunard's second generation container ship, *Atlantic Conveyor*. Other consortia were formed such as Johnson Scan Star, which included Blue Star Line and the Johnson Line of Sweden. The Head Donaldson Line was in partnership with Canadian Pacific, who operated a joint container service between Gladstone Dock and Canada. United States Lines used a number of converted general cargo ships for a little while until new specialised container ships could be brought into service.

Towards the end of the 1960s, given the turbulent rate of change that was now being experienced on the dock estate, a number of other, separate, but related issues were affecting the port's operations, and the future viability of the port itself was beginning to be questioned. By 1965, Liverpool's share of the import and export trade in the United Kingdom had fallen to an all-time low of 18.3 per cent, with 16.2 per cent of the imports and 20.7 per cent of the exports passing through the port. Other ports, both at home and in Europe, had better cost structures and more efficient systems of cargo handling. Due to the influx of more container ships to the port, and the all-important need for those vessels to be in port for the shortest time possible, it became the rule rather than the exception that work on container vessels necessitated a twenty-four-hour operation; this in itself caused a number of labour relations difficulties. However, on the positive side of the balance sheet, many initiatives had been taken to change the industrial base of Merseyside, chief of which was the new car manufacturing factories that had been established on Merseyside. The Ford factory, based at Halewood, was gaining more export orders; the graving docks at Langton Dock were filled in to create a marshalling yard; and an export car compound was built in the North Mersey Goods Yard. The cars were then transferred to the transatlantic carriers. Fiat was also importing large numbers of cars from Italy through Seaforth terminal's S6 berth. Then, in 1969, after a problem with lock gates on the Manchester Ship Canal, Manchester Liners transferred their operations to Liverpool, albeit on a temporary basis. The dock estate was now experiencing a much-needed transformation.

By now, other ports were beginning to become established in the fast developing container market, adapting their port facilities with specialised container handling equipment. London consortiums were seen to be taking the lead in this respect, but Southampton and Felixstowe both had vibrant container facilities. Towards the end of the 1960s and the beginning of the 1970s, the market was fast moving away from Liverpool. The port was faced with a financial crisis and came very near to complete closure. The world of shipping was changing radically, and the blunt fact of the matter was that the MDHB was not keeping abreast of the changes in technology and methods of working. Significant debts were being incurred and the Mersey Docks and Harbour Board was forced into liquidation. The Conservative Government of the period, under the leadership of Ted Heath, decided that, strategically, the Port of Liverpool was too important to be allowed to lose its place in the nation's economy. A bill was brought before parliament that altered the nature and constitution of the Port Authority, making it a statuary company. The Mersey Docks and Harbour Act was passed in 1971. The effect of the act was to dissolve the former Mersey Docks and Harbour Board and create The Mersey Docks and Harbour Company (MDHC). With a completely different constitution from the former Mersey Docks and Harbour Board, the MDHC held its first board meeting early in August 1971. Following a number of personnel changes at senior level and an apparent improvement in labour relations, the company actually turned a profit in its first year of operation. It was also during that year that the first ship to enter the Seaforth terminal unloaded its cargo. However, the port had not shed its difficulties with its labour force and on this occasion the issues were completely out of the hands of the company; the Industrial Relations Act was passed by the Conservative Government. The act made it mandatory to hold strike ballots before any strike could become official. There were also clauses in the bill that required a cooling-off period before strike action could be taken, and there were to be tighter controls on union membership. The act was repealed on 16 October 1992.

The strikes that followed as a direct result of the introduction of the act spread throughout the country, but they were particularly harmful to the port's economy and recovery. The national dock strike started towards the end of July and lasted most of the way through August. The port was also beset with disputes over pay and conditions at the grain terminal and the container berths, and, to make matters worse, other ports such as Port Talbot in South Wales could already accommodate bulk carriers up to 100,000 tons, whereas Seaforth's maximum tonnage was a mere 75,000 tons. This coupled with the inexorable increase in size of these bulk carriers—ships of over 300,000 tons were already being built—meant that, once again, the Port of Liverpool was operating at a distinct disadvantage. Faced with a continuing decline in trade and a history of poor labour relations, it was easy to understand why the company was returning operating losses. The port went into a prolonged period where cutbacks became the inevitable outcome. The newly formed company, through making these cost saving cutbacks, were to eventually move into a modest profit and, recognising that future prosperity of the port might be aided by a programme of diversification, expanded into a raft of new developments, many of which were not shipping related. It was also recognised by the company that, if progress was to be made in rebuilding trade, trust, and profit, radical changes would have to be made. It was at this point that the company brought in outside management consultants to give a lead as to where those changes would have to be made. The consultants' report recommended that the company should be reorganised into five operational divisions. The recommendations were accepted by the board and five divisional directors were appointed: Director of Port Services, Personnel Director, Operations Director, Personnel Director, and Commercial Director. The new organisational structure did not, however, solve the company's difficulties. One of the unforeseen outcomes of the appointments was that yet another layer of bureaucratic management was imposed upon the company, which in itself led to sluggish responses in management decision making and this during a period of fast changing developments in the shipping industry. However, by the beginning of the 1980s, much of this bureaucratic machinery had been shed and a new management team had been appointed; the majority of the new managers were conversant with the docks and the port's labour force.

The embryonic Seaforth Container Port began to take form. Being built north of Gladstone Dock, the new area would have deeper docks and much longer berths to accommodate the larger ships that were now being built. The quayside areas were built with far more space than previously, as the whole concept of container berths and handling was very different from early methods of discharging cargo. The grain terminal, which was designed as an integral part of the container port complex, had specially built sheds for handling bulk grain and could accommodate bulk carriers of up to 75,000 tons deadweight. There was also incorporated into the design a mechanical system, whereby grain could be discharged directly into adjacent silos. Provision was also made for discharging grain into barges if required, with an inlet dock that could receive vessels of up to 10,000 tons deadweight. Three mills were now being served by the grain terminal on the Liverpool side of the river and other, smaller mills, were using Birkenhead's East Float. Kellogg's had opened their Seaforth mill in 1973 and the terminal was also used by Allied Mills and Cargill. The terminal also had specialised handling equipment for perishable cargoes, with the S2 berth in the dock being specially equipped for the handling of refrigerated cargoes. On 6 December 1971, the *Tasmania Star*, a refrigerated general cargo ship owned by Blue Star Line became the first vessel to sail through Gladstone Lock to discharge refrigerated cargo.

With the opening of the new container terminal, which had access via an entrance that had been cut through the north wall of Gladstone Dock, both the Gladstone Container Terminal and also the Hornby Container Terminal were closed and the business transferred to the new facility. New container cranes were built for berths S3, S4, and S5, and the two container cranes from the Gladstone Terminal were also taken to the new S5 berth.

It was a measure of the terminal's success that, even before completion, most of the berths had been allocated. S7 was to be used by West Coast Stevedoring, which served ports in South America, whereas S8 and S9 were forest products terminals managed by the MDHC. Indeed, the opening of the new Royal Seaforth Dock in July 1973 by the Princess Royal marked a new chapter in the development of the port. The new facility was now able to accommodate much larger ships and the highly specialised container ships. The dock also had facilities for handling bulk carriers. The Port of Liverpool was undergoing a renaissance, acknowledging that cargo handling was changing, as was sea transport and also cargo transport on land. Turnaround times in port were now much quicker.

Over in the docks on the Birkenhead side of the river, the new company resourced the modernisation of a number of general cargo berths. A group of transit sheds and offices were built for Ocean Group at their base at Vittoria Dock. Clan Line also had warehouses and offices built for them on the opposite side of the dock. However, in general, the port was undergoing a prolonged period of unrest within its labour force. A demarcation dispute between different branches of the Transport and General Workers Union (TGWU) meant that the newly completed grain terminal was, as yet, unable to unload cargo. Also, the benefits of being a member of the EEC were not as apparent in Liverpool as they were in other ports. Although there was a marked increase in imports of grain, many of the cargoes were destined for east coast ports.

With the continuing unrest in the port, the economic pressures were being felt by many of the stevedoring companies, prompting the MDHC to take under its wing some of the remaining stevedoring companies, including A. E. Smith Coggins, Ocean Port Services, and the Port of Liverpool Stevedoring. There were still a number of stevedoring companies on the dock estate, but there were only three major players: Harrison Line, the West Coast Stevedoring Company, and Liverpool Maritime Terminals.

As there had been considerable changes in shipping operations and ships themselves since most of the docks had been built, it was evident that many of the docks—particularly the southern docks—were past their sell-by date and fast becoming unfit for purpose. The Mersey Docks & Harbour Company had responded by creating the Royal Seaforth Dock, but it was evident that further fundamental decisions would have to be made by the company if the docks' market share was to be maintained. The South Docks System was finally closed in 1972–1973, and companies using those docks were given alternative berths in the northern system. The main arguments for closure being that the cost of dredging in order to maintain the channels to the dock entrances was too high; general cargo liners could be berthed in other, more northerly, docks within the estate; and finally, the overheads and general operating costs were becoming prohibitive. As the south docks at Liverpool and an area of the Birkenhead docks were no longer used for shipping, ownership and management responsibility was transferred to the Merseyside Development Corporation in 1980 as a result of direct government intervention. Under the general direction of the corporation, many of the redundant docks were drained, cleaned, and refilled. Albert Dock, one of Hartley's many masterpieces, has been transformed into a shopping and restaurant complex. The complex also has a television studio, many apartments, and is the home of the Tate Gallery in Liverpool. The Merseyside Maritime Museum has also relocated to a site near to Canning Dock. The Mersey Docks and Harbour Company, working in conjunction with the David Maclean Group, was redeveloping an area around Prince's Dock; this development area would include a number of luxury apartments, a hotel, and office accommodation. Similar plans were scheduled for the warehouse buildings at Wapping Dock and Waterloo Dock. In this development, the MDHC were in partnership with Barratt Developments (the builders).

Although much of the port's traditional trade was experiencing a marked decline, the port was still managing to stave off the general downturn in trade. This was not helped by the fact that trans-Atlantic air travel was beginning to gain the ascendency in passenger numbers, with the advent of jumbo jets and cheaper air fares. Elder Dempster had a regular service between Liverpool and West Africa, but this service was transferred to Southampton. Similarly, Canadian Pacific had a regular service between Liverpool and Quebec, but the port's scheduled trans-Atlantic passenger trade ended when the company's liner, *Empress of Canada*, sailed into Liverpool on 23 November 1971. For a short period, Shaw Savill operated cruises from the port, but the venture was not viable and was terminated. Other services were developed from the port, such as the jetfoil service which B&I Line planned to operate between Liverpool and Dublin, but, when the twice-daily service started in 1980, the company soon found that the high running costs, together with the poor sea state that was often encountered on that particular crossing, rendered the service uneconomic—the service was suspended, and there didn't appear to be much prospect of it resuming in the near future. However, the British and Irish Line did retain their Dublin route by introducing roll-on and roll-off vessels to the service, the so-called Ro-Ro passenger ferries. In order to be able to berth these vessels, suitable modifications were made in Trafalgar Dock and, similarly, West Prince's Dock was also modified for the Belfast Steamship Company's service to Belfast. There was also operating at the time, a nightly Ro-Ro service between North East Hornby Dock and the Isle of Man. This service also carried containers that were packed and unpacked at the dock. However, beset with financial difficulties, the Irish government-owned B&I Line ended its long-standing link with Liverpool on 6 January 1988. Later in the year, Sealink started a replacement service, which operated seven days a week. Norse Irish Ferries introduced a daily freight service between Belfast and North Brocklebank Dock. This new service was in addition to the P&O service that operated between Liverpool and Dublin. As the lengthy Prince's and George's Landing Stage was no longer required for passenger liners, it was demolished and replaced by a smaller structure. The new landing stage was specifically designed to accommodate the Mersey ferries and the regular scheduled service to the Isle of Man.

The North American container trade was seen as being an opportunity to establish Liverpool as the gateway to Europe, now that Britain had entered the Common Market. The investment made in the container port looked to be a shrewd business decision, but the geographical location of the Royal Seaforth Dock, together with the unsatisfactory labour relations history, was beginning to work to the detriment of the port. With more business being diverted from Liverpool, continental ports were gaining strength as were some of the newer ports on the east coast of England. The Port of Felixstowe was being privately developed with modern facilities, with none of the historic poor labour relations and disputes that had plagued Liverpool. The port was set to take advantage of new container trade opportunities. Also, because Felixstowe and a number of the other smaller east-coast ports were not included in the National Dock Labour Scheme, they were not bound by any of the labour agreements under that scheme; in effect, if they wished, they could revert to casualisation of labour—perhaps having some resonance with the zero-hours contracts that are popular in today's work-based economy. Seeing these economic advantages, companies such as the

United States Lines soon moved their larger container ships away from Liverpool, preferring to take advantage of the faster turnaround time that the east-coast ports offered. There were other companies who made the move away from Liverpool, including Ellerman Lines, but there were some that came back to the port. As the transit time through the Manchester Ship Canal was proving to be too time consuming and costly, Manchester Liners moved to the Royal Seaforth Dock.

It was now becoming accepted 'custom and practice' that the packing and unpacking of containers was deemed to be within the remit of dock workers. However, with the publication of the Jones-Aldington Report, the situation changed, allowing container handling to be conducted away from the dockside. The Aintree Container Base, many miles inland, was purpose-built for container packing and had both suitable rail and road connections. Similarly, in the early days of container shipping in the 1960s, dockside sheds had been used for packing and unpacking containers, but, as methods changed, more and more shipments were made up of house-to-house containers. To a large extent, the quayside transit sheds were rapidly becoming redundant. With new working practices such as these occurring away from the docks, the effects soon impacted upon the labour force. There was no longer the need for so many staff, so, after somewhat protracted negotiations, a number of voluntary severances were agreed. There was also a two-year pay settlement on offer, but this was dependent upon accepting these new working practices.

In 1980, the port had a trading loss of £3.86 million and future prospects were not looking too good. The turn of the decade had seen the ongoing labour relations problems carried forward, with an even greater number of days lost through disputes and strikes. In 1979, the number of man-days lost was 21,235, but, by 1980, that figure had risen to 35,006. It was clearly becoming an intolerable situation, which resulted in Bulk Cargo Handling Services and T&J Harrison ceasing to trade from the port. There was also the looming threat of a national dock strike. Due to a number of factors, such as a recession in the building trade, the number of timber containers passing through the port was significantly down, as was general cargo, with only 736,000 tons passing through the port in 1980, whereas previously, in 1979, the comparable figure had been 1,138,000 tons. There was also a significant drop in the number of vessels using the port; 5,366 vessels had passed through the port in 1979, but the figure dropped to 4,540 by 1980. However, the following year (1981) must be recorded as being one of the worst years in the history of the port. During that year, the port lost trade that was worth more than £9 million. The east coast port of Felixstowe was proving to be severe competition. Both Johnson Scan Star and Manchester Liners transferred their business to that port. However, there were other closures which adversely affected the operation of the port. Tate & Lyle, the sugar refiners who had been long-established in Liverpool, decided to move their operational headquarters away from the city, and the Central Electricity Generating Board closed their operation at Birkenhead. The Tranmere Oil Terminal also experienced a downturn in trade, when Burma Oil, one of the terminal's main users, pulled out. The loss of business from Manchester Liners and Johnson Scan Star had a big impact on the container terminal at Seaforth Dock and the economic viability of the terminal was continually being tested by a series of stoppages and other industrial disputes. The decline in trade was even more marked on the Birkenhead side of the river, with only one or two docks continuing in use for deep sea cargo vessels. Another blow was dealt to the port on 12 October 1981, when the P&O service between Liverpool and Northern Ireland was withdrawn after almost 150 years.

During the next ten years, the volume of trade passing through the port had declined at an alarming rate. In 1982, only 9.3 million tons of cargo passed through the port as a whole. There was a number of reasons for this decline, but the main two factors were the chronically poor labour relations on the dock estate and the effects of Britain's entry into the Common Market. Far from being the gateway to Europe, as had been heralded, many shipping companies were either sailing directly into European ports or using ports on the east coast of England.

The extremely competitive container shipment business was always moving forward. In 1984, ACL launched their new generation Ro-Ro container vessels. The vessels were of such a size that entry to the terminal was governed by the tides. This, in turn, necessitated new working patterns having to be introduced, with the labour force agreeing to weekend working, in order to ensure that ships were not kept waiting. It was critical for ships to enter the Gladstone Lock system two hours before high water and leave again before the next high tide. This gave approximately eleven hours for all loading and unloading operations to be completed. A new generation of straddle carriers had also been introduced into the terminal, capable of stacking containers three high; the older straddle carriers were only capable of stacking containers two high. Unfortunately, ACT, a container-carrying consortium that included several large shipping companies such as Cunard and T&J Harrisons, moved their operational base to Tilbury docks in London. Having transferred their operations from Southampton to Liverpool, Atlantic Container Line (ACL) remained in the terminal. Although, working to Liverpool's advantage was a number of industrial disputes at Southampton container port during 1984 and 1985. These disruptions prompted both Overseas Containers Limited (OCL) and Southern Africa Europe Container Service (SAECS) to relocate to Liverpool. With containerisation now becoming normal practice in sea transportation, docks that had formerly handled mainly general cargoes from countries in West Africa and South America were now adopting a dual approach, handling both containers and general cargo. The Huskisson Dock and Canada Dock area handled mixed cargoes, with container traffic being handled on North 3 Canada and North 1 Huskisson handling general cargo. Companies trading with Central and South America, such as the Pacific Steam Navigation Company, moved to carrying both containers and general cargo using older vessels. A number of other companies sailing out of Liverpool adopted similar policies, companies such as Lamport & Holt Line and T&J Harrisons.

With industrial relations on the dock estate appearing to be much healthier, with not one single day being lost to industrial disputes in 1986, the MDHC was more confident in focussing on development in the port, with new rail track being laid in the Freightliner terminal at Seaforth, such that containers could be loaded and unloaded directly. The forward-looking policies being adopted by the company were obviously paying dividends, as the company made reasonable profits throughout most of the 1980s. However, with changing methods of working, both on the dockside itself and also in the administrative side of the business, there was a much reduced need for personnel. This transition to more reliance upon technology also affected allied industries on the estate, including ship repair and ship supplies. Although the future of the port was dependent upon profitability, the port also needed significant amounts of investment to survive.

An indication of the rejuvenation that was occurring throughout the dock estate can be gained by considering some of the many developments that were happening or being planned. From 1982 onwards, scrap metal was being exported from Liverpool. The metal went to destinations in Europe and also the Far East. Throughout the 1980s and 1990s, the trade continued to prosper with the apparently insatiable world demand for metal. There were now large mounds of scrap metals deposited on quaysides from Seaforth along to Huskisson Dock, with many companies now using bulk carriers for their export. Scottish granite was also being imported to Seaforth's S10 berth; the granite was mainly used for road building in the north-west. Further along the dock estate, the transit sheds adjacent to Harrington Dock, Brunswick Dock, and Toxteth Dock were transformed into a business complex. The areas that were formerly the docks themselves have been filled-in and now provide vehicular access and abundant parking facilities. Other docks were now being considered for future development. The Waterloo grain warehouse, adjacent to the Dock Road, was converted into luxury apartments following the closure of the Waterloo river entrance. Vessels still using the port were now using the more modern docks at the north end of the dock estate. As Prince's Dock had long ceased to be used for seaborne trading, office accommodation and hotels were planned for the in-filled dock area. Also, and again because of economic necessity, the MDHC moved from their prestigious headquarters in the former Port of Liverpool Building to more modest accommodation nearer to the centre of activity at Seaforth Dock. Although being dormant for many years, Vittoria Dock on the Birkenhead side of the river was reinvigorated with general cargoes now returning, including steel and timber imports. Also, now that the M53 link motorway had been built, many specialist, heavy-lift cargoes were exported from the dock. Another development involved Bibby Edible Oils Limited, a long-established company in the city, who were seeking a move to more conducive premises. Following negotiations with the MDHC, the Brocklebank Dock, the Brocklebank Graving Dock, and Carriers Dock were in-filled so that a suitable site could be created for their new complex. Seaforth Container Terminal continued to grow, with new business arriving. One of the main advantages of having Freeport status, which much of the north docks and Seaforth now enjoyed, was the exemption on paying VAT on stored goods, until that is the cargo was sold and finally left the port. Ocean Transport & Trading moved purely to container trading and the Balt–Canada Line moved its operation to Seaforth from Felixstowe. Coastal Containers that had daily services to Belfast also transferred from Garston docks, further inland down the Mersey to S6 berth at Seaforth. With offshore activities in the Liverpool Bay field assuming greater importance, many offshore supply vessels were now using the port; this factor no doubt helped to contribute to the record profits and turnover that the MDHC achieved between 1991 and 1998. During that period, profits increased annually from £13.2 million to £47.6 million, with a corresponding rise in tonnage using the port from 24.7 million tons to 33 million tons.

In 1989, Margaret Thatcher's government decided to bring to an end what was known as the National Dock Labour Board Scheme. This agreement had effectively meant that registered dockworkers were guaranteed jobs for life. Almost inevitably, this announcement was immediately followed by a national dock strike. The government had a number of contingency plans, one of which was to fund redundancy packages at all of the affected ports coming under the agreement—the so-called 'scheme' ports. Large numbers of registered dock workers (RDWs) were offered substantial sums, approximately £35,000 each, to quit the scheme. The government hailed the initiative as being a huge success, when many RDWs accepted the package and left the docks. The national strike ended after six weeks, with workers at all ports returning to work, except workers at Liverpool docks. Liverpool dockers were still seeking union recognition and guarantees of future employment. One week later, the men marched in solidarity to the dock gates, a symbolic gesture to mark the end of the strike at Liverpool. During the strike period, however, many Liverpool dockworkers had accepted the government's severance package. While the dispute had continued, the MDHC had also drawn up a number of plans that they proposed to implement as soon as the strike came to an end. One of the main changes that the company wanted to make was a move away from the system of centralised labour control, which had its base at Hornby Dock. They proposed permanent localised groups working in specific dock areas. This change in working patterns formed the basis for the new contracts of employment. The contracts also included clauses that specified rates of remuneration and manning levels—the main emphasis of the new contracts being aimed at achieving improved working flexibility. Coincidental with the ending of the National Dock Labour Scheme, new trading patterns were beginning to emerge along the dock estate, including more coal being imported through Gladstone Dock in anticipation of the Powergen (now E.ON UK) facility, which was to be built on the dock estate.

The picture that was now emerging from the container port was more encouraging, with a total of some 28,863,000 tons passing through the complex in 1999. The terminal also attracted new services—the Forest Products Terminal attracting new services from Brazil, South Africa and Canada. There was also increased trade coming from both Belfast and Dublin, and, by the turn of the millennium, the port was handling as much tonnage as it was in the early '70s; however, employed labour now totalled 600, whereas the number employed in the early '70s was in excess of 14,000.

The port has now become one of the major exporters of scrap metal and, similarly, is the main destination for the importation of edible oils, fats, and timber. With one of England's biggest coal-fired power stations nearby at Fiddlers Ferry, the bulk terminal now imports over 6 million tons of coal *per annum*, which is then transported by rail directly to the power station.

The company was now a major employer within the region and, together with the Capital Expenditure Programme scheduled for 1992–1998, was expected to create at least another 15,000 jobs in the immediate area. A bulk terminal and a unit for animal feed were built at Canada Dock. Also, Phase 2 of what was known as the Bulk Industrial Zone—part of Liverpool Freeport—was completed in 1994 at the West Float in Birkenhead. With business in the port beginning to show signs of improvement, in 1995 planning applications were made to Sefton Council to create a 70-acre site in an expanded port and Freeport. The plans included additional warehousing and industrial units. It also necessitated the partial closure of the Dock Road. Planning consent was given and work on the development started in 1997.

With the cruise trade becoming more prominent in the holiday and tourism industry, a number of large passenger liners began to return to the city. The port took a proactive stance when it sent representatives to the Seatrade Cruise Exhibition, which was held in Miami, in an effort to promote the port and the city as a cruise destination. As early as 1992, companies such as CTC Cruise Lines and the Royal Caribbean Line were visiting the city as a cruise destination in their itineraries and, following the undoubted success of CTC Lines cruise programme, Direct Cruises also announced a programme of cruises with departures from Liverpool. After a very lengthy absence, the Cunard Line also started to visit the Mersey again, culminating in the company's then flagship, the *QEII*, visiting the Mersey in 1994 as part of her silver jubilee celebrations. By 1997, Direct Holidays announced a cruise programme, starting in 1998, which would be using Liverpool as its main departure terminal. The cruise programme was to visit destinations such as Iceland, the Norwegian Fjords, Greenland, and the Mediterranean. In an effort to consolidate their earlier success, Direct Cruises launched another cruise ship that would also operate out of Liverpool. However, because of difficulties with both liners, Direct Cruises were forced to cancel much of its 1998 programme. The company itself was acquired by Airtours in 1998, and the cruise programme, as advertised, did continue for some time, but then, in 1999, the company announced that, from 2000, their scheduled cruise programme would not be operating from any British port. The news did much damage to the port as a cruise terminal. Then, for a number of political, legal, and economic reasons, the proposed new landing stage, which should have been operational from 1999, was not built. It had been envisaged that the landing stage and passenger terminal would have a throughput of upwards of half a million cruise passengers and passengers using the Irish Sea crossing. However, a new cruise terminal opened in 2007 and since then has received more than a quarter of a million cruise passengers and crew, thus renewing the port's links with passenger-carrying shipping companies. After the terminal's opening, the number of liners calling at the port rapidly increased and a number of other companies decided to offer Liverpool-based cruises, including Thompson Cruises, Fred Olsen, and Cruise & Maritime. The port was awarded the accolade of being the 'Best UK Port of Call' in the 2013–2014 season.

To mark the company's 175th anniversary, Cunard organised a number of special events in their spiritual home in Liverpool, from where their first scheduled transatlantic liners sailed in 1840. On 25 May 2015, Cunard's three queens, the *Queen Elizabeth*, *Queen Victoria*, and the company's flagship *Queen Mary II*, joined together on the River Mersey in a special 'Three Queens' salute in front of the Cunard Building; the company's headquarters from 1917 until 1967. Later in the year, on 4 July 2015, *Queen Mary II* sailed from Liverpool on a transatlantic crossing to commemorate the original maiden voyage of Cunard's then flagship, *Britannia*, which sailed from Liverpool to Halifax and Boston on 4 July 1840.

Liverpool City Council bought the Cunard Building in the hope that it could be converted and used as a cruise liner terminal, but the plans have been temporarily shelved on the grounds of being prohibitively expensive—conversion would cost somewhere in the region of £15 million—when factors such as secure check-in facilities and border control facilities as required by the Home Office had been taken into account. Another difficulty would have been creating a secure route for passengers between the registration point and the embarkation point. The council is now considering a number of alternative sites in the city to be converted into a cruise terminal.

During 2015, a total of fifty-four cruise liners were scheduled to bring more than 80,000 cruise passengers to the city—an increase of 40 per cent on 2014.

With a different constitutional base, the company was now ready to expand into shipping and shipping management. The year 1991 marked one of the first ventures in this market, with the acquisition of the Coastal Container Line. Then, in 1993, the company took a 50 per cent share in Merchant Fleets Limited, which operated a daily Ro-Ro service between Heysham, Fleetwood, and Warrenpoint in Northern Ireland. The overall contract had a number of other enshrined agreements, which included acquiring a 50 per cent share in the freight forwarding company, MTS Shipping, which Merchant Fleets owned, and there was also a long-term agreement with the Belfast Harbour Commissioners, giving access to the port's Victoria Terminal. In addition to acquiring the 50 per cent share in Merchant Fleets Limited, the company also acquired Medway Ports Limited for £103 million. In many respects, it was a logical addition to the company's business portfolio, in that it extended the company's geographical base and brought a further degree of diversification; the port being one of the leading ports for the importation of forestry products, cars, and fresh fruit. The

Serried rows of quayside cranes at Royal Seaforth Container Terminal.

acquisition of Medway Ports Limited also included the ports of Sheerness and Chatham. There was a further extension to the services that Coastal Container Lines offered in 1995, when a service between Liverpool, Belfast, and Greenock was started. The following year (1996), the Rotterdam-based BG Freight Line was bought by the Mersey Docks and Harbour Company. This further extended the geographical base of the company, with BG Freight operating to Antwerp, Belfast, Cork, Dublin, and Rotterdam. The company then invested a further £5 million in Sheerness in order that refinements could be made to the temperature-controlled facility where fresh produce was stored; this followed the announcement of a 60 per cent rise in profits during the 1994 financial year. At the same time, the company announced firstly that they had secured a ten-year contract with Volkswagen-Audi to import cars through Sheerness, and secondly that Hyundai were planning to transport up to 15,000 vehicles through the port every year. The wider concept of embracing many different forms of transport became a reality when, in 1994, the Euro-Rail Terminal at

Seaforth began direct rail services between Liverpool and several European cities including Paris, Brussels, Stuttgart, Milan, and Bordeaux. Also in 1994, the Hamilton Oil Company moved their operational base to the Port of Liverpool. The company had berths in both West Hornby and Alexandra Docks. Another milestone was reached in May 1995, when the Isle of Man Steam Packet Company opened their new passenger terminal at Liverpool landing stage. Some initial work was done on building a Ro-Ro berth to cater for boats coming from Ireland. When the plans were announced in 1995, it was anticipated that the operational base would be located at Trafalgar Dock, and work commenced on in-filling the dock. However, in 1999 it was decided to conduct a feasibility study regarding the proposed berthing arrangements, as it was considered that other options might be more suitable than having to build a completely new floating landing stage. Taking further cognizance of the changing needs of business being generated by coastal traffic and, in particular, the increasing trade from Irish Sea operators, the MDHC took over Twelve Quays from Forth Ports in 1997 and set plans in motion for further development work to begin in 2001. The new developments would improve facilities for both shipping and haulage companies. At the start of 1996, it was becoming evident that the Mersey Docks and Harbour Company was continuing to attract a good share of the market, as it was steadily climbing up the ranks of the top-rated companies in the United Kingdom. The company was now handling over £1 million through the Seaforth terminal, which it claimed—with some justification—was the largest Freeport in Britain. At the turn of the millennium, there were four distinct divisions in the company's portfolio: the Port Operations Division, the Shipping Division, the Property Division, and finally a new Logistics and Transport Division. The Ports Operations Division comprised the Port of Liverpool, Medway Port, and Marine Terminals in Dublin. The Shipping Division now included the Coastal Container Line, Concorde Line, BG Freight Line, and the Seawing organisation, and the Property Division managed the company's property portfolio. Further expansion was envisaged and, in 2001, the Port of Heysham was brought into the portfolio, and, later, in 2002, the company acquired a 50 per cent holding in North West Ship repairers.

By 1997, oil and gas production platforms in the Irish Sea were supplying 70,000 barrels of oil and 8.5 million cubic metres of gas every day. This followed an investment of over £1 billion by the Liverpool Bay Development Partnership in four gas and oil fields.

In 2005, the Mersey Docks and Harbour Company was taken over by Peel Holdings, and in June 2013 work started on Liverpool2. The construction of this £300 million deep-water container terminal is the centre piece of Peel Holdings' development plans for the port. It is estimated that the terminal should be opening towards the end of 2016 and be able to accommodate two 400-metre post-Panamax container vessels, each having a maximum capacity of 13,500 TEUs (the term TEU derives from the time in the Korean war when, for ease of movement, the US military 'stuffed' equipment into 20-foot long containers;

TEU is a '20-foot equivalent unit', even though most containers are now 40 foot long). The current terminal can accommodate ships having a maximum of 4,500 containers, but this new in-river container terminal will double the port's container capacity and, in doing so, create at least another 500 port-based jobs and up to another 5,000 in the region as a direct result of this development. The design capacity of the new terminal will add a further half a million TEUs to the port, increasing capacity to upwards of 2 million containers per year. The company's design estimates of road and rail usage indicate that up to 150 million miles will be saved in any one year. This saving will have a positive impact upon the carbon footprint in the region and, by building an additional 3,500 metres of road, help to reduce congestion—easing future expenditure on transport networks. Located in the River Mersey, the terminal has been designed to be able to berth up to two 13,500 TEU vessels at any one time, although no vessel size restrictions will be imposed, which is the case with the current terminal that has a traditional closed dock system.

Lend-lease, which had been named by Peel Holdings as the principal contractor, will be responsible for most of the major construction operations, including ensuring that all projects and sub-contractors within the compass of the overall project will operate at optimum efficiency. Lend-lease will also work in close co-operation with Peel Holdings in the appointment of the quay-wall contractor. The overall plan envisages a completely new quay wall of some 854 meters in length. To assist in this aspect of the project, the *Sea Jack*, a massive self-powered Danish barge, is being used to drill and lift piles into position. As the proposed opening date for the new terminal approaches, dredging continues twenty-four hours a day, seven days a week in the river. The existing channels are being dredged to a depth of 16.5 metres, which will give berthing pockets directly adjacent to the quay wall and enable the world's biggest container ships to enter the terminal. It is estimated that, by the time the dredging is completed, more than 5 million cubic metres will have been taken from the river bed, with most of the material being taken and dumped offshore. Some of the dredged material will, however, be used as landfill, creating a land mass that will enable the new container standing area to accommodate over 600,000 containers and the bank of ship to shore quay cranes with cantilever rail-mounted gantry cranes (CRMGs). The decision to turn to CRMGs rather than the more traditional straddle carriers was prompted by a more efficient use of space and a faster ship turnaround. The ship-to-shore cranes, costing somewhere in the region of £100 million, are being manufactured by the Shanghai-based, Zhenhua Heavy Industries. The contract was awarded for seventeen mega cranes to be built including five 3,000-ton ship-to-shore cranes. The new cranes will be capable on unloading a container in just over half a minute.

With Liverpool2 creating exciting new challenges and opportunities for the port, coupled with the increasing numbers of cruise passengers now visiting the city, another dimension was added to the port's resurgence, and that was the return of narrow boats to the city's canals. In the early days of transportation by canal, the Port of Liverpool received and despatched materials and manufactured products through the Stanley Dock Branch. However, with the ever-increasing demand for speed, coupled with the advance of technology at the time of the Industrial Revolution, more and more cargoes were being transported via rail networks and road. At the same time, a number of docks were becoming unfit for purpose, mainly due to changes in marine technology and the increasing size of vessels entering the port. George's Dock and its basin were in-filled to create building land at the Pier Head. The Port of Liverpool Building was built on this land and became the very grand headquarters of the then Mersey Docks and Harbour Board. This building was followed shortly by the building of the Cunard Building and the Liver Building. One notable outcome of this building programme was the severing of the canal link between the north and south dock complex. The Leeds and Liverpool Canal, at the Liverpool end, had its original terminal close to the Stanley Dock Branch—a useful location for the nearby Tate and Lyle sugar refinery. The canal's route finally ended close to the Pier Head near to Prince's Dock, but, in 1987, this stretch was in-filled almost back to the original terminus.

It was the development of leisure cruising that created the need for better canal links into the heart of Liverpool and the newly transformed Albert Dock complex. British Waterways, later to become known as the Canal and River Trust, muted the idea of opening a new canal link, the Liverpool Docks Link, between the north and south docks complex. As the concept of the new link gained traction, three plans were considered, each having some advantages, but each also having major cost implications. The plan that was finally adopted took the proposed link along a route via two locks and a number of tunnels and cuttings going past the 'Three Graces' and eventually to the Canning Basin. The new link would reconnect the northern dock complex with the southern dock complex, which had not been possible since 1898. When the scheme was given final approval in 2005, funding was raised from a number of sources including the European Regeneration Fund and the English Regeneration Fund. The overall cost of the 1.4-mile link has been estimated at £22 million. Construction of the link commenced in May 2006. After making progress through the outer city environs, the canal route passes under the St Nicholas Tunnel and then through the Cunard Tunnel before entering the Museum Tunnel under Mann Island. The route eventually enters Canning Basin, through Canning Half-Tide Dock, and on to Albert Dock. The final terminal for canal craft is then through to Salthouse Dock. Further linkages can be made through Duke's Dock, Wapping Dock, King's Dock, Queen's Dock, Coburg Dock, and the Liverpool Marina at Brunswick Dock. The canal route passes not very far from the newly opened Prince's Landing Stage Cruise Ship Terminal and Floating Landing Stage. With much of the construction work being completed by the summer of 2008, the official opening ceremony was performed on 25 March 2009, when the Lord Mayor of Liverpool and the Chief Executive of British Waterways traversed the new link aboard the *Pride of Sefton*.

With so many ambitious and diverse developments happening on the dock estate, Liverpool may yet be experiencing another renaissance and, although many of the change agents are outside of the port's control, if the indomitable spirit of the people of Liverpool has any bearing on the situation, the future may still be bright.

Select Bibliography

Baines, T., *History of the Commerce and Town of Liverpool in 1859*, (London: Longman & Co, 1859); *Liverpool in 1859*, (London: Longman & Co, 1859); *The Port and Town of Liverpool in 1860*, (London: Longman & Co, 1860)

Brook, R., *Liverpool As It Was, 1775-1800*, (Liverpool Libraries and Information Service, 2003)

Brown, A., *Smith's Strangers' Guide to Liverpool, its Environs, and Part of Cheshire, for 1843*, (Liverpool: Benjamin Smith, 1843)

Collard, I., *Mersey Ports: Liverpool & Birkenhead*, (Stroud: Tempus, 2001)

Enfield, W., *An Essay Towards the History of Liverpool 1774*, (London: J Johnson, 1774)

Forwood, W. B., *Recollections of A Busy Life; Being the Reminiscences of A Liverpool Merchant 1840-1910*, (Liverpool: Henry Young & Sons, 1910); *Reminiscences of A Liverpool Ship Owner, 1850-1920*, (Liverpool: Henry Young & Sons, 1920)

Howley, F., *Slavers, Traders and Privateers. Liverpool, the Africa Trade and Revolution, 1773-1808*, (Birkenhead: Countyvise, 2008)

Hussey, J., *Cruisers, Cotton & Confederates*, (Birkenhead: Countyvise Publication, 2008)

Hyde, F. E., *Liverpool & the Mersey*, (Newton Abbot: David & Charles Publishers, 1971)

Lane, T., *Liverpool: City of the Sea*, (Liverpool: Liverpool University Press, 1997)

Lynch, A., *Weathering the Storm - The Mersey Docks Financial Crisis 1970-1974*, (Liverpool: Liverpool University Press, 1994)

Muir, R., *A History of Liverpool 1907*, (Liverpool: Henry Young, 1907); *Bygone Liverpool 1913*, (Liverpool: Henry Young, 1913)

Noakes, R., *Liverpool's Historic Waterfront*, (London: HMSO, 1984)

Paul, D., *Thetis: Submarine Disaster*, (Stroud: Fonthill Media, 2014)

Pickton, J., *Memorials of Liverpool, Including A History of the Dock Estate 1873 Vol 1.*, (London: Longmans, Green & Co, 1875)

Postance, R., *Old Liverpool: Written In Manuscript 1889*, (Liverpool: The Liverpool Printing and Stationary Co. Ltd, 1928)

Richardson, D., Schwarz, S., and Tibbles, A., *Liverpool and Transatlantic Slavery*, (Liverpool: Liverpool University Press, 2007)

Wallace, J., *A General and Descriptive History of the Ancient and Present State, of the Town of Liverpool*, (Liverpool: J McCreery, 1796)

Walvin, J., *Black Ivory*, (London: Blackwell, 1992)

Wilkinson, C., *Liverpool Characters and Streets*, (Liverpool: The Bluecoat Press, 2009)